IMAGES
of America

LeRoy

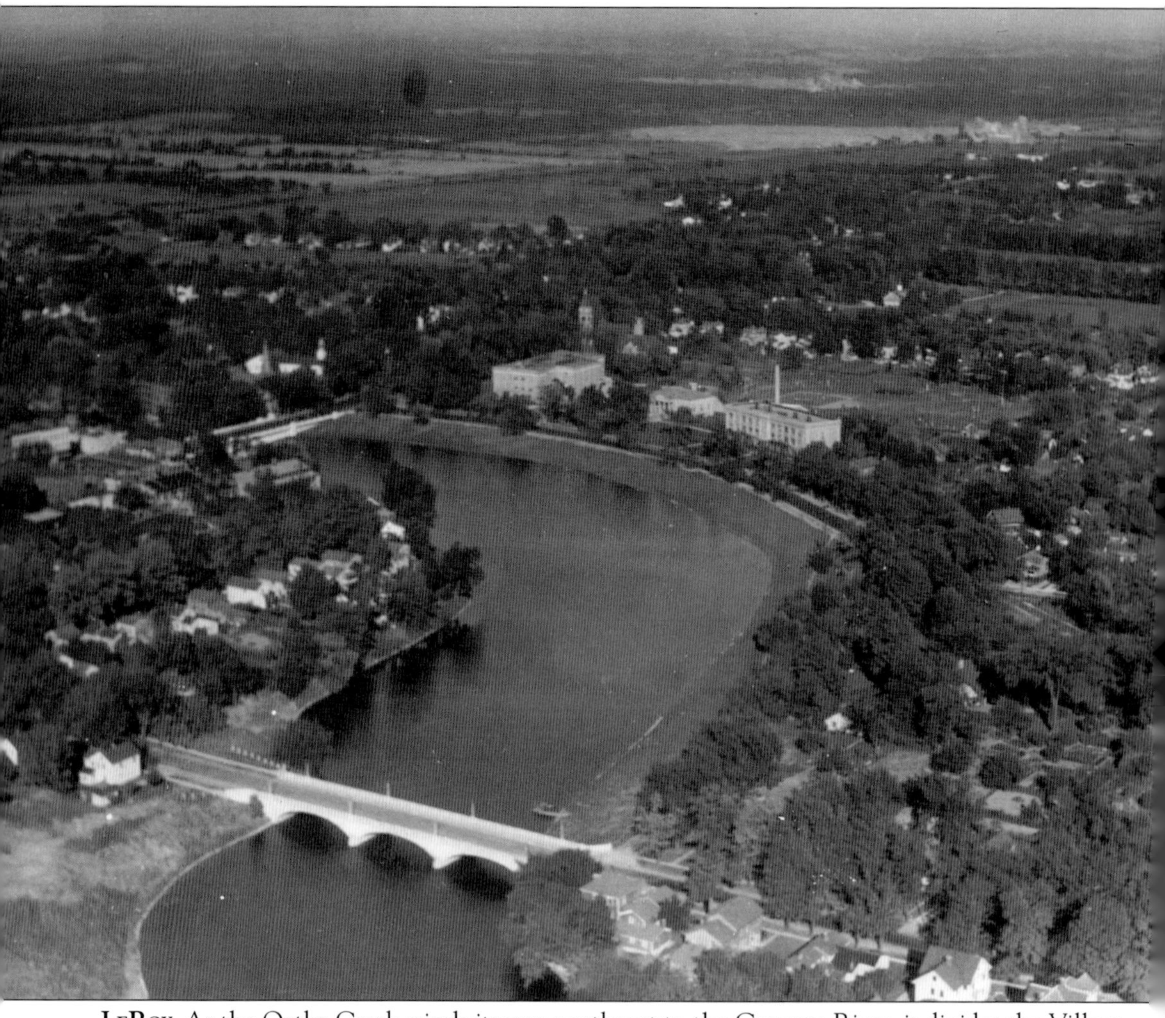

LeRoy. As the Oatka Creek winds its way northeast to the Genesee River, it divides the Village of LeRoy east from west. This aerial view looking north was taken in 1940 and shows the Clay Street bridge in the foreground, the millpond, the school campus, and the Main Street bridge. (Courtesy of the LeRoy Historical Society.)

On the Cover: Students and faculty of Ingham University pose on the front steps of University Hall, located at the corner of Wolcott and East Main Streets. Ingham University was founded in 1837 and became a nationally acclaimed university for women. (Courtesy of the LeRoy Historical Society.)

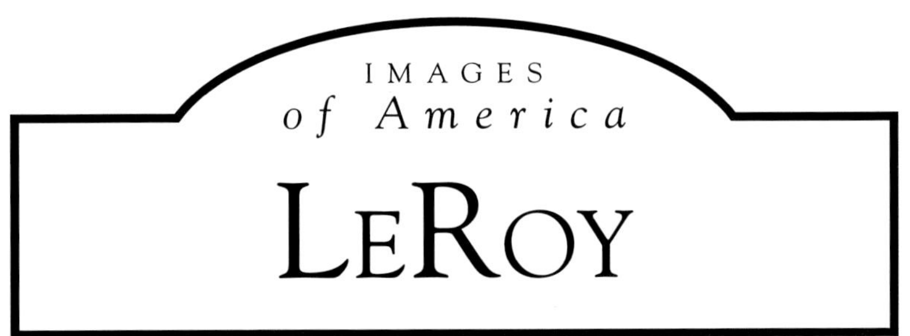

Lynne J. Belluscio

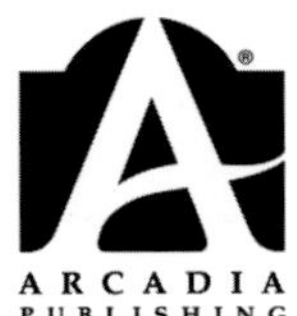

ISBN 978-0-7385-7299-4

Published by Arcadia Publishing
Charleston SC, Chicago IL, Portsmouth NH, San Francisco CA

Printed in the United States of America

Library of Congress Control Number: 2009940132

For all general information contact Arcadia Publishing at:
Telephone 843-853-2070
Fax 843-853-0044
E-mail sales@arcadiapublishing.com
For customer service and orders:
Toll-Free 1-888-313-2665

Visit us on the Internet at www.arcadiapublishing.com

Dedicated to the memory of Seely F. Pratt, whose love for the rich heritage of LeRoy was contagious.

Contents

ACKNOWLEDGMENTS

Through the years, people from LeRoy have believed that it was important to collect and preserve the photographs and archives that chronicle the history of this community. Without their foresight and dedication, this book would never have been possible. Before the LeRoy Historical Society was organized in 1940, the Te-car-na-wun-ah Chapter of the Daughters of the American Revolution acquired and maintained a sizable collection of photographs. Eventually that collection was donated to the LeRoy Historical Society. In addition, the LeRoy Historical Society has been fortunate to receive other valuable photograph collections from Phil Tompkins, the Woodward family, and Alvin Stripp. Many people have donated small collections, or even single photographs, that have proved to be extremely important to the photographic record. Several years ago, William Lane began the monumental task of sorting and identifying the collection. Recently, Marianne Lee continued the project. As donors bring in more photographs, the identification and filing continues. Several books have provided invaluable information, including *History of Genesee County, New York 1890-1982*, published in 1985, and *The Heritage of LeRoy: A Pictorial History of the Village of LeRoy, New York*, published in 1984. Unless otherwise noted, all images appear courtesy of the LeRoy Historical Society.

A special thank you to Ruth Harvie, Brenda Beal, Mary Bryant, Wilfred Vasile, Brian Duddy, and Terry Gilford who have assisted in the preparation of this book. All royalties from the sale of this book will be donated to the LeRoy Historical Society to be used for the preservation of the photograph collection.

INTRODUCTION

As the Town of LeRoy prepares to celebrate its bicentennial in 2012, it faces the challenges that confront hundreds of other American communities. Few people live in the towns where they grew up. The mobility of society has created generations of people who know little about the history of the places in which they work and live. And those people who still live in their hometown wonder if anyone will preserve their family's legacy. The task is left to local historical societies, museums, and municipal historians to collect and preserve photographs, genealogical records, and artifacts. With this publication, Arcadia Publishing offers an opportunity to preserve and share the visual heritage of our home, LeRoy.

LeRoy's location has influenced its history for hundreds of years. Situated on the eastern edge of Genesee County in Western New York, it is about 25 miles southwest of Rochester and less than an hour from Buffalo. The incorporated village of LeRoy is centered on the intersection of Route 19 and Route 5 and has a population of 4,500. The village is surrounded by the town of LeRoy, which has a population of 7,200. The town is bordered on the east by Livingston County and on the west by the town of Stafford. The Oatka Creek rises in the hills of Wyoming and slices through LeRoy, spilling over Buttermilk Falls and winding its way north to the Genesee River

Before roads and railroads crisscrossed the land, Native American trails passed through the dense forest and along the Oatka Creek. When the Iroquois came to the area, the Woodland People had already left behind evidence of their encampments at Fort Hill and along the banks of the Oatka. Early settlers wrote about burial sites and collections of arrowheads. The Iroquois camped along the creek and had contact with the settlers. As pioneers streamed into the region after the Revolution, the old trails were overrun by thousands of wagons and the Native Americans found refuge in nearby reservations.

Early in 1793, Hinds Chamberlain traveled into the region and camped overnight by the creek, which at that time was called Allen's Creek. The water spilled over the black shale and Chamberlain remarked that it looked like buttermilk, so the area became known as Buttermilk Falls. In 1797, Charles Wilbor arrived and built a cabin on the Mill Tract. Located on the east side of town, the Mill Tract was the earliest of the three land tracts and attracted the first settlers. Open for settlement next was the Triangle Tract, which was surveyed in 1801. Ezra Platt bought 500 acres of the Triangle Tract for the future village of LeRoy. The third tract was the Craigie Tract located on the west side of town. It was promoted by Thomas Tufts, who arrived in the area in 1810.

When Capt. John Ganson bought Charles Wilbor's cabin in 1798, he established a tavern and inn. Its reputation spread far and wide and the area became known as the Ganson Settlement. A bridge was built across the creek in 1801 and 1802, and a dam was built to harness the waterpower of the rapids. Richard Stoddard and Ezra Platt built the first gristmill on the west side of the creek. In 1812, the settlement became known as Bellona after the Roman goddess of war, but in less than a year the town was named for a wealthy New York merchant, Herman LeRoy.

The early settlers established churches and schools throughout the area. In 1837, Marietta and Emily Ingham founded the LeRoy Female Seminary. In 1857, the seminary was granted a charter to become a university. In the 19th century, Ingham was one of seven nationally recognized women's universities. It closed in 1892 because of financial difficulties.

LeRoy's early industries were dependent on the agricultural economy and the natural resources in the area. Flour, salt, limestone, wool, apples, beans, cattle, and poultry all came from LeRoy. Entrepreneurs built shops for furniture, carriages, railroad cars, stoves, patent medicines, cigars, hats, agricultural implements, milled lumber, malt, dynamite, silos, porcelain insulators, organs, automobile parts, airplanes, and most notably "America's Most Famous Dessert"—Jell-O. But the thriving community changed. The LeRoy Salt Company closed shortly after World War I. LeRoy Plow Company closed after World War II. Most of the patent medicine companies ceased operation. Jell-O moved to Dover, Delaware, in 1964. People in LeRoy were driving to Rochester and nearby communities for work. Today there are very few LeRoy industries that have been in business for more than 20 years.

In Western New York, before the opening of the Erie Canal, farmers and merchants depended on a network of overland roads that were often impassable during the spring and intolerable in the hot summer months. The Erie Canal passed 17 miles north of LeRoy. Lake Road led directly to the canal at Brockport. The road was filled with wagons until the first railroad arrived in LeRoy in 1853. By the end of the century, three railroads had stations in the village and two others skirted the town. Today only one railroad is still in operation. Passenger service was discontinued in 1953. The decline of the railroad was matched by the growth of the automobile and the improvement of roads and highways. Route 5, which passes through LeRoy, was the main east-west road through New York between Buffalo and Albany. With the advent of the interstate highway system in the 1950s, LeRoy became Exit 47 of the New York State Thruway and the western exit for Rochester. Exit 47 is connected to downtown Rochester by Interstate 490.

Obviously the earliest history of LeRoy was not captured by photographers, but as early as 1841, a photographer had a studio at the Eagle Hotel. A succession of photographers plied their trade recording the people, landscapes, and events of this community. The most complete photographic record of LeRoy was made in 1940 by Oscar Wieggel as part of a community project. He assembled over 500 images, which were bound in a large album that is now in the collection of the LeRoy Historical Society. The challenge for this Arcadia Publishing book has been the search to find the images that best tell the story of LeRoy.

One

Early History and the LeRoy Family

The Great Niagara Road led pioneers and travelers into Western New York across the Genesee River at Avon and through a wide fertile plain before rising to Caledonia. From there, the road turned westerly and traversed an area of limestone outcroppings that was dotted with low scrubby trees. Gradually the road rose, then dipped to a rapids at Allen's Creek. The water churned over the black shale and was as white as buttermilk. The area became known as Buttermilk Falls.

Settlement began in 1797 when the Native Americans signed the Big Tree Treaty at Geneseo. In that year, Charles Wilbor built a log cabin one mile east of Allen's Creek on the Mill Tract. He soon moved west and Capt. John Ganson bought the cabin and established an inn and tavern. The area became known as the Ganson Settlement.

Although there were several land tracts in the area, the most prominent in LeRoy was the 87,000-acre Triangle Tract that extended north from a point in LeRoy to Lake Ontario. In 1801, Richard Stoddard surveyed the Triangle Tract and became its first land agent. On June 8, 1812, the town was officially named Bellona for the Roman goddess of war, but less than a year later, at the first town meeting on April 6, 1813, the town petitioned the state to change the name to LeRoy, for Herman LeRoy, a wealthy New York merchant and land speculator and one of the owners of the Triangle Tract.

Herman LeRoy and his business partner, William Bayard, had purchased the Triangle Tract from Robert Morris. Herman LeRoy's nephew, Egbert Benson Jr., became the third land agent. He was replaced by Herman's son, Jacob. The community continued to grow and prosper. On May 5, 1834, the incorporated village of LeRoy was established. Joshua Lathrop became the first mayor.

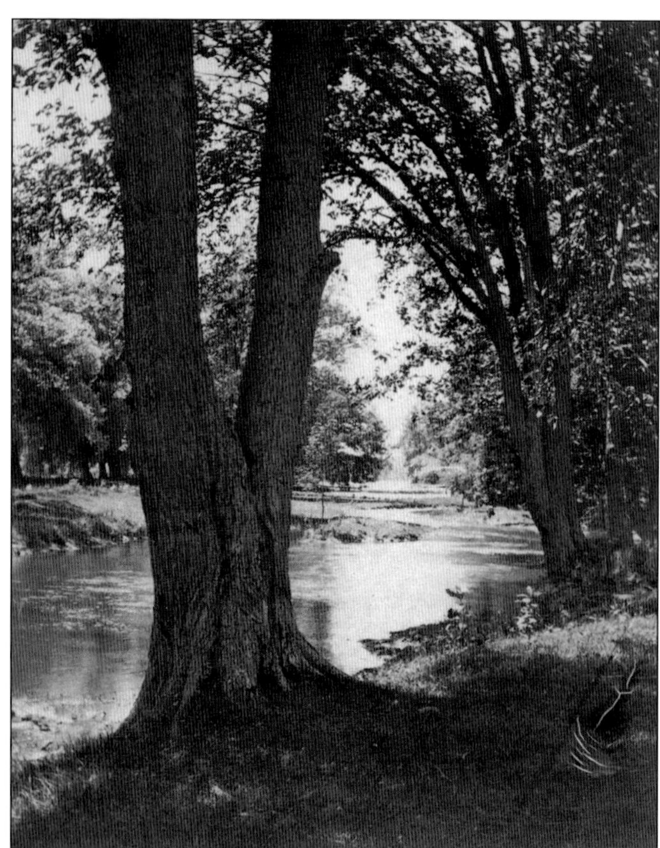

I Am the Oatka. "I am the Oatka: I have held my course for ages / I shall flow on endlessly / I have seen tribe succeed tribe, race follow race / They are despoilers all, careless desecraters of the beautiful / In spite of them, I am still beautiful." (Unknown author.)

The Mill Pond. In the village, the creek fell 11 feet over rapids that were known to the earliest settlers as Buttermilk Falls. Soon after the Main Street bridge was built in 1801, the creek was dammed. It formed a large millpond that provided headwater for Platt and Stoddard's flour mill. Silt built up behind the dam, and in 1933, the millpond was drained and dredged.

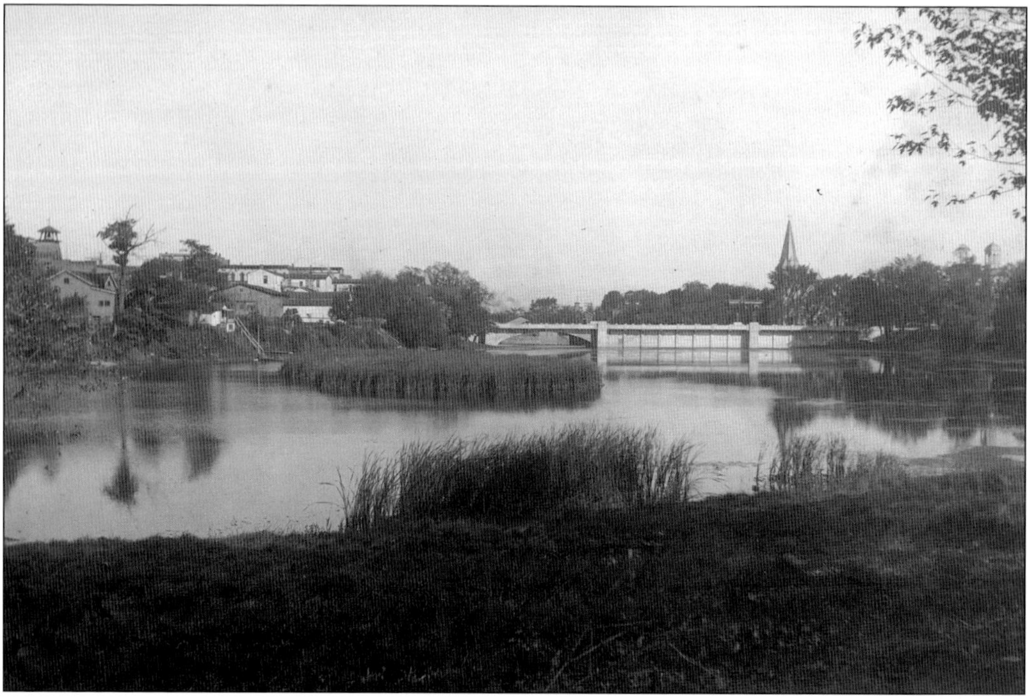

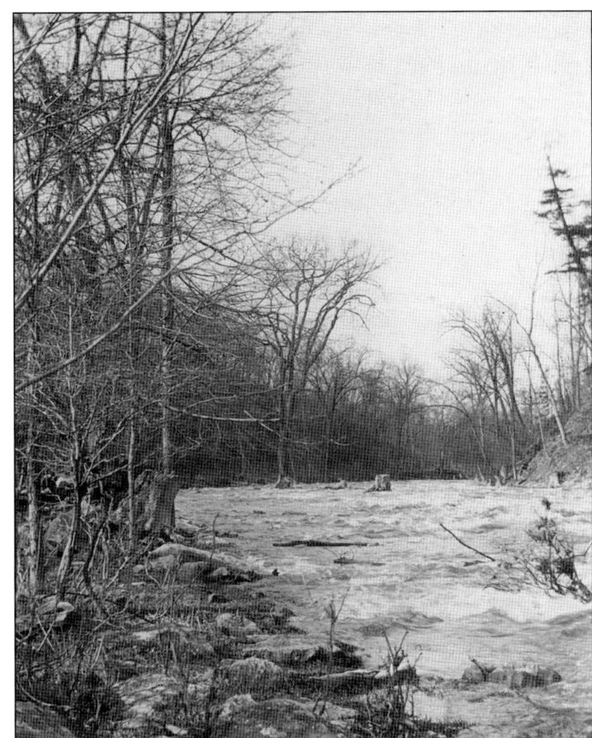

The Creek. Known to the settlers as Allen's Creek, it was named for Ebeneazer "Indian" Allen, who settled near the mouth of the creek on the Genesee River at Scottsville. In 1850, J. R. Anderson of LeRoy suggested that the name of the creek be changed. He asked Ely Parker, a noted Seneca, for the Native American name of the creek. Parker replied "O-At-Ka" which means "leaving the highlands" or "approaching an opening" in reference to the creek's origins in the hills of Wyoming and its confluence with the Genesee River.

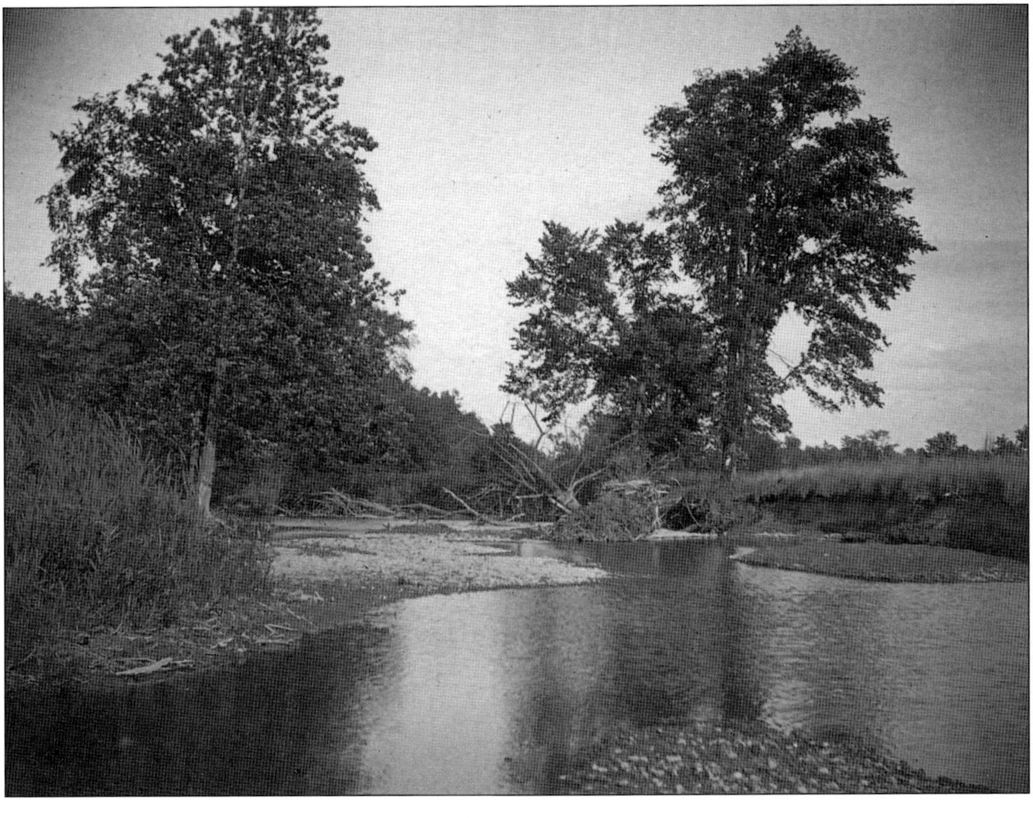

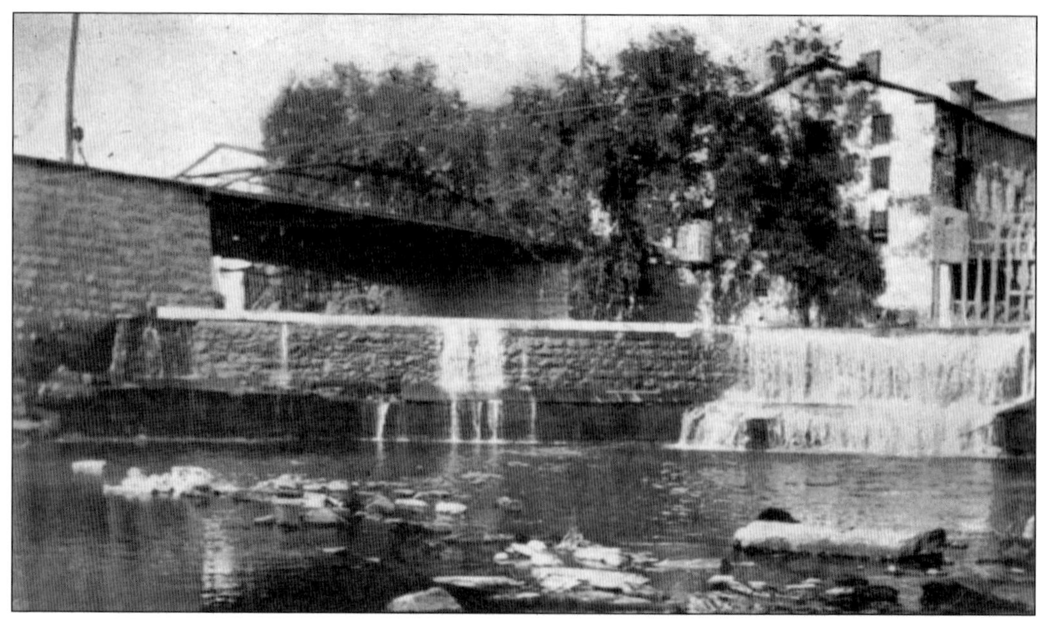

The Old Dam. The original dam was on the north side of the bridge. Remnants of it can still be seen. The dam was rebuilt south of the bridge after the Creek Project in 1933. Oatka Creek often reaches flood stage in the spring. The photograph below was taken on May 11, 1916, during one of the worst floods recorded.

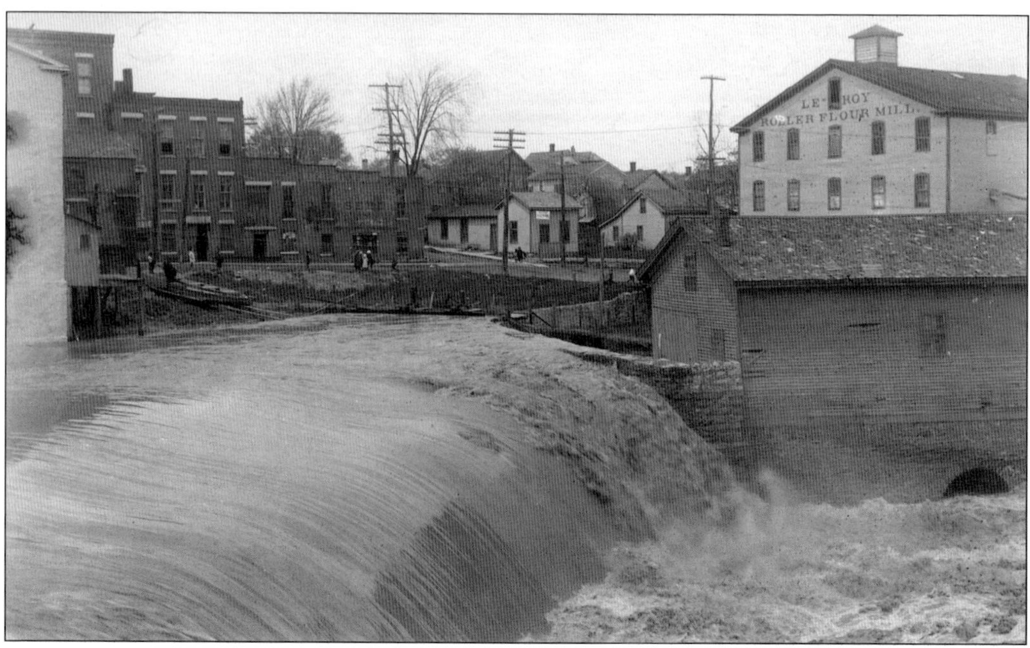

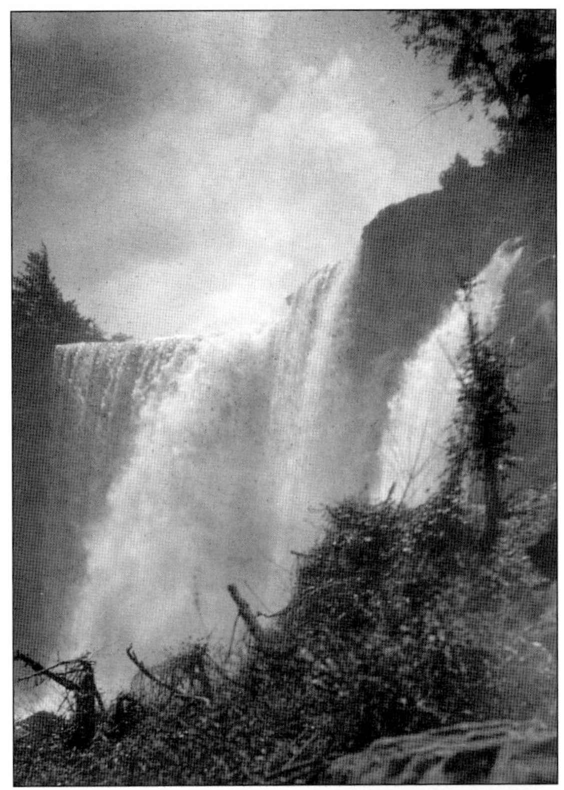

Buttermilk Falls. Oatka Creek spills 63 feet over a thick ledge of Onondaga limestone north of the village. Originally, these high falls were known as the Great Falls, and the rapids in the village were known as Buttermilk Falls. When the rapids were dammed in 1802, the Great Falls became known as Buttermilk Falls. The limestone creek bed is filled with fissures and cracks. During the summer, the water level drops upstream and the water disappears into the fissures above the falls and travels a long distance downstream before reappearing.

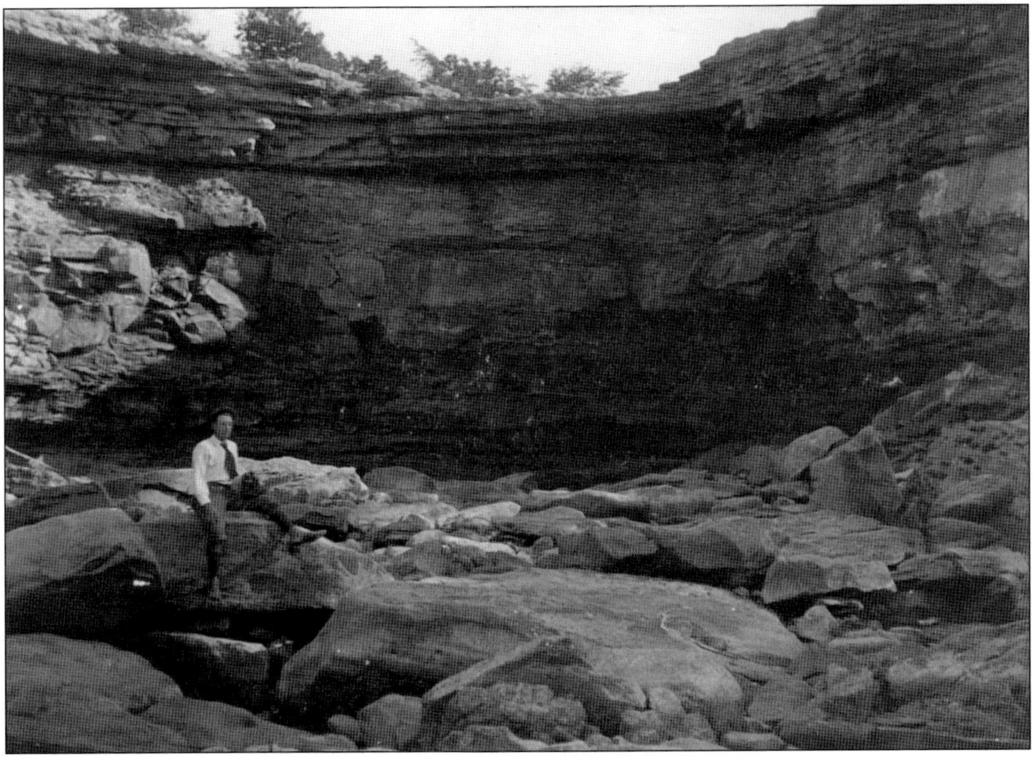

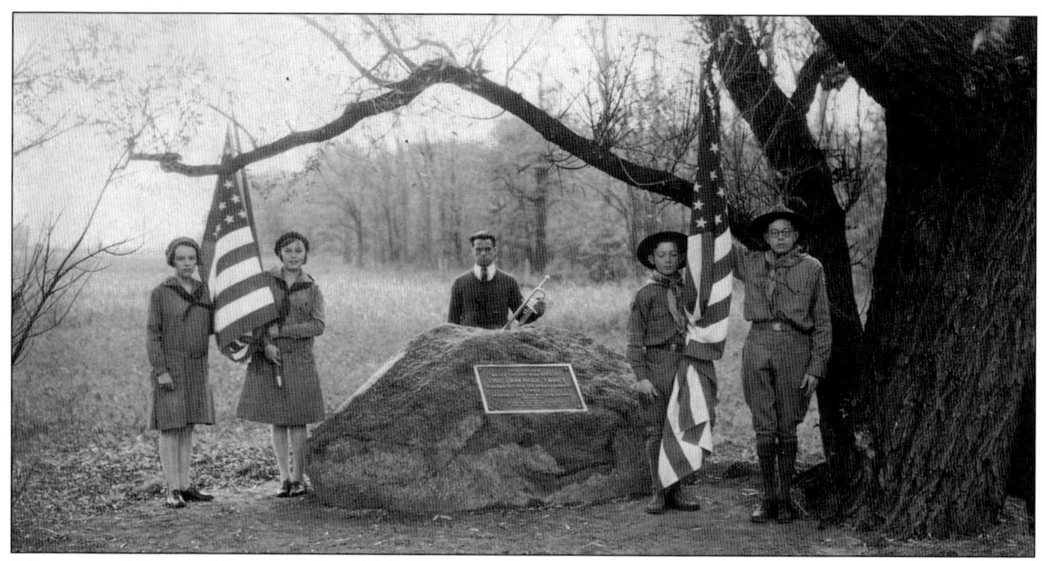

Triangle Tract Marker. In 1793, New York investors Herman LeRoy and William Bayard purchased 87,000 acres from Robert Morris. The Triangle Tract extended from a point south of the village of LeRoy to Lake Ontario. It was surveyed in 1801 by Richard Stoddard, who became the first land agent. This boulder on Summit Street was dedicated in 1930 and marks the exact location of the apex of the triangle.

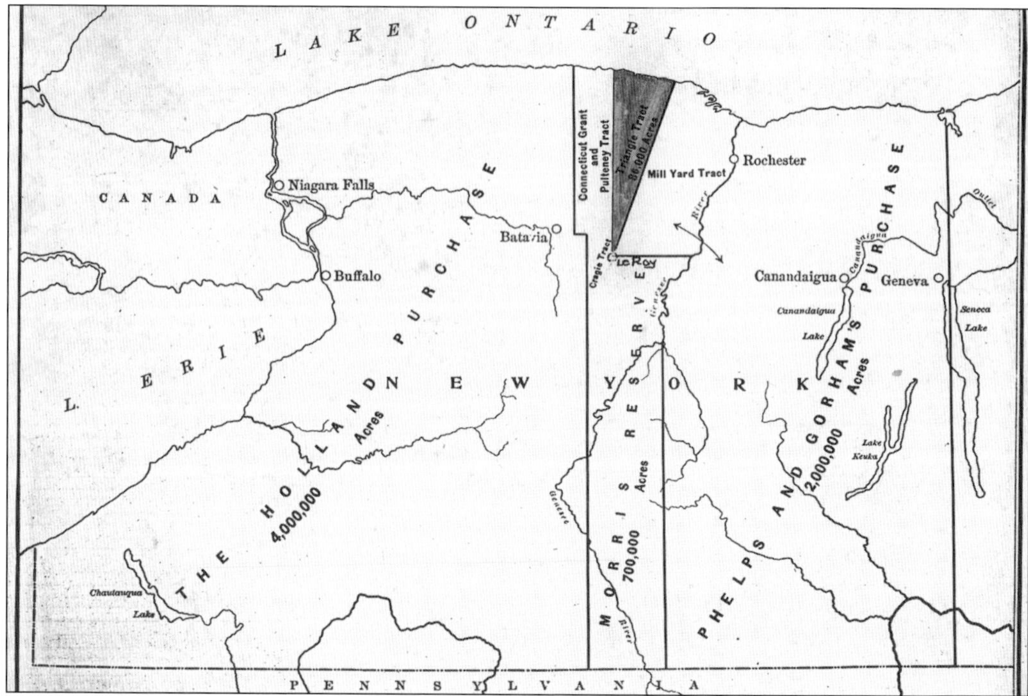

Map of the Triangle Tract. The Triangle Tract was the result of an error made when the Mill Tract was surveyed by Col. Hugh Maxwell. Erroneously, the measurement was made from the Genesee River in Avon, not from the mouth of the Genesee River at Lake Ontario. The mistake took 87,000 acres from the Native Americans. A new survey by Judge Porter corrected the error and created the Triangle Tract.

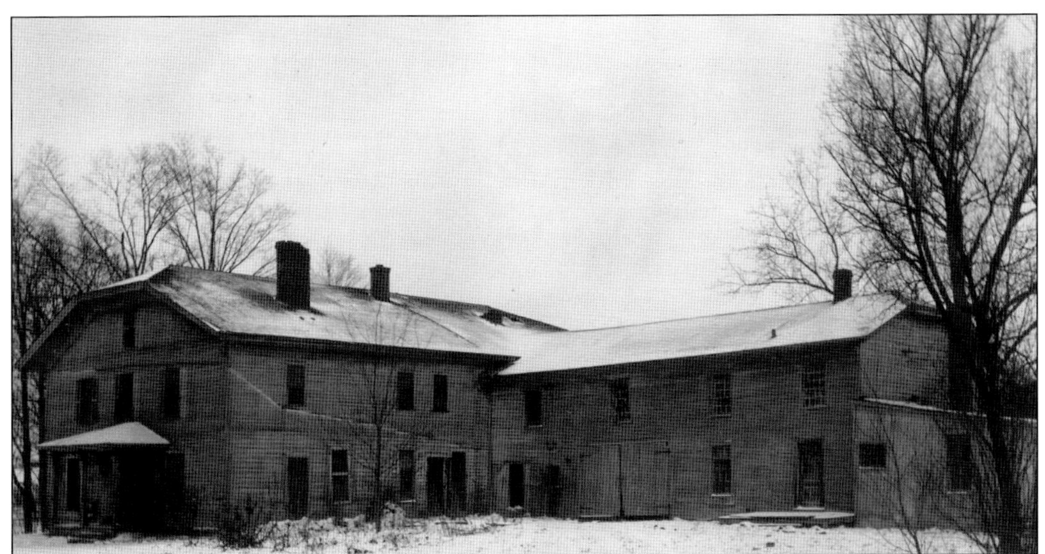

The Ganson Inn. In 1797, Charles Wilbor built a log cabin a mile east of the creek on the Great Niagara Road. A year later, he sold the cabin to Capt. John Ganson, who established an inn and tavern, which he later enlarged. The area became known as the Ganson Settlement. The Ganson homestead was razed in 1934. The site is commemorated by a historical marker.

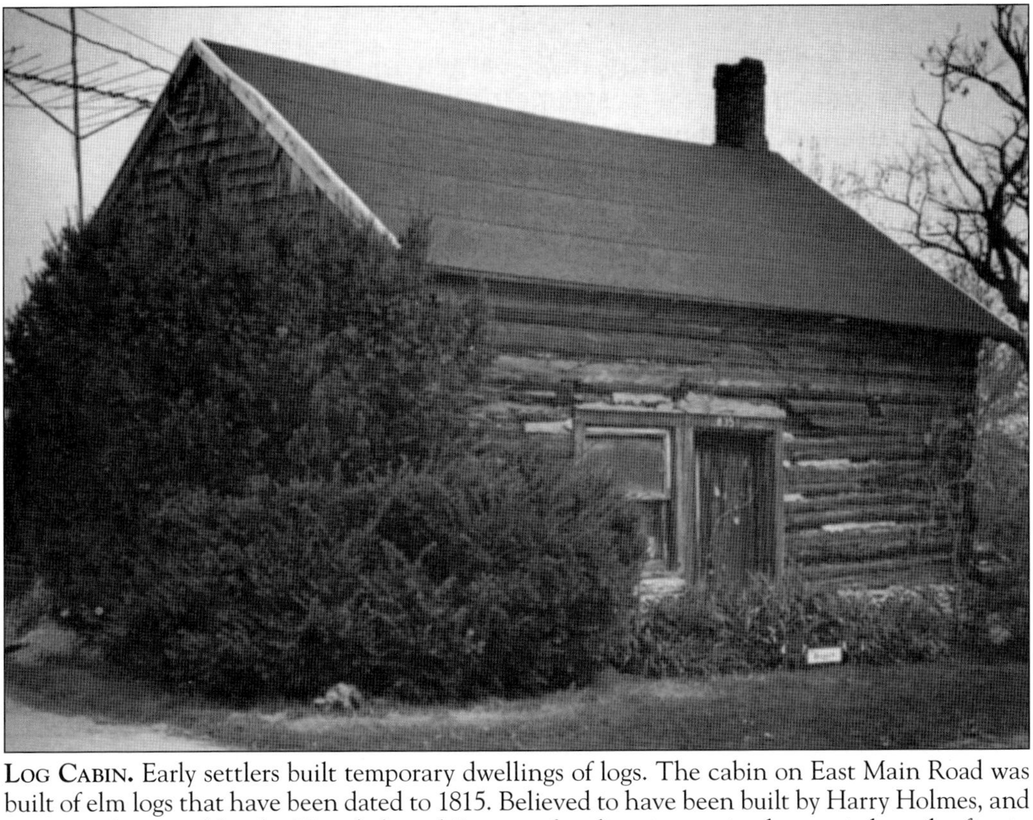

Log Cabin. Early settlers built temporary dwellings of logs. The cabin on East Main Road was built of elm logs that have been dated to 1815. Believed to have been built by Harry Holmes, and successively owned by the Heimlich and Sprague families, it remained occupied until a fire in 2005. It was condemned and razed in 2009.

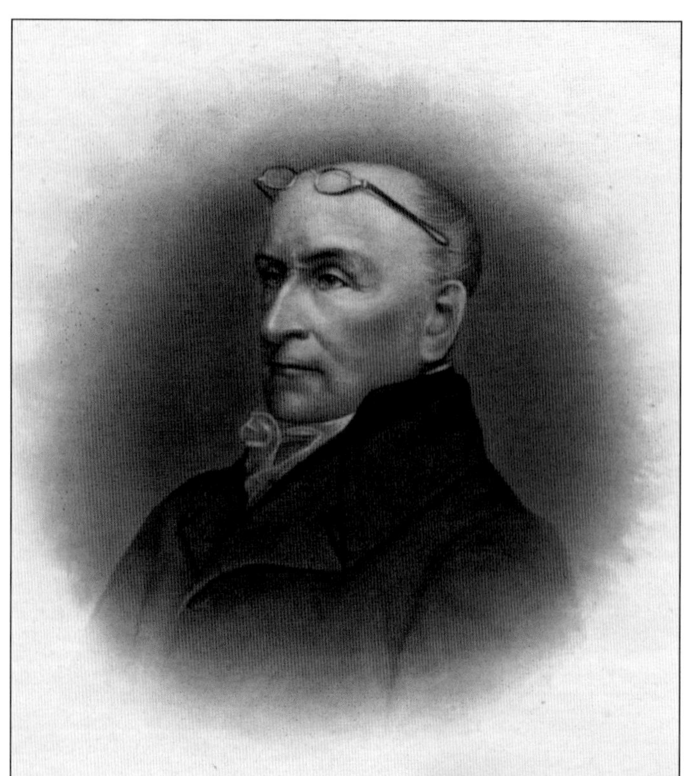

Herman LeRoy (1758–1841). The town was named for this wealthy New York City merchant and land speculator. He served as president of the Bank of New York from 1802 to 1804 and was a member of one of the old Knickerbocker families. There is no indication that he ever visited the town that carried his name. His brother Daniel bequeathed Herman "generosity and gratitude, both of which he is of need of."

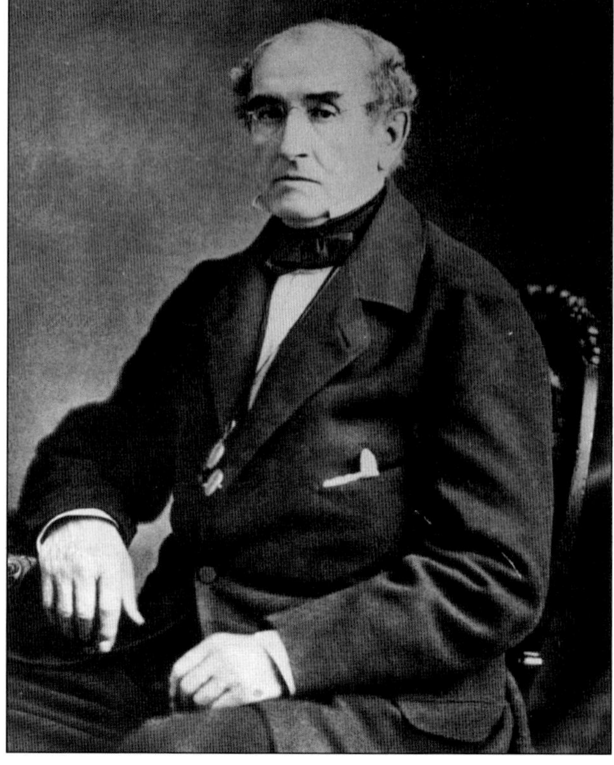

Jacob LeRoy (1794—1861). Son of Herman LeRoy, Jacob moved to town in 1822 and served as land agent for the Triangle Tract until he returned to New York City in 1837. He married Charlotte Otis, and 9 of their 10 children were born in LeRoy House. Two of Jacob's brothers, Daniel and Edward, followed him to the area. Jacob served as the first president of the Genesee County Agricultural Society.

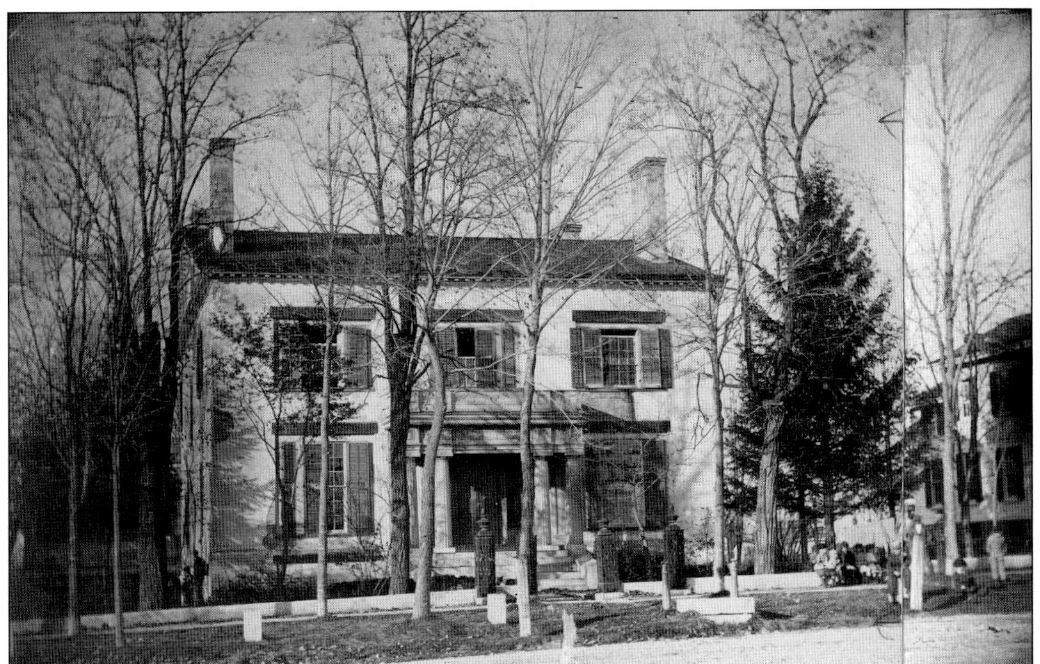

LeRoy House. This building served as land office for the Triangle Tract office. It was enlarged in 1822 by Jacob LeRoy and made into a residence with a ballroom. The garden was surrounded by a wall covered with broken glass to discourage intruders. It became the home of Rev. Samuel Cox, chancellor of Ingham University in the 1850s. In the 1870s, it was a boardinghouse for students and faculty of the LeRoy Academic Institute.

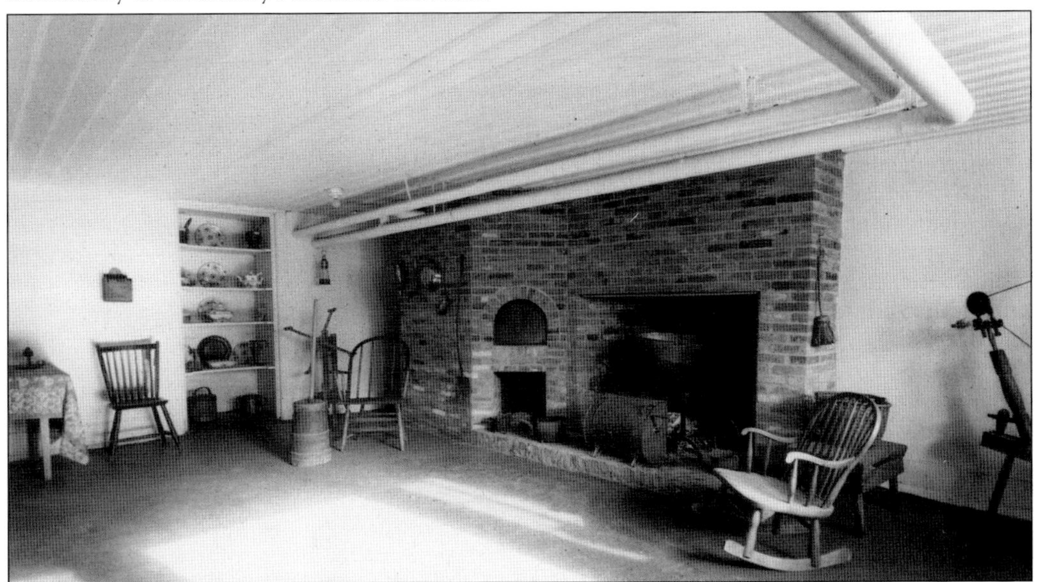

LeRoy House Kitchen. Since 1943, LeRoy House has been a museum. The basement kitchen, with open hearth and brick oven, was restored in 1946. Charlotte LeRoy's 1822 manuscript cookbook is in the LeRoy Historical Society's archives. It contains recipes for lemon cakes, puddings, boiled calf's head, and mock turtle soup. Mrs. LeRoy had servants, including a cook and a governess for the children.

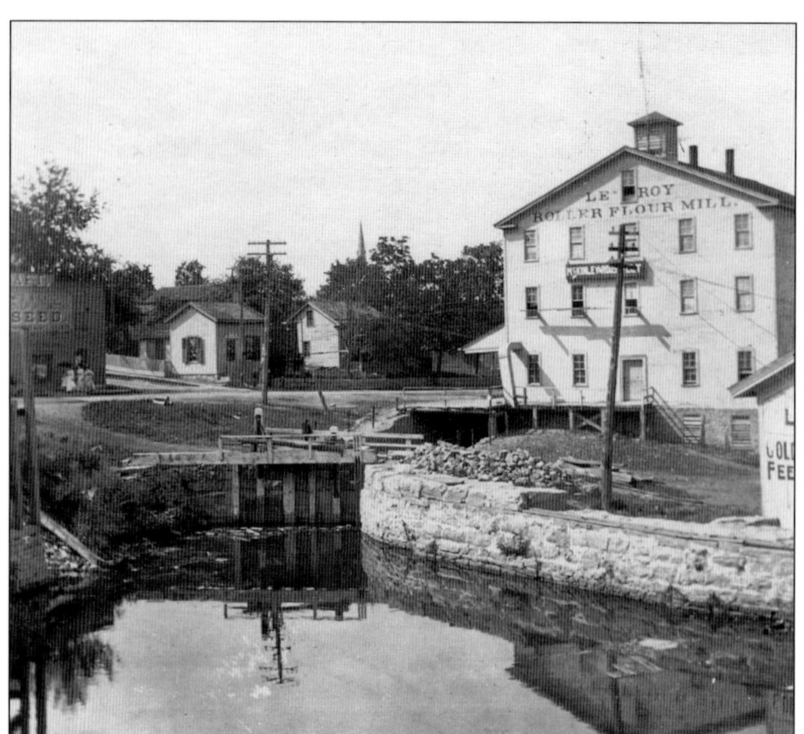

LeRoy Mill. Ezra Platt and Richard Stoddard built the first mill in 1802. In 1822, it was enlarged by Jacob LeRoy. Joshua Lathrop acquired the mill and sent a barrel of flour to Queen Victoria in 1851. Charles Prentice bought the mill in 1865. He used the mill to generate electricity in 1884. It was razed in 1923 and the cornerstone, dated 1822, was placed in Ernest Woodward's garden wall.

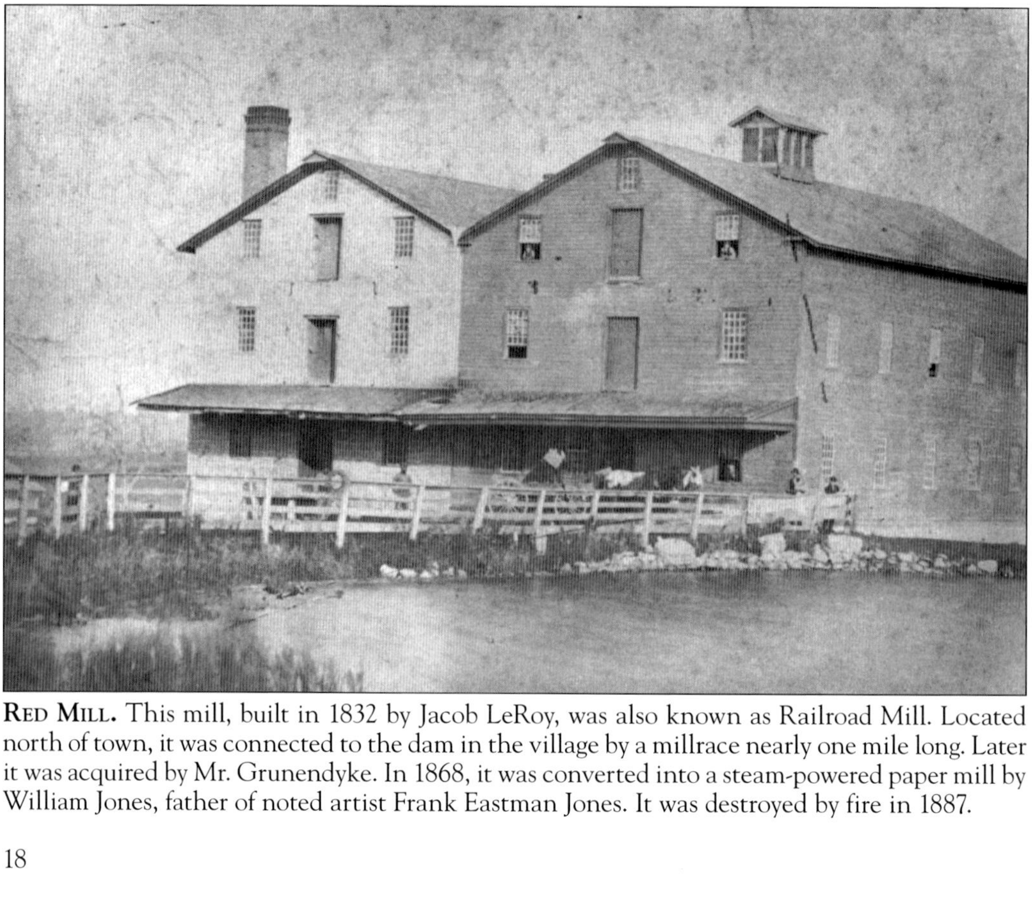

Red Mill. This mill, built in 1832 by Jacob LeRoy, was also known as Railroad Mill. Located north of town, it was connected to the dam in the village by a millrace nearly one mile long. Later it was acquired by Mr. Grunendyke. In 1868, it was converted into a steam-powered paper mill by William Jones, father of noted artist Frank Eastman Jones. It was destroyed by fire in 1887.

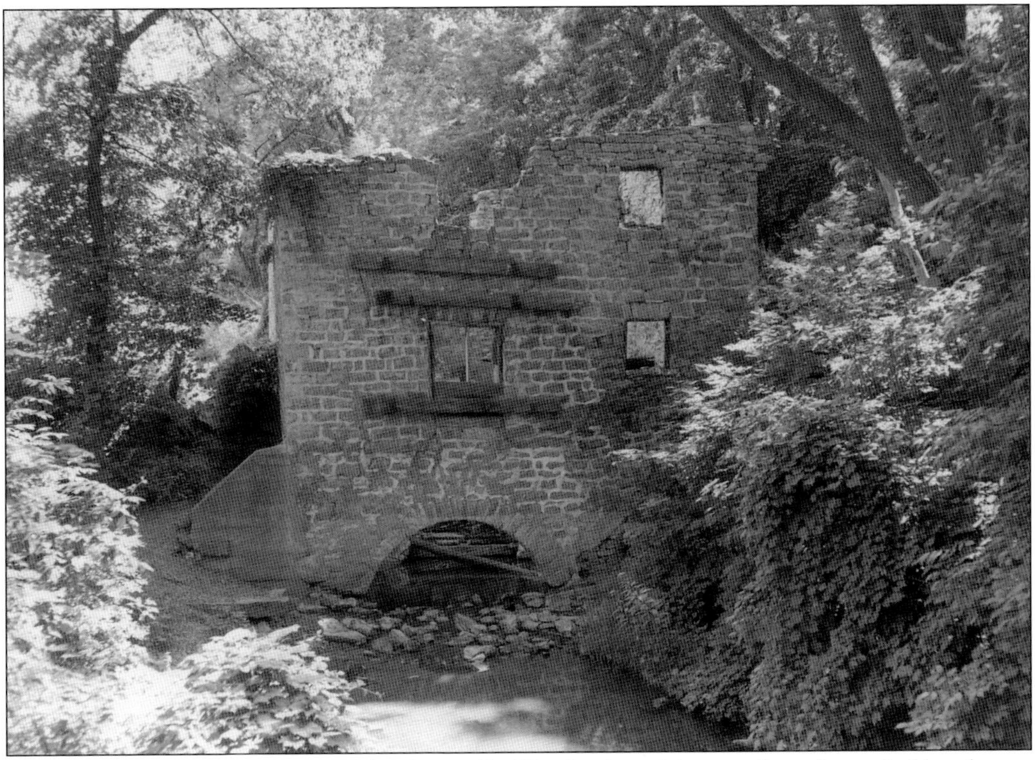

Haskins Mill Ruins and Dam. The dam at Red Bridge (now Munson Street) supplied headwater for mills on both sides of the creek. On the east was Knowlton Rich's stonecutting mill, which cut limestone for the Genesee County courthouse in Batavia. On the west was a carding mill that was converted to a flour mill by John Haskins. It was in operation until the late 1800s. The dam was rebuilt in 1850 but washed out in a flood in 1856 and was rebuilt again. The ruins of Haskins Mill were destroyed when the Munson Street bridge was rebuilt.

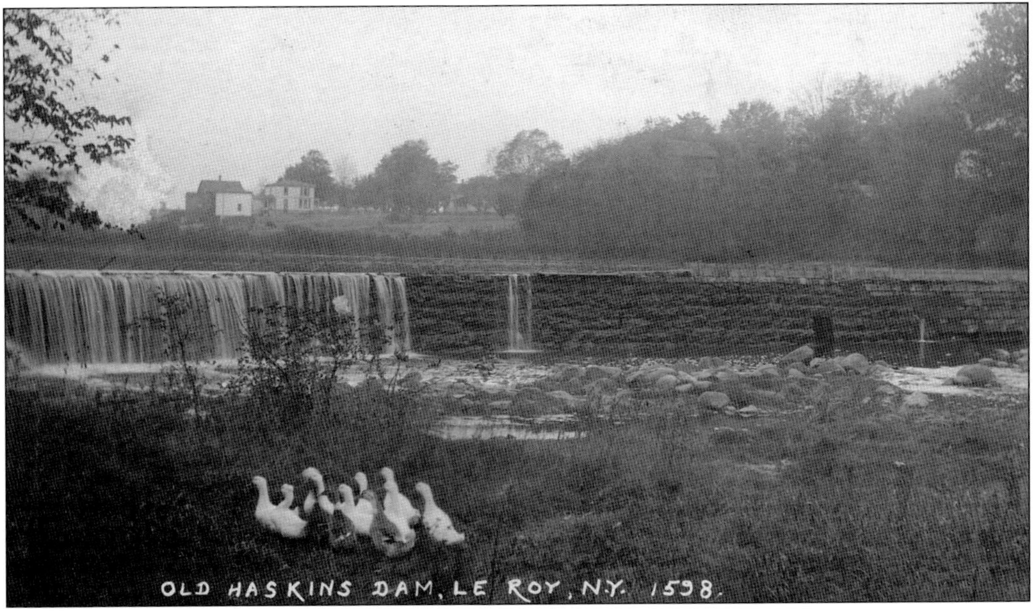

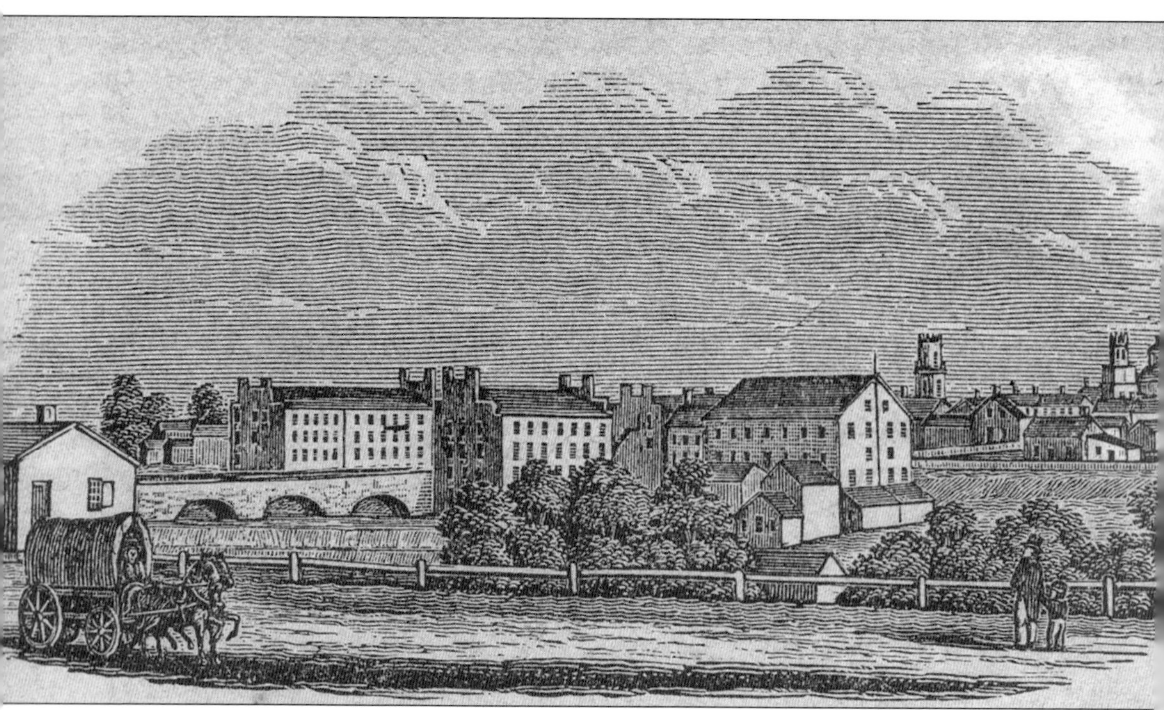

View of LeRoy, 1840. This view is taken from the *Historical Collections of the State of New York*. In the foreground is Church Street. On the left, at the east end of the Main Street bridge, is a factory that was later dismantled and the stone used for St. Mark's Episcopal Church. The three large buildings are, from left to right, Ballard's hat "manufactory" (now the Creekside), which is connected to the Eagle Hotel, the "Dock" (site of the post office), and the LeRoy Flour Mill. The three steeples are, from left to right, the Presbyterian Church, the tower of the Round House, and the dome of the Round House. The three-arch bridge was the second bridge over the Oatka and was replaced by the 1855 iron-arch bridge.

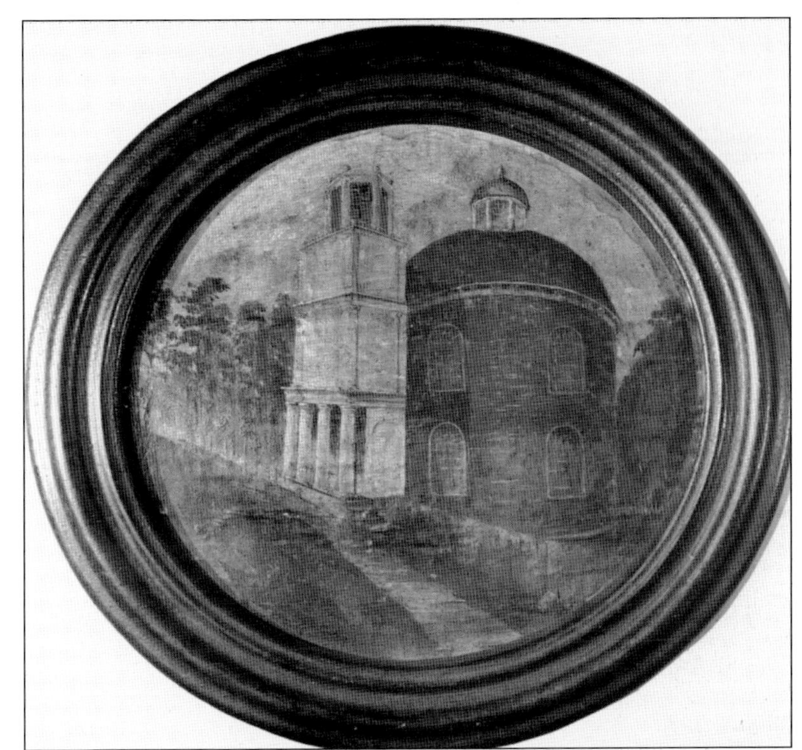

The Round House. The Round House was erected in 1825 as a Masonic lodge. There are no known photographs of this historically significant building. It became a school and meetinghouse and was never used as a Masonic lodge because of the disruption caused by the Morgan Anti-Masonic affair in 1826. The Universalist Society bought the building in 1859 and had it torn down. (Painting owned by the Olive Branch Masonic Lodge.)

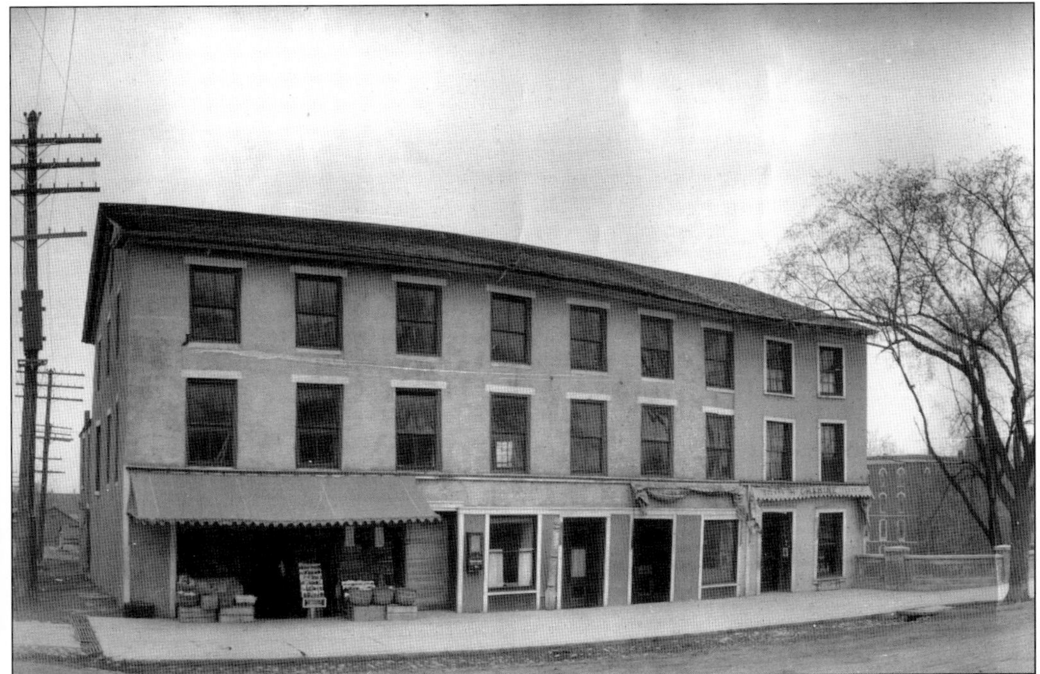

The Dock. This building is shown in the center of the "1840 View of LeRoy" at the west end of the bridge. There were a variety of merchants and shops in the dock, including the office of Sidney Grannis, who claimed that Fredrick Douglass stopped here while traveling on the Underground Railroad. The building was razed for the post office.

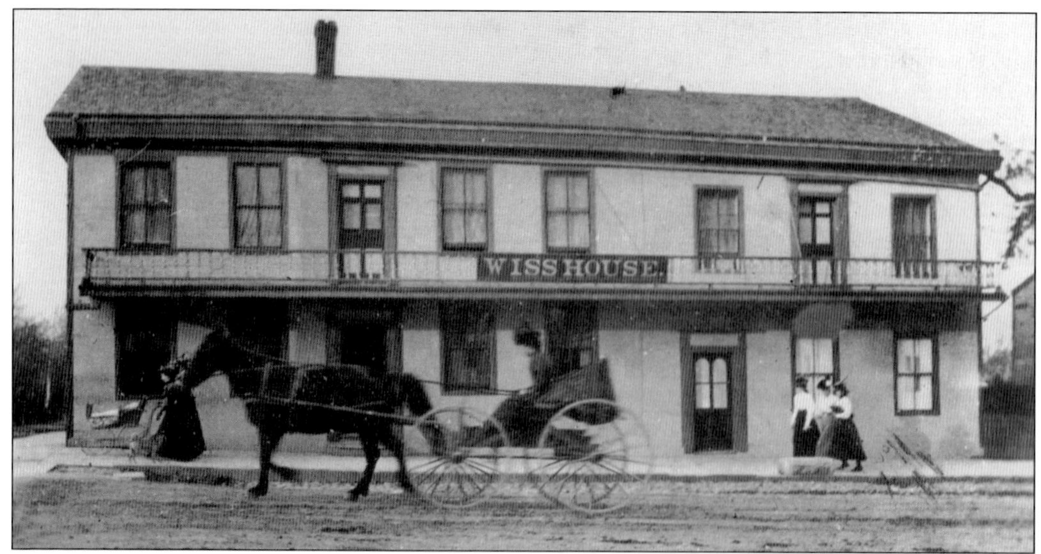

Wiss Hotel, c. 1900. Located on the corner of Main and Lake Streets, the frame building was built in 1802. Originally a store, it became the Globe and Eagle Tavern, noted for its sign with a large golden eagle perched on a globe. It has been known as the Graves Tavern, Ballard's Tavern, the Collins House, and Michel House. In 1869, it was purchased by John Wiss. It closed in 2005.

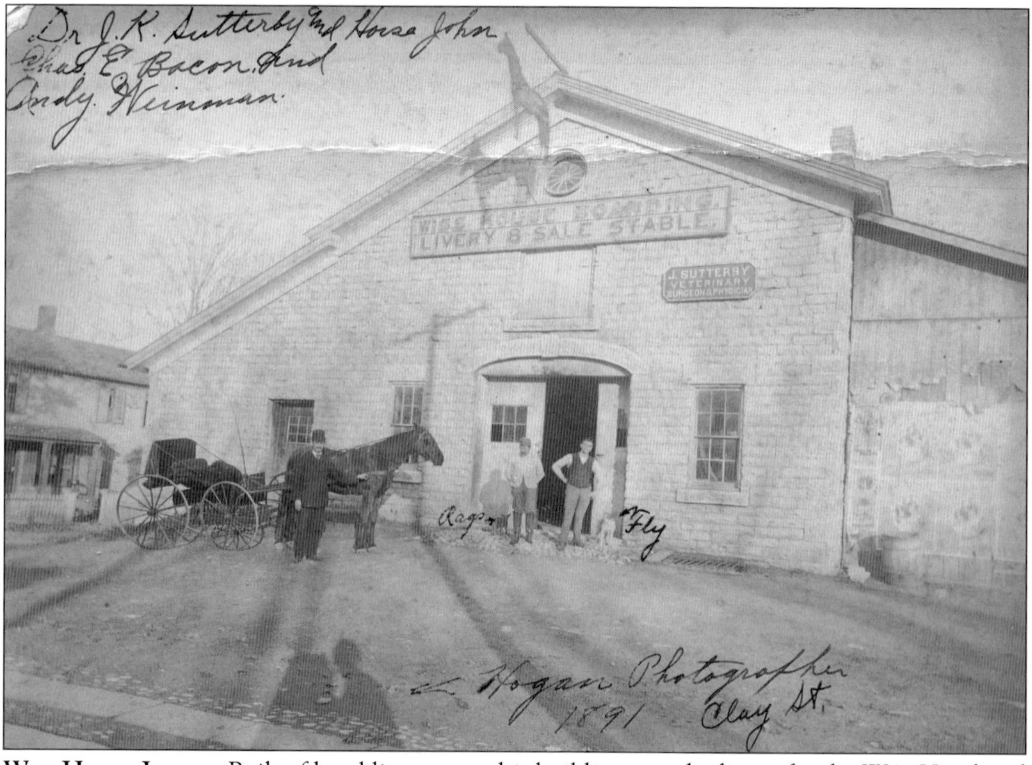

Wiss Hotel Livery. Built of local limestone, this building was the livery for the Wiss Hotel and Dr. Sutterby's veterinary. The picture taken in 1891 shows, from left to right, Dr. J. K. Sutterby with his horse, John; a small black dog, Rags; Charles Bacon; Andy Weinman; and a white dog, Fly. Later the building became a gas station and garage. Today it is leased by NAPA Auto Parts.

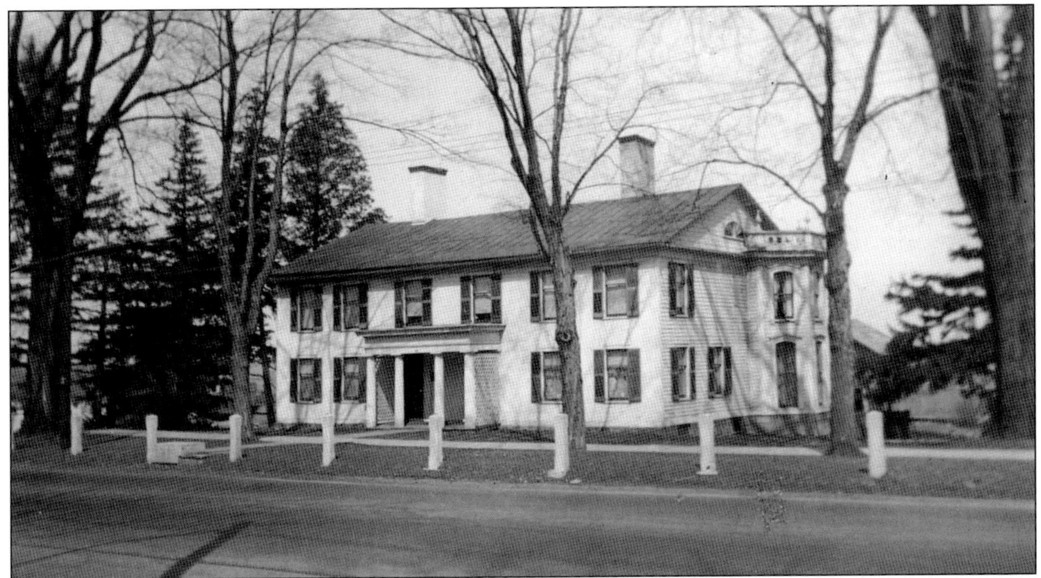

LENT TAVERN. Built about 1810 by Thomas Tufts, land agent for the 20,000-acre Craigie Tract, the structure was bought by John Lent in 1813, who then opened this tavern. He was involved with financial investments in the area and was a bank president. At the time of his death in 1861, Lent was considered the richest man in LeRoy. Located on West Main Street, the tavern is now a private residence.

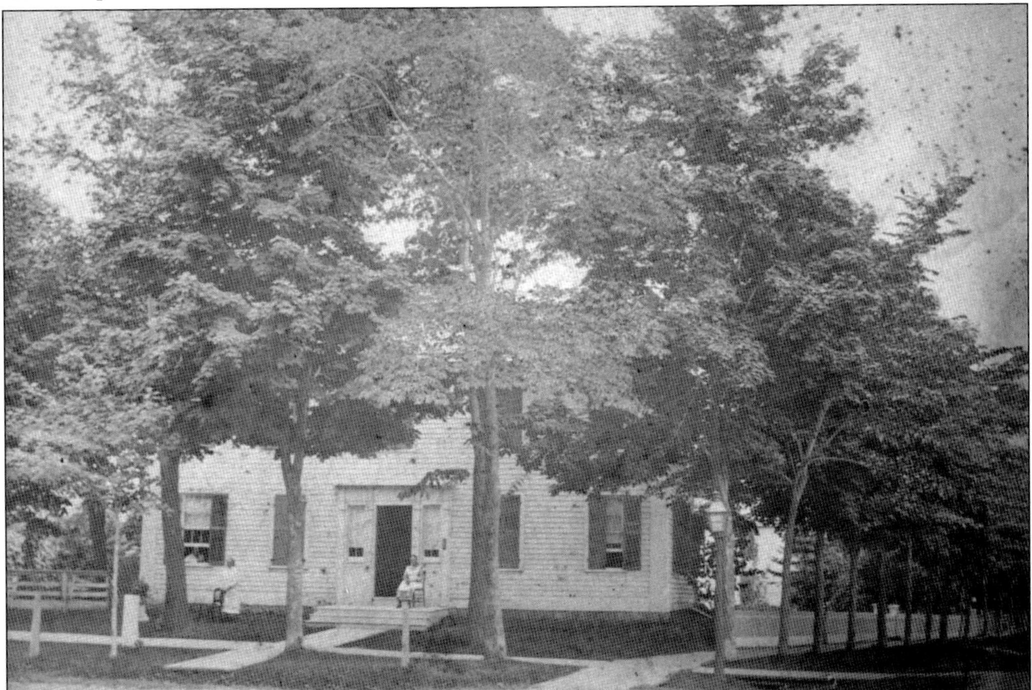

FRONTIER INN. James Ganson built a residence on the corner of South Street (known as Frontier Road) and East Main Street in 1819. Shortly afterwards, it was converted into an inn and tavern. Later it was sold to Sydney Hosmer, and it became known as the Hosmer Inn. In the late 1800s, a mansard roof was added. It is now an apartment building.

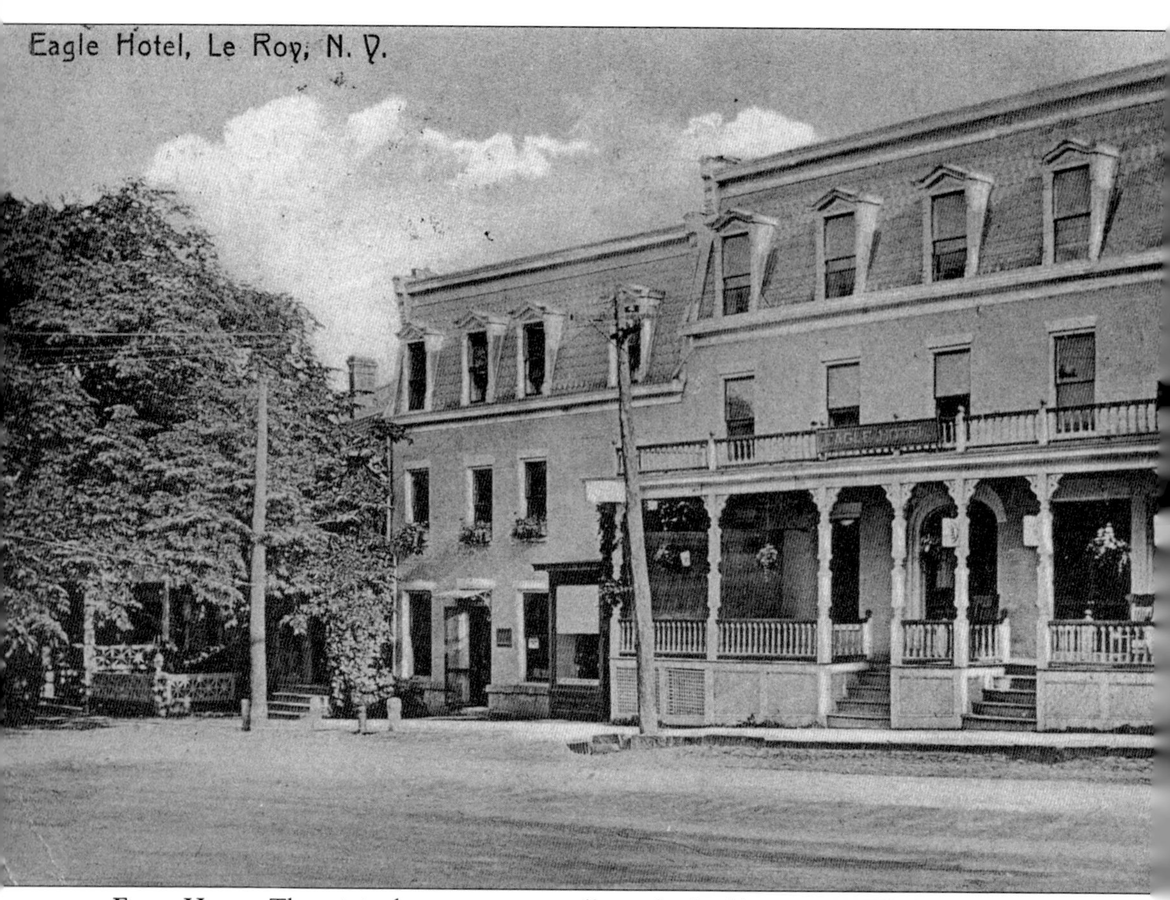

Eagle Hotel. The original tavern was a small wooden building operated by "Auntie" Wemple. In 1825, James Ganson erected this building with bricks manufactured by LeRoy's first brickmaker, Uni Hulbert. The addition to the east was added two years later with a passage between the two buildings to allow stagecoaches to enter the livery in the rear. The passageway was removed in 1848. The first village meeting was held at the Eagle Hotel on May 5, 1834. The large porch on the front was removed in 1937.

Two

Churches and Cemeteries

LeRoy's landscape is dotted with church steeples. Three years after the first settlers arrived, missionaries held services at Ganson's Tavern. Early congregations met at schoolhouses until they could raise funds to buy land and erect church buildings. The first religious organization was formed on February 4, 1812, by a group of Congregationalists. Two years later, they united with the Presbyterians. The Episcopalians met on April 8, 1817, and formed St. Mark's Episcopal Church. Shortly after, on June 25, 1818, a group of Baptists met at the Langworthy School to organize a church. Early in 1823, twelve people organized the First Class of the Methodist Episcopal Church of LeRoy. The First Universalist Society was organized in 1831 and held meetings at the Round House on West Main Street. The First Congregational Church, also known as the Church of God in LeRoy, was organized on April 16, 1843. They met in a building on the site of the present-day Municipal Building but disbanded in the early 1870s. The German Lutherans were organized on March 23, 1895. The Roman Catholic congregation first met at the Round House for Holy Mass in April 1849 and established St. Francis Church. It would later become St. Peter's Church. On February 15, 1907, Fr. Joseph Gambino arrived in LeRoy to lead St. Joseph's Church. A day later, he held services at the Lime Rock school and established St. Anthony's Church. The Second Baptist Church began in 1915 in the home of Emma Alexander. Calvary Baptist Church was founded on November 8, 1972.

There are 10 cemeteries in LeRoy and 8 of them are listed as abandoned and are under the care of the town. The oldest is located on East Main Road. The Fort Hill Cemetery on Parmelee Road is the final resting place of Roswell Parmelee, a veteran of the French and Indian War. The old Presbyterian burying ground is located on Myrtle Street, and Old St. Mark's Episcopal Cemetery is located on Church Street. The two active cemeteries are Machpelah Cemetery on North Street and St. Francis Cemetery on Exchange Street.

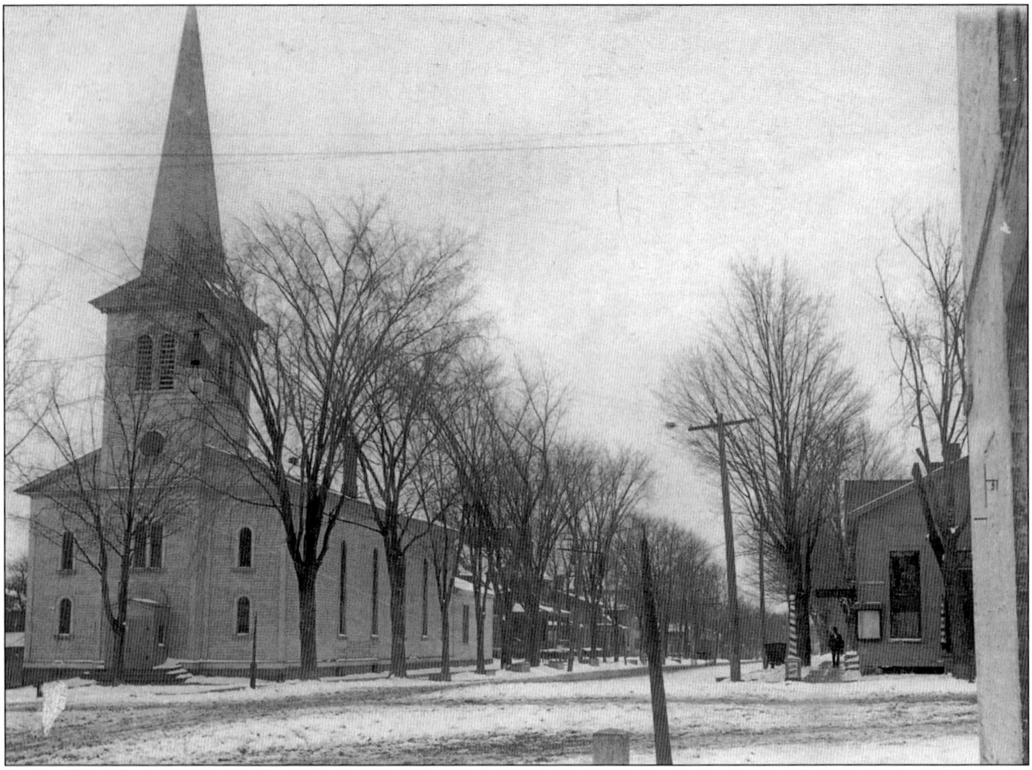

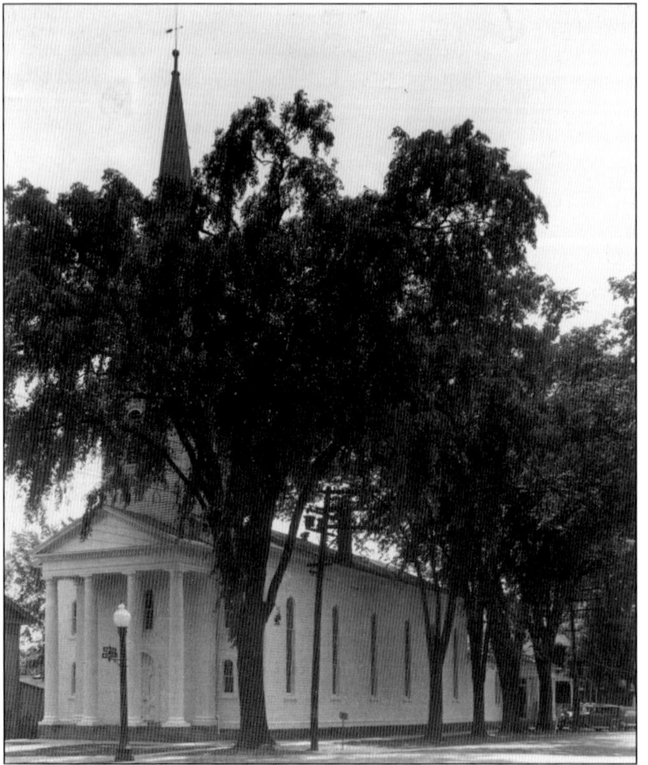

First Presbyterian Church. The church, located at the corner of Clay and Main Streets, was dedicated in 1826. The steeple was added to the bell tower in 1866. The Greek Revival portico and columns were added in the 1920s (left). It was the site of several abolition meetings and was affiliated with Ingham University.

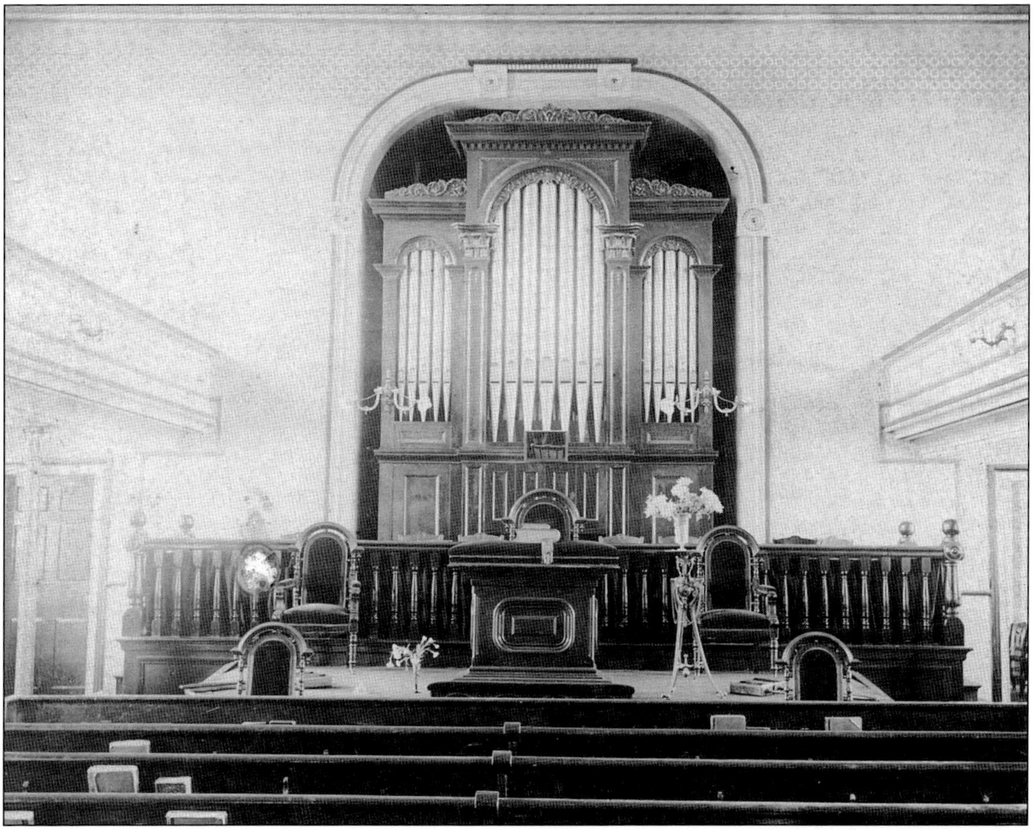

INTERIOR OF PRESBYTERIAN CHURCH, 1900. Music at the First Presbyterian Church was accompanied by a melodeon until 1866. The first pipe organ was installed in the north end of the upper gallery. In 1898, the organ was moved to the front of the sanctuary. In 1906, the old organ was replaced by a Beaudry organ manufactured in LeRoy.

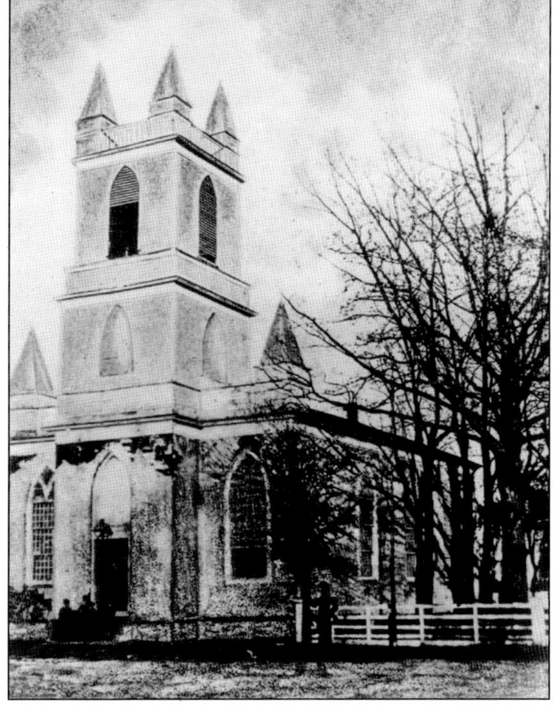

OLD ST MARK'S EPISCOPAL CHURCH. This building, located on Church Street next to the cemetery, was consecrated in 1827. Jacob LeRoy was a member of this parish. At first, the church had a huge iron triangle, but it was replaced by a bell in 1828. By the 1860s the physical condition of the building had deteriorated. When it was razed, the rubble was used for fill on Wolcott Street.

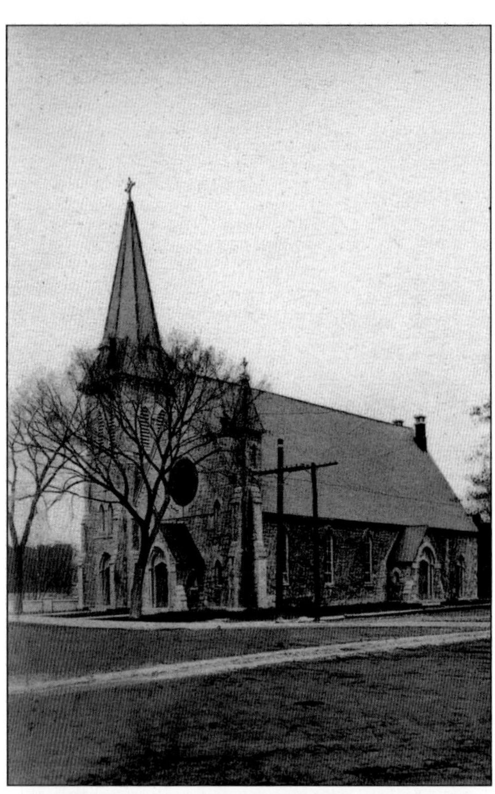

ST. MARK'S CHURCH. The cornerstone of St. Mark's Episcopal Church was laid in 1869. Stone for the new church was taken from the old factory that stood on the site. Services were held in 1870; however, the church was not consecrated until 1876. The Canon Plumley Parish House was added in 1957 with a donation from the Woodward family.

INTERIOR OF ST MARK'S. In 1876, an organ was installed in the altar niche. A boys' choir was begun in 1881.

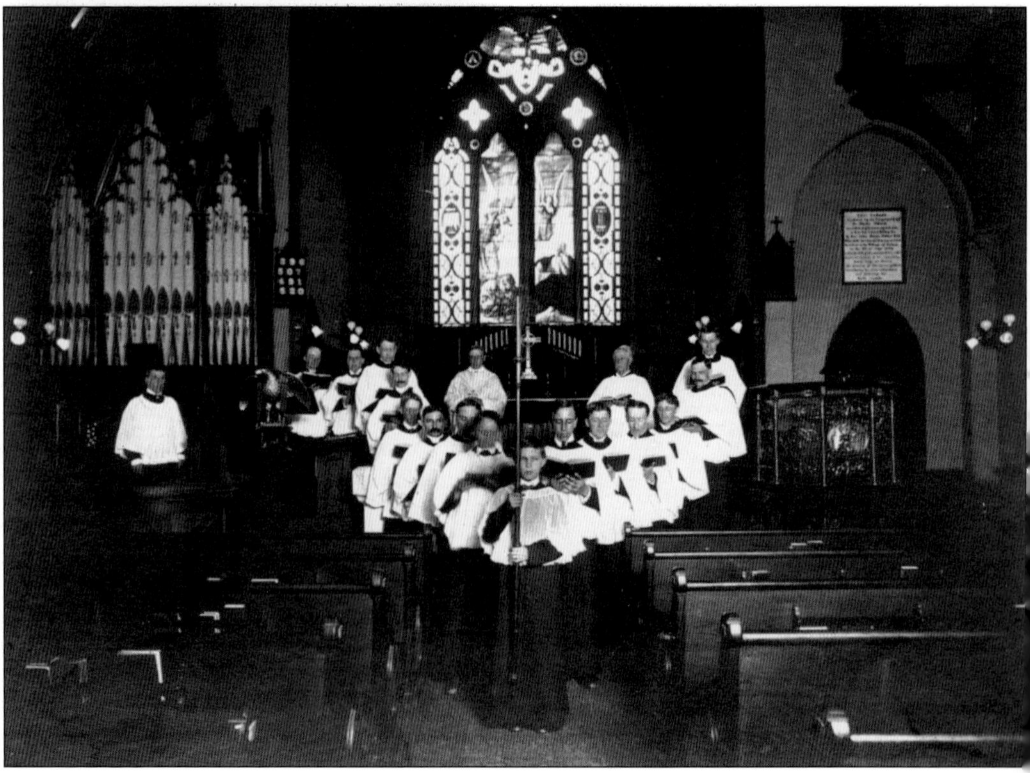

OLD BAPTIST CHURCH . The Baptist congregation was organized in 1818, and the first church was completed in 1829. It was located on the north side of lower East Main Street. In 1835, the building, shown in this photograph, was moved with teams of oxen to the east side of Church Street. In 1843, the town installed a clock in the tower.

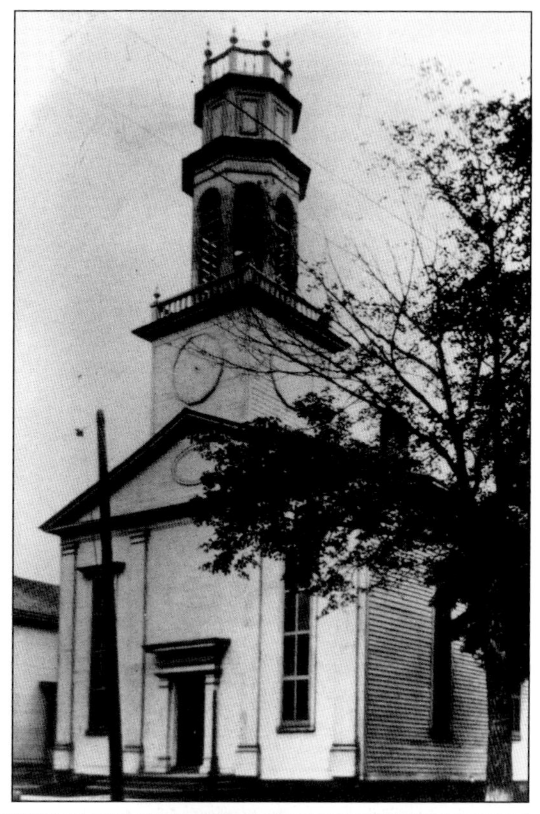

FIRST BAPTIST CHURCH. The Baptist church was moved for the second time in 1902 to its present location on East Main Street. In 1925, the church underwent extensive remodeling and the stained glass windows were removed. The church was rebuilt in the classic Colonial Revival style and the rear Sunday school building was added.

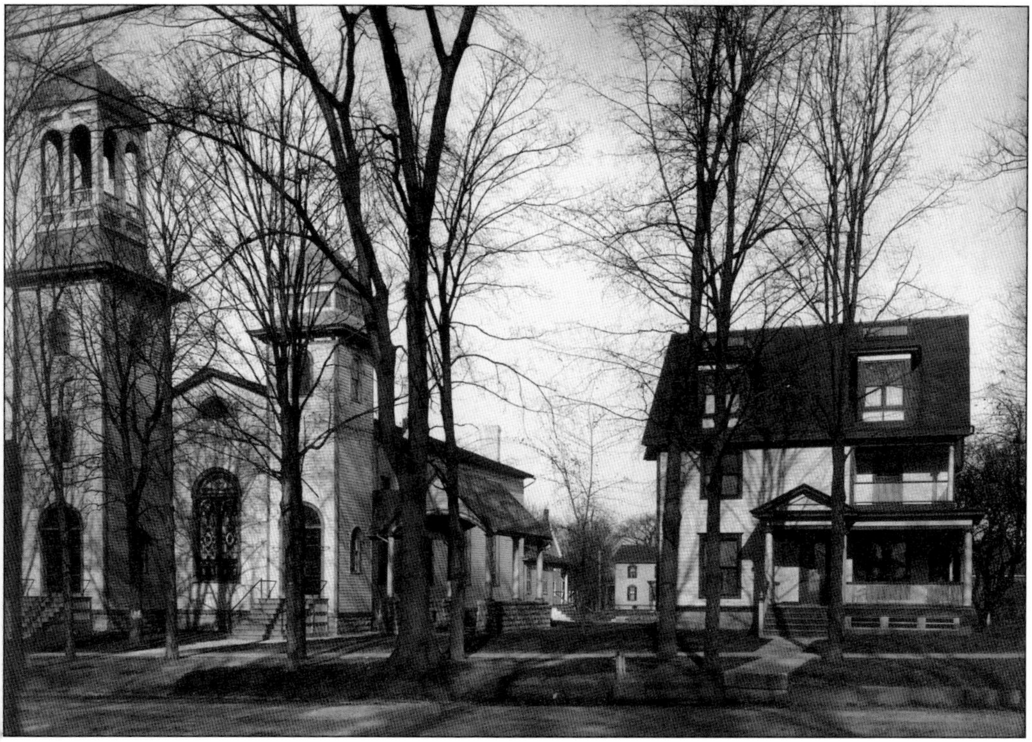

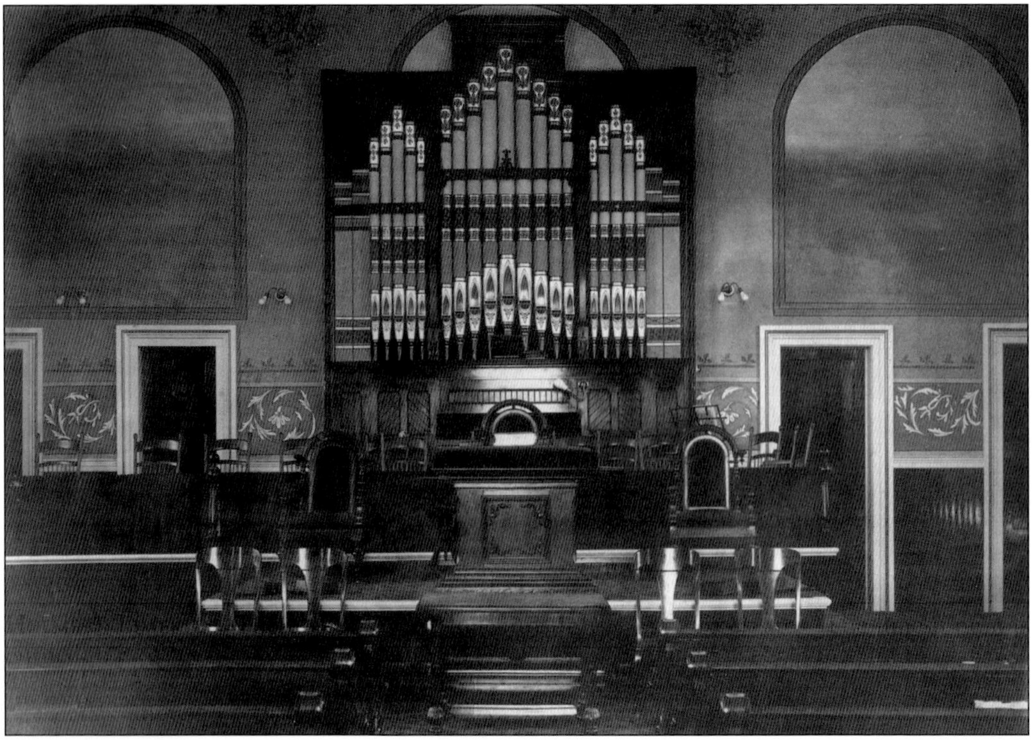

Interior of Baptist Church 1904. This photograph shows a very ornate painted interior and a massive pipe organ. The walls were painted with frescoes with a heavy Egyptian influence. These elements were removed when the church was remodeled and updated in 1925.

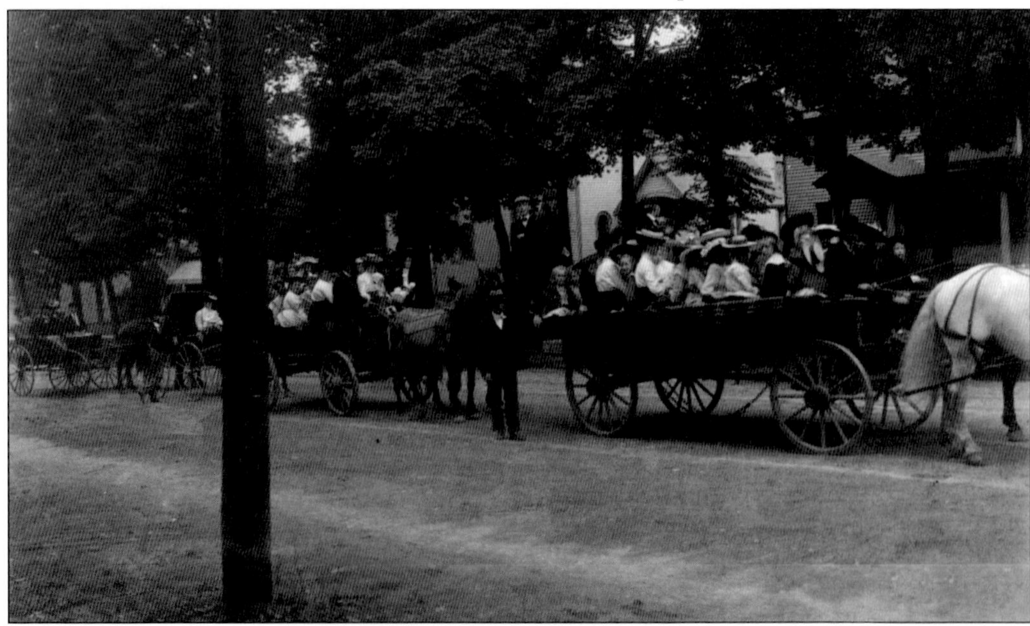

Baptist Church Picnic. In 1886, the Baptist Social Union was formed to raise money for a new organ. The Social Union held concerts, lectures, sleigh rides, maple sugar festivals, boating parties, ice cream socials, and picnics to raise money.

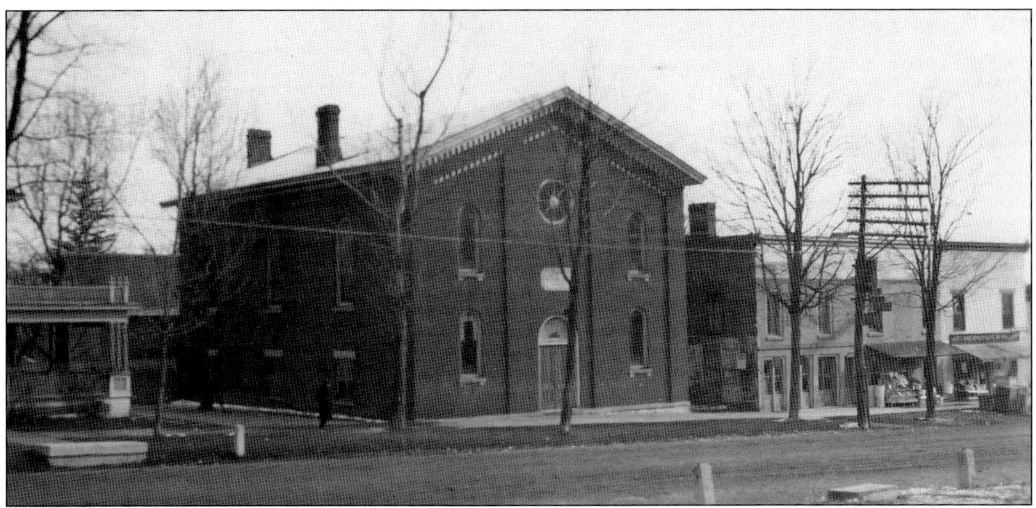

THE UNIVERSALIST CHURCH. Organized in 1831, the Universalists purchased the Round House on West Main Street in 1859 and had it torn down. It was replaced by this brick structure, which was dedicated in 1860. The society was active until the early 1900s. In 1906, the building was purchased by the Free and Accepted Masons. In 2008, the building was sold and razed. Walgreens drugstore is now on the site.

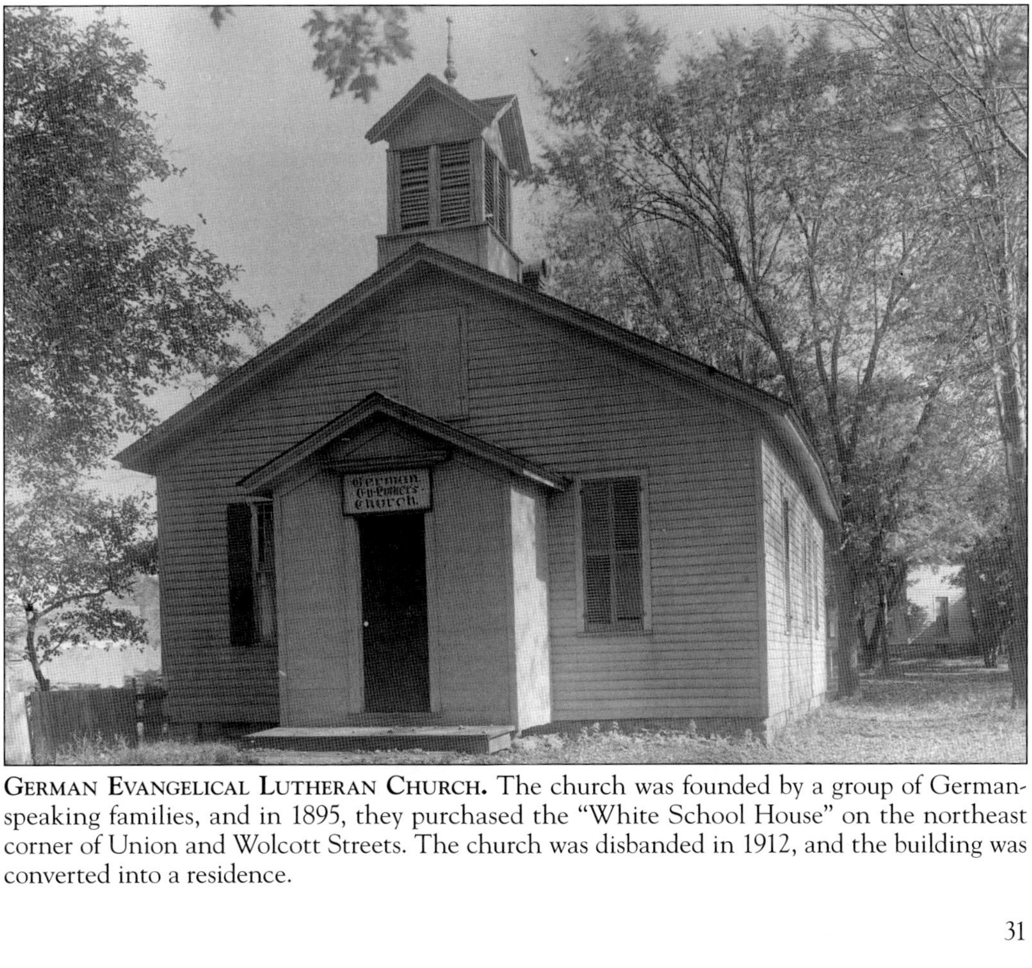

GERMAN EVANGELICAL LUTHERAN CHURCH. The church was founded by a group of German-speaking families, and in 1895, they purchased the "White School House" on the northeast corner of Union and Wolcott Streets. The church was disbanded in 1912, and the building was converted into a residence.

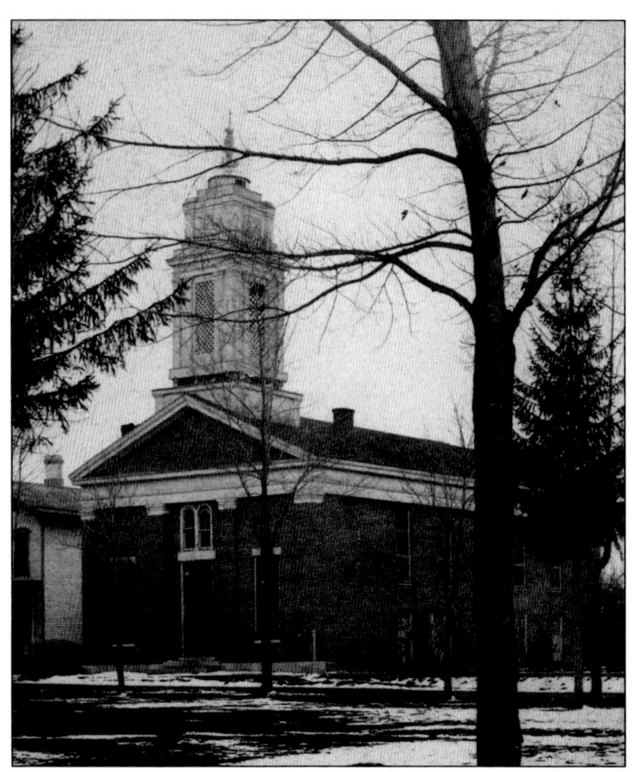

Methodist Episcopal Church. The first Methodist congregation met in 1823. In 1829, the brick church (left) was dedicated. Located on Trigon Park, it was destroyed by fire in 1884. Two years later, the limestone Richardson Romanesque building (below) was completed. The steeple was struck by lightning in 1945 and was removed, but it was restored in the 1990s.

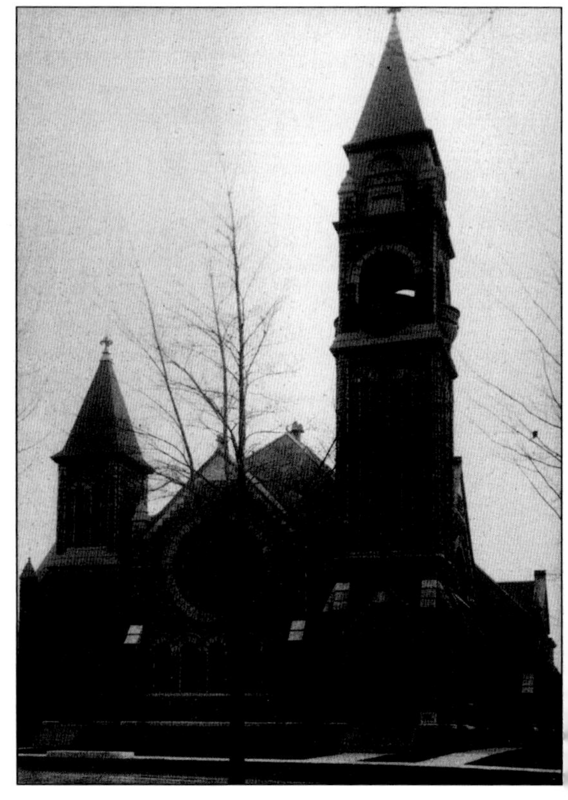

INTERIOR METHODIST EPISCOPAL CHURCH. The new church was built in the "Akron Style" with an open sanctuary surrounded by Sunday school rooms on two levels. In 1917, Cora Woodward presented the church with a pipe organ. In 1923, the Children's Chimes were donated by Donald Woodward in memory of his mother, Cora. However, structural problems in the bell tower prevent the chimes from being played.

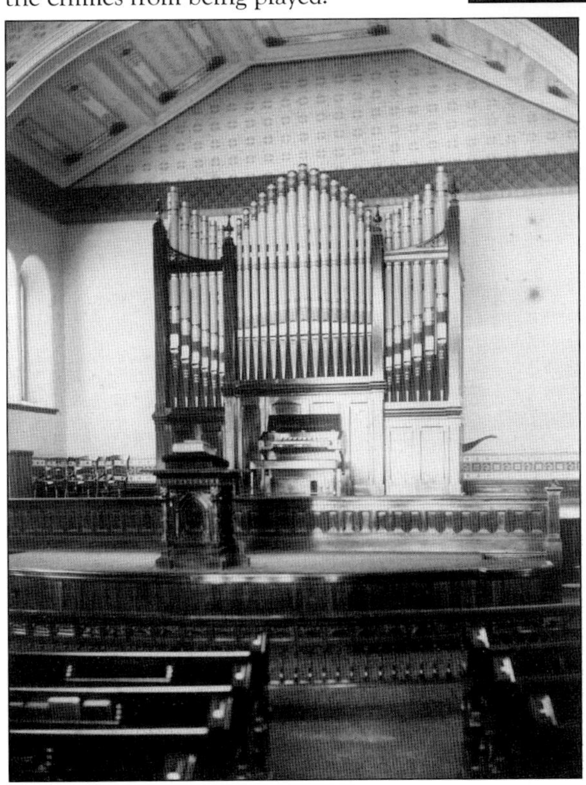

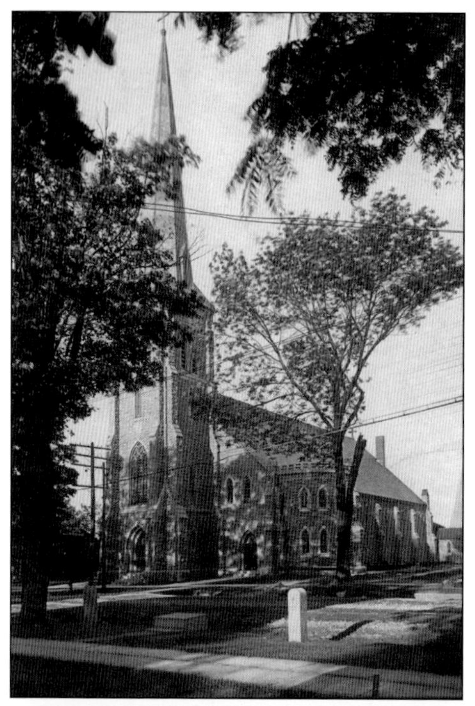

St. Peter's Catholic Church. The first Catholic Mass was held in the Round House in April 1849. Shortly afterwards, St. Francis Church was built on lower Pleasant Street and a High Christmas Mass was held in the new church in December 1849. The congregation outgrew the little church. In 1870, the cornerstone for St. Peter's Church on Lake Street was laid. Built of local limestone, the church was dedicated in 1873. The vestibules flanking the main entrance were added in 1910. In 1929, the Stations of the Cross were installed. The steeple was removed in 1930 after being hit by lightning four years earlier. St. Peter's and St. Joseph's churches were joined together in 2009 under the name of Our Lady of Mercy Parish.

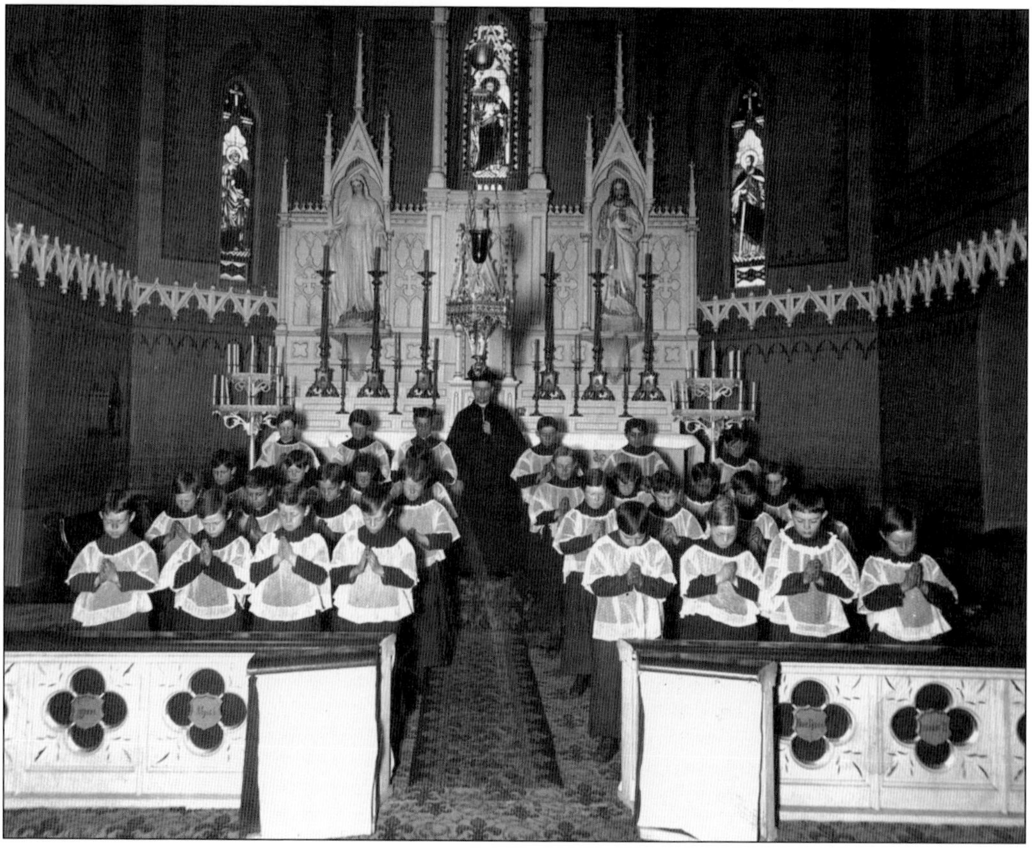

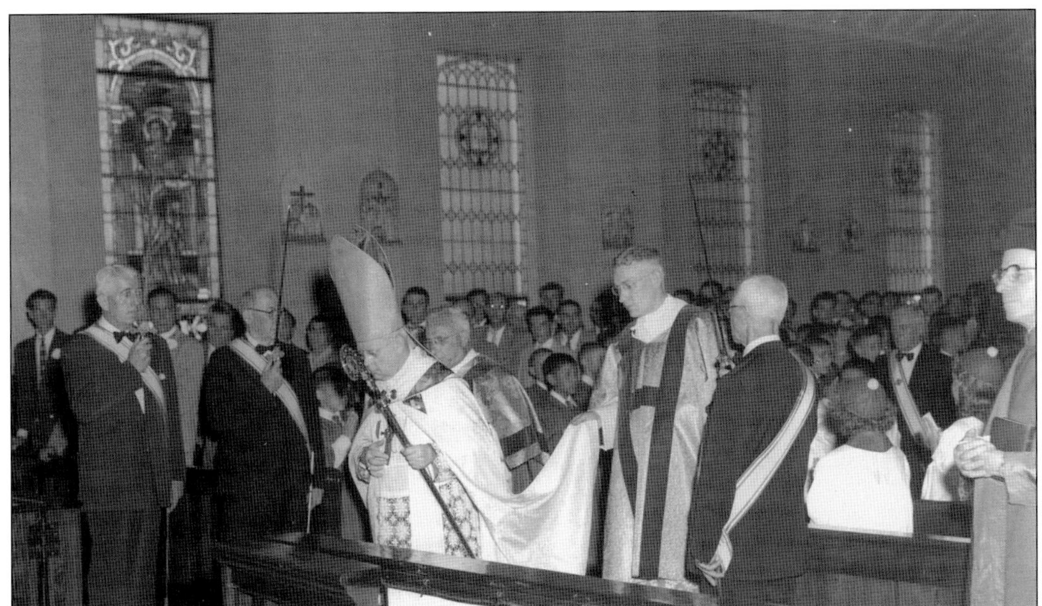

St. Joseph's Catholic Church. St. Joseph's Catholic Church Society was established in 1907 for the LeRoy Italian community under the guidance of Fr. Joseph Gambino. Ninety-eight families formed the first congregation. The church building was dedicated in 1909. The church celebrated its 100th anniversary in 2009 and is now part of Our Lady of Mercy Parish.

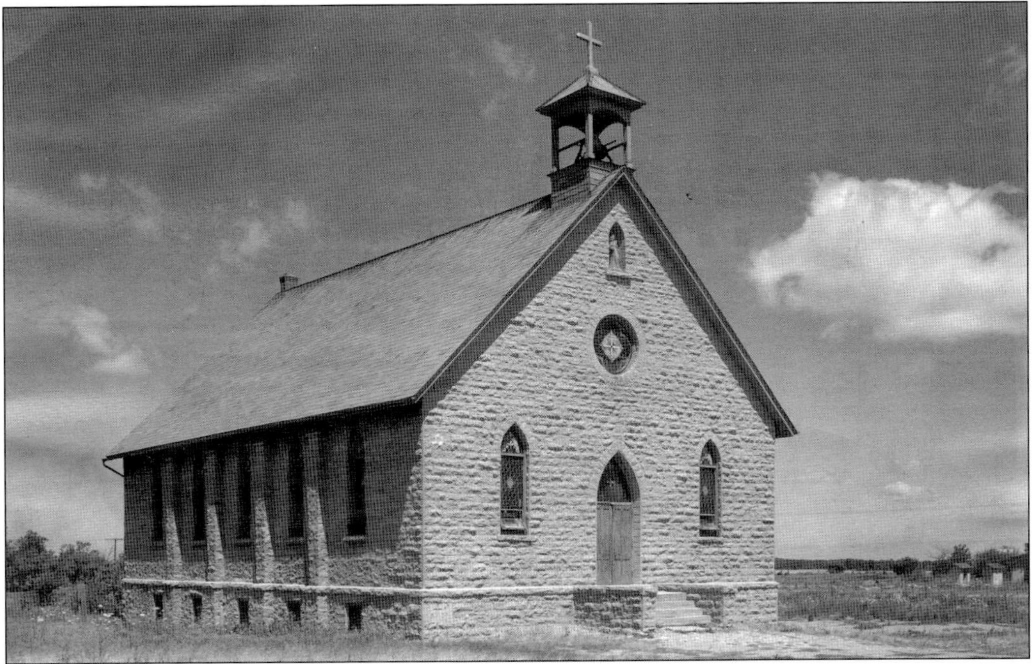

St. Anthony's Catholic Church. Located in Lime Rock, the church was built by local Italian stonemasons. Dedicated in 1909, it became a mission attached to St. Joseph's in LeRoy until 1911 when it became a separate parish. In 1925, it became attached to St. Peter's Catholic Church. It celebrated its 100th anniversary in 2009. The Buffalo Diocese closed the church the same year and the building was sold.

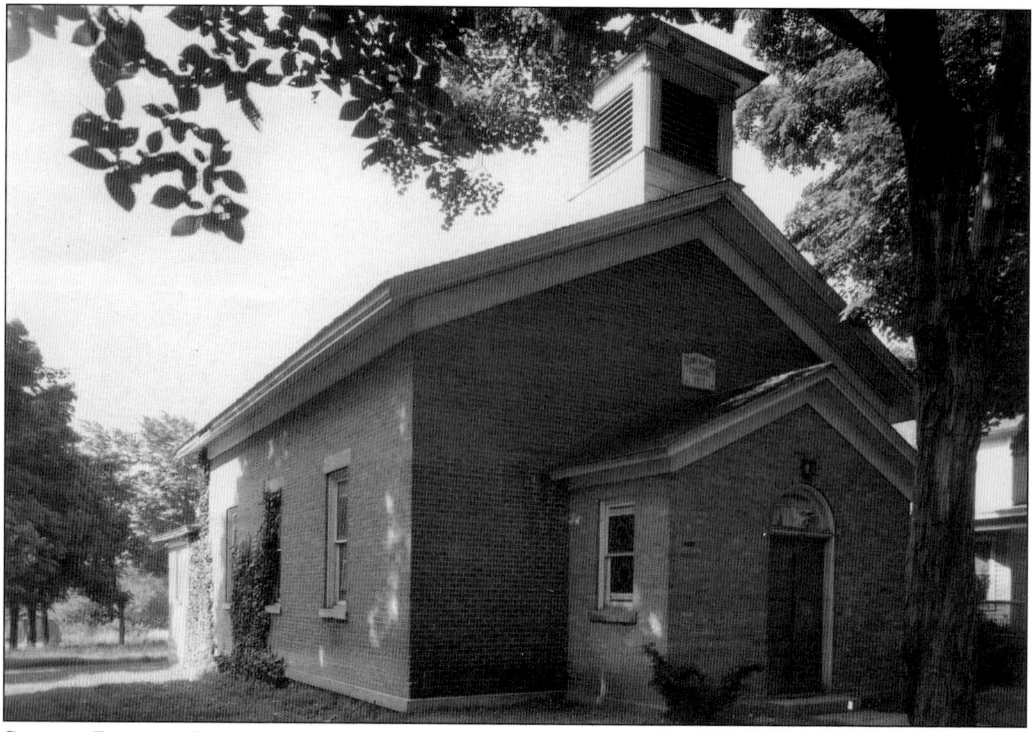

Second Baptist Church. In 1915, a small group of people met at the home of Emma Alexander and this group eventually formed the Second Baptist Church and Sunday school. In 1917, the congregation purchased the Myrtle Street School and converted it into a church. The first pastor was James E. Rose in 1915, who eventually moved to Rochester and was a pastor at Mt. Olivet Baptist Church. In 1940, the Second Baptist Church congregation is, from left to right, (first row) Mrs. W. S. Clark, Mrs. J. Green, the Reverend St. Clair Lang, Mrs. C. M. Sterverson, Mrs. M. Clark, Mrs. P. Sellers, and Mrs. S. M. Arrington; (second row) W. S. Clark, C. G. Griffin, C. E. Layne, G. I. Williams, S. M. Arrington, C. Perry, and Dorothy Burrell, organist.

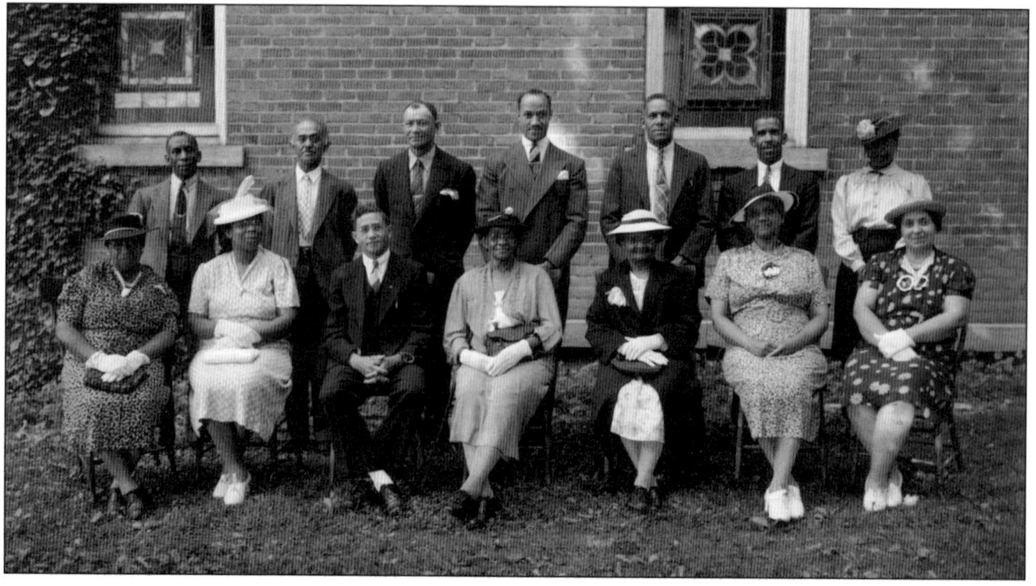

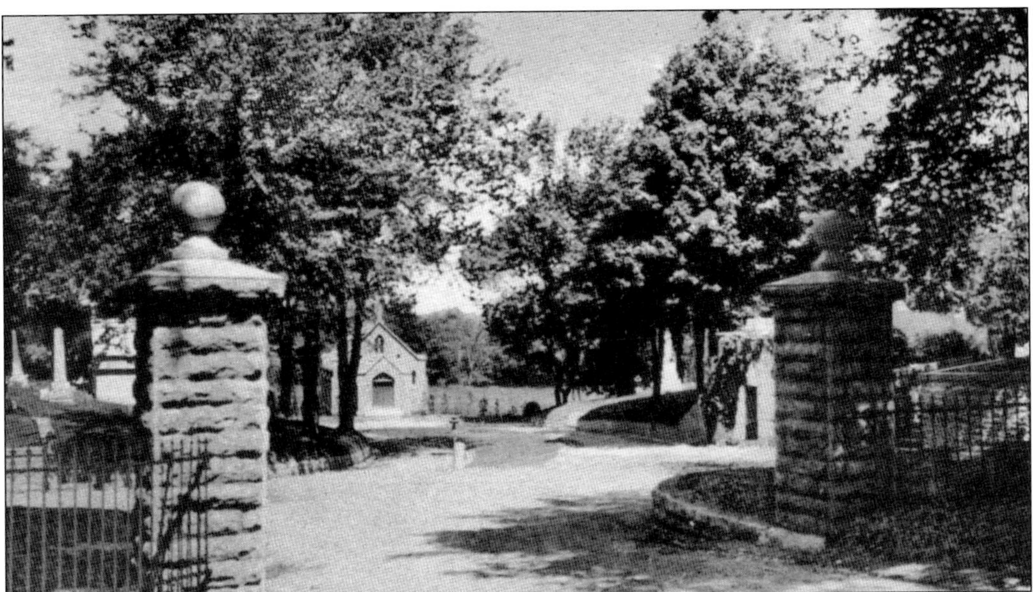

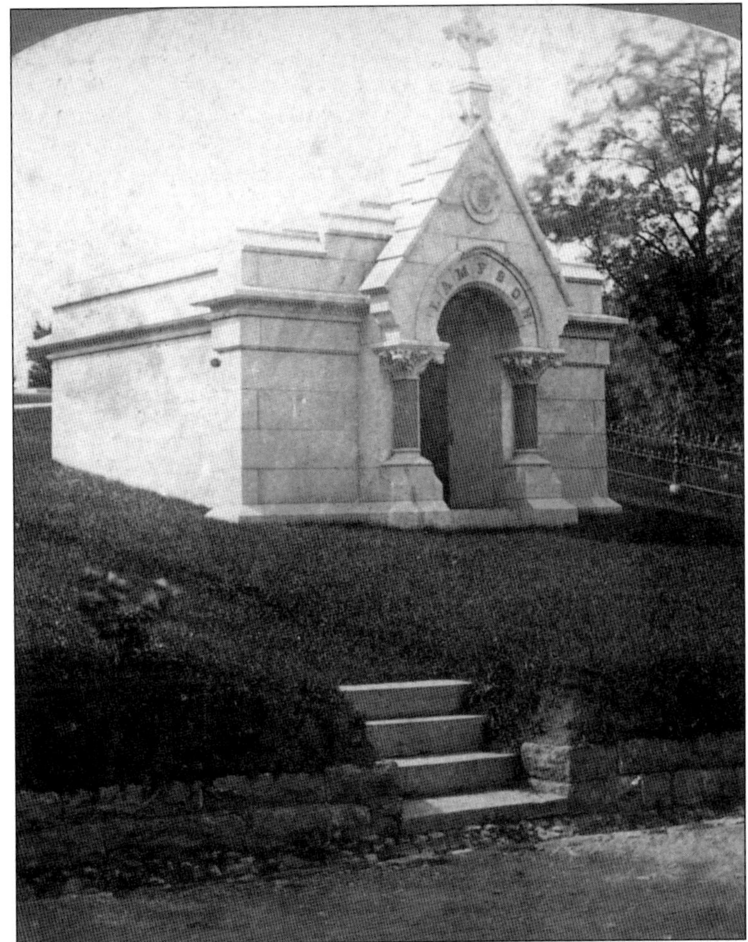

Machpelah Cemetery. The cemetery was laid out in 1858 by George Boldgett and was incorporated in 1873. The unusual name was the suggestion of Reverend Cox and is a reference to the burial place mentioned in the Old Testament, Genesis 49: The Death of Jacob. In 1870, the Lampson tomb (right) was erected by the heirs of Miles P. Lampson. Built of granite, the roof and cornice are locked together by their own weight. In 1906, when Orator Woodward died, his body was temporarily placed in the Lampson tomb until the Woodward mausoleum was erected in the southern section of the cemetery.

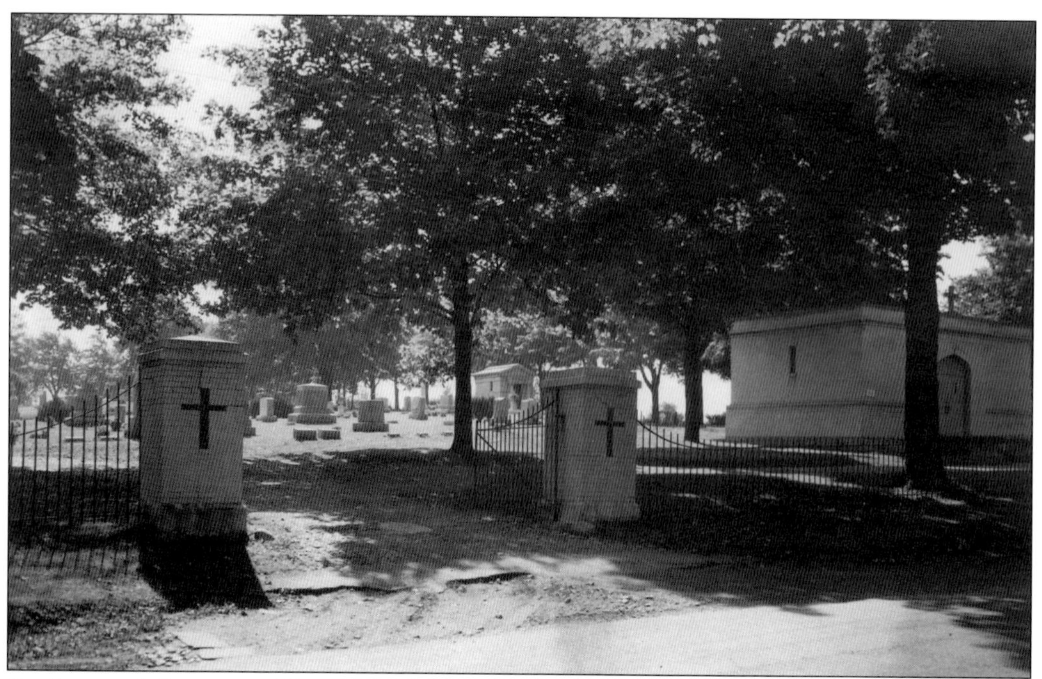

St. Francis' Cemetery. Named for the first Catholic church in LeRoy, the cemetery property was purchased in 1863. A cemetery association was formed in 1875 and formal plans were laid out based on Holy Sepulcher in Rochester and Forest Lawn in Buffalo. The cemetery was consecrated on July 10, 1881. Improvements, including the erection of the iron fence and the mausoleum, were completed in 1925.

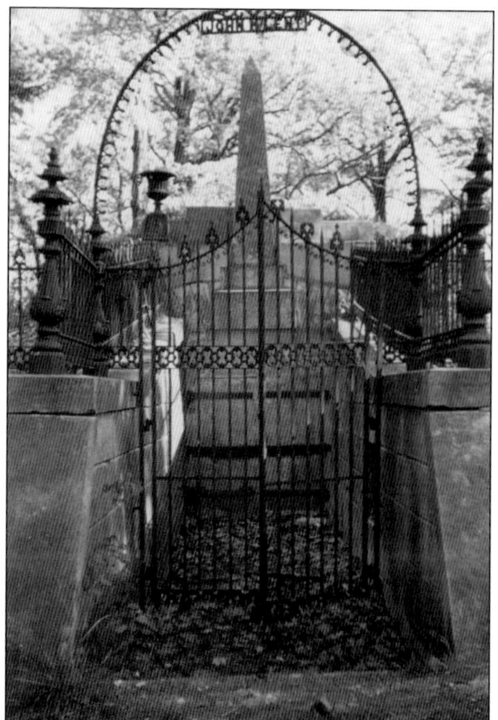

Lent's Tomb. In 1846, John Lent built a tomb on West Main Street. Fourteen family members were buried there, including his mother, Phoebe; both of John's wives, Lydia and Olive; and his son, John Howland Lent. The last person interred was John Howland Lent's wife, Harriet, who died in 1920. After the tomb was burglarized, it was sealed with cement. The fence posts were installed in front of LeRoy House.

Three

Schools and Ingham University

LeRoy has always been committed to providing educational opportunities. The first school west of the Genesee River was built in 1801 on East Main Road. It is commemorated by a historical marker. Settlers at Fort Hill north of the village organized the first school in the Triangle Tract in 1805. The first school in the village was a small wood-framed building on the public square—now Trigon Park. Another school, known as the "School on the Hill," was located on Craigie Street. Later it was moved to Cooper Street (Myrtle Street). The village was divided into four school districts, each with its own schoolhouse. During this time, advanced classes were held at the Round House on West Main Street.

In 1837, Marietta and Emily Ingham from Saybrook, Connecticut, founded the LeRoy Female Seminary on the corner of Wolcott Street and East Main Street. This school of higher education for women would eventually become Ingham University. It received its charter from the New York State Board of Regents in 1857. Thousands of students attended Ingham, and many became pioneers in the fields of education, science, art, and music. Ingham closed in 1892.

The LeRoy Academic Institute was founded in 1864. Classes were held in the former Tufts house, now the American Legion. In 1865, a new two-story school was built behind LeRoy House. In 1891, the LeRoy Academic Institute was sold to the Union Free School. A new high school on Trigon Park opened in 1911. In 1924, the Wolcott Street Elementary School was built. The Union Free School was consolidated into the LeRoy Central School in 1949. In 2003, a new high school was built on South Street Road next to Hartwood Park. St. Peter's Parochial School was established in 1889 and replaced in 1955 by Holy Family Parochial School.

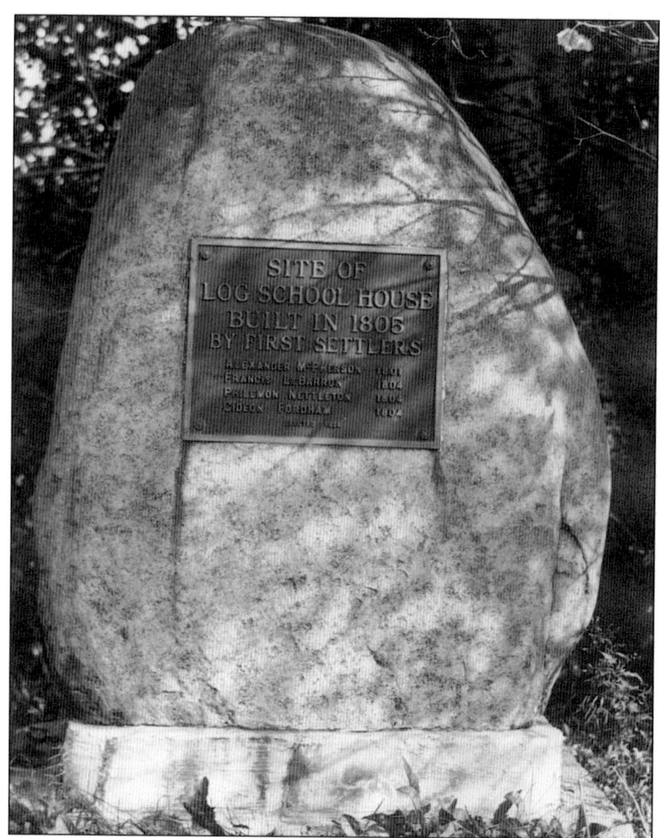

Fort Hill School Marker. The first school built in the Triangle Tract was a log cabin located north of the village. Erected in 1805, it was eventually replaced by a frame building. This boulder on the east side of Parmelee Road is dedicated to the first settlers, Alexander McPherson, Francis LeBarron, Philemon Nettleton, and Gideon Fordham.

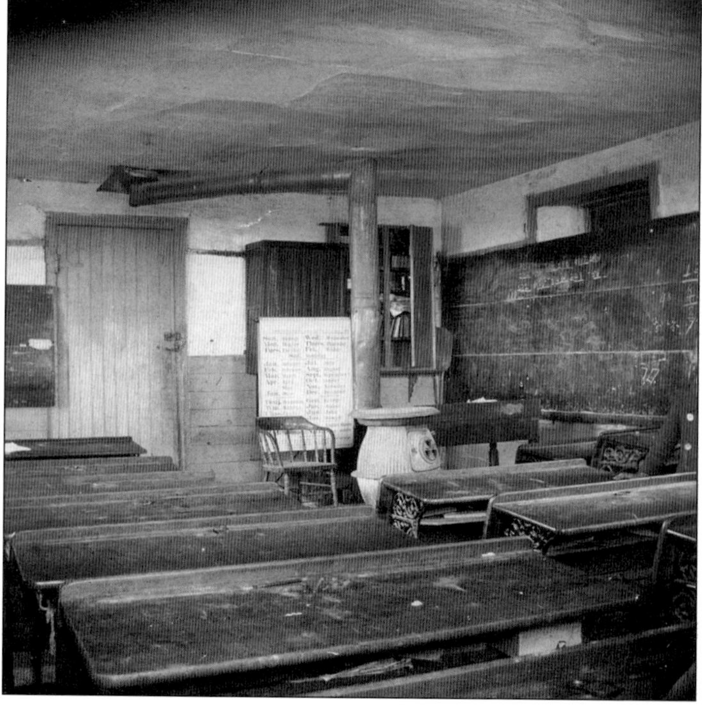

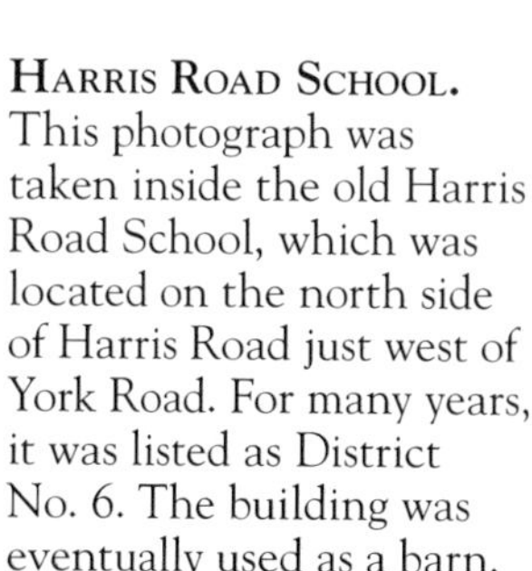

Harris Road School. This photograph was taken inside the old Harris Road School, which was located on the north side of Harris Road just west of York Road. For many years, it was listed as District No. 6. The building was eventually used as a barn.

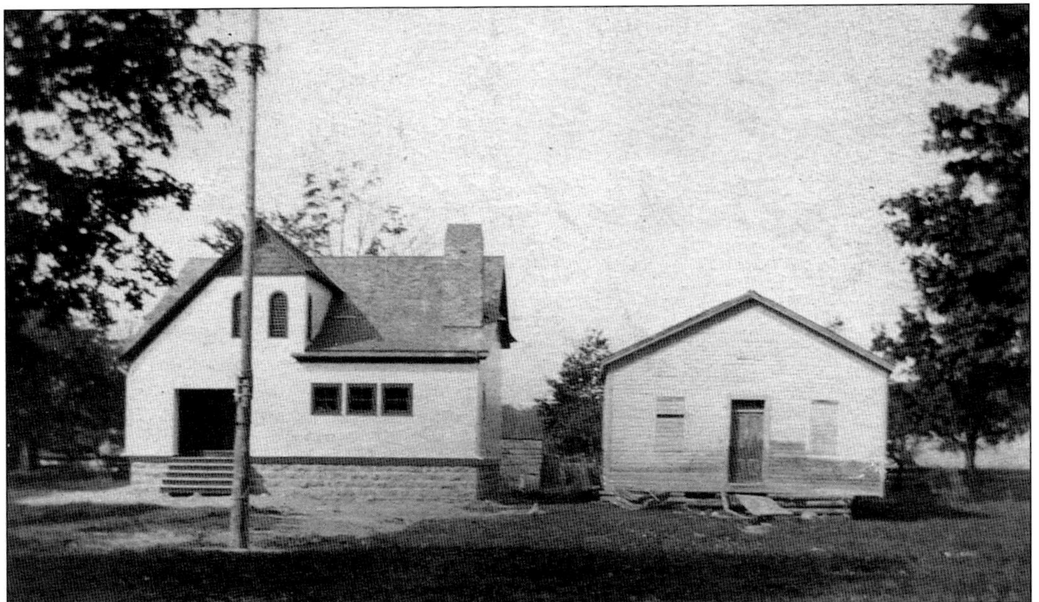

Fort Hill School. Located on Parmelee Road at the end of Oatka Trail, the Fort Hill School was listed in 1866 and 1876 as District No. 7 and District No. 4 in 1904. This photograph shows the old school, at right, which was later moved and used as a blacksmith shop. The new school, on the left, was used through the late 1940s and was razed in 2000.

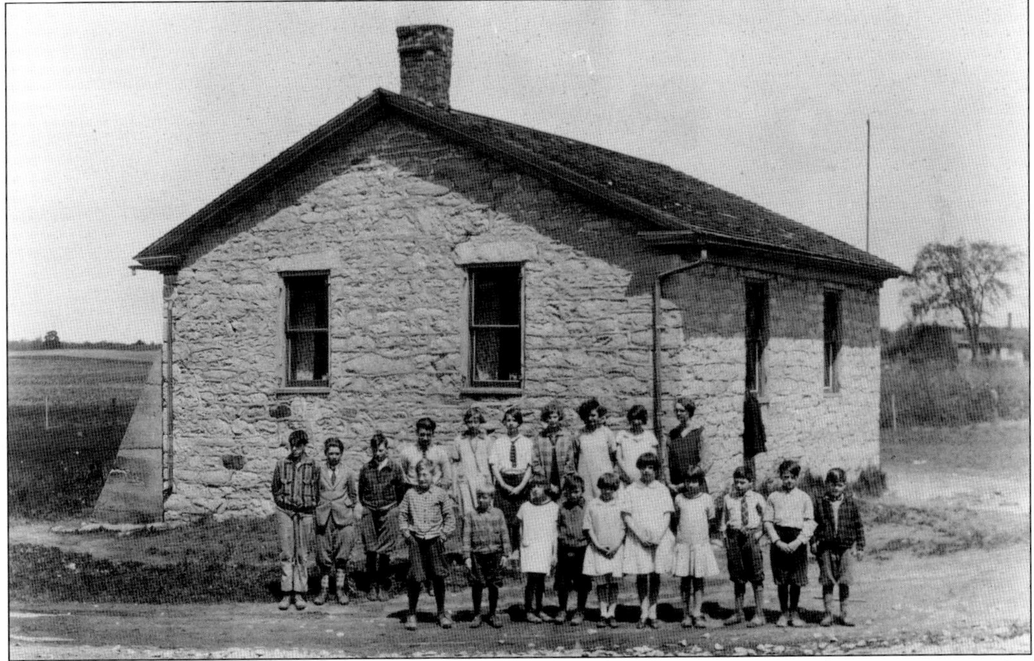

The Stone School House. This stone school was located two miles west of the village on the northeast corner of West Main Road and Nilesville Road. Listed as District No. 8, it was called the Paul District. It was one of two stone schools in LeRoy. The other was located in Lime Rock on the south side of Route 5, opposite Church Road. The Lime Rock School survives as part of a house.

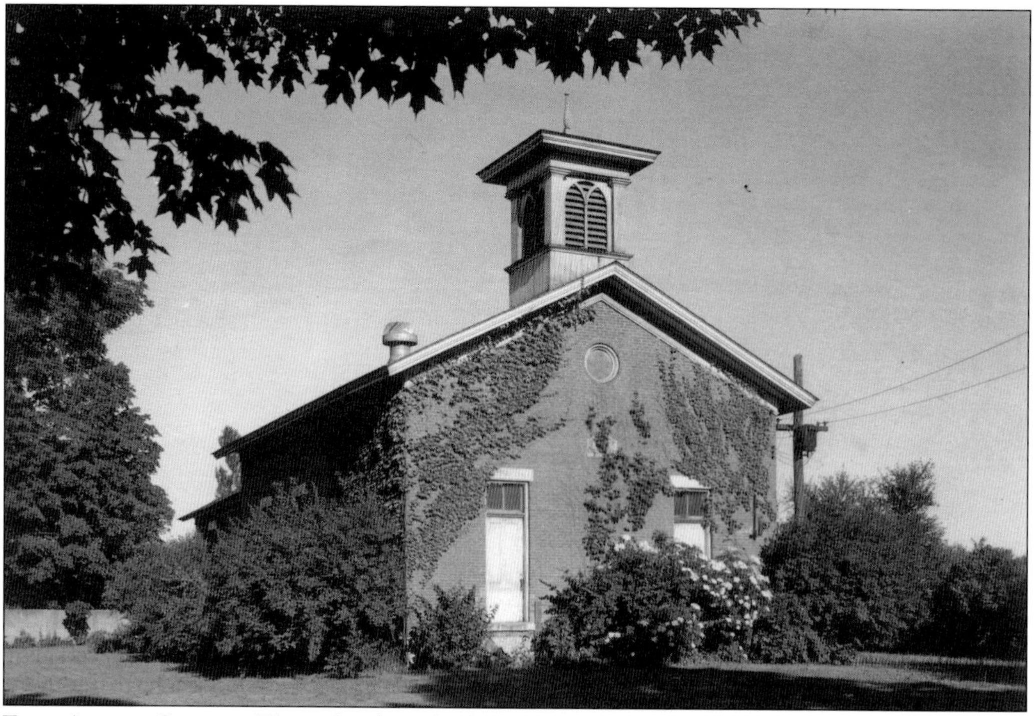

East Avenue School. This school was built of brick taken from a school located on East Main Street (below) that was razed in 1879. It served as District No. 10 and was in use until the formation of the Union Free School. In the early 1900s, it was used by Daniel and Sydney O'Shea for the manufacture of a grain-based coffee substitute known as Co-fe-no. It is now a private residence.

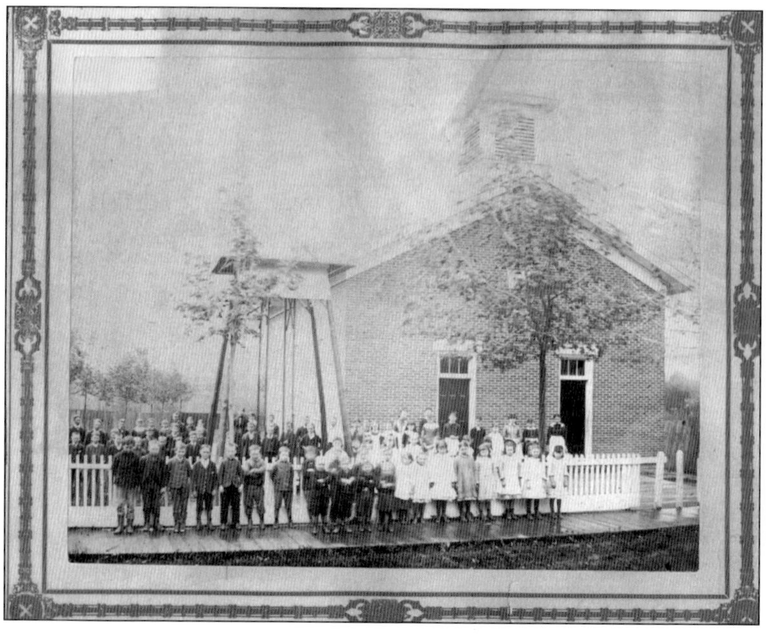

The Myrtle Street School. This brick school, built about 1879, replaced an earlier wooden school that had been moved from Craigie Street. The large wooden structure in the photograph is a swing. Known as the Shepard School, it was named for teacher Edwin Shepard. It served as an elementary school after the formation of the Union Free School. In 1917, it was purchased by the Second Baptist Church.

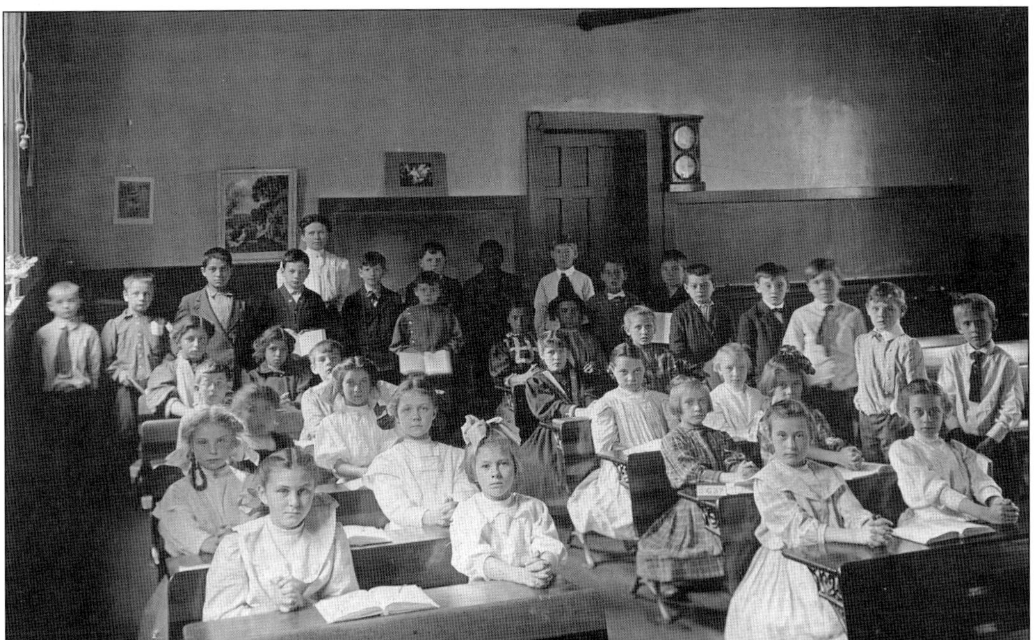

Lake Street School. The teacher is Miss Wightman. She is pictured with her third grade students, among whom are Cora Nongard, Marion Whittaker, Hazel Seyfer, Frank Johnson, Kenneth Howk, Pearl Matia, Alice Roth, Dorothy Walker, Alice Chase, Josephine Barone, Rose Mangoose, Rex Perkins, Lee Hutchinson, Walter Kellog, Adman Murry, Dawson Kendle, Robert Green, Dewey Price, Dean Wright, John Scanlon, Lester Hyman, Clarence Shepard, Joseph Barone, James Delong, and Milton Brown. The other students have not been identified.

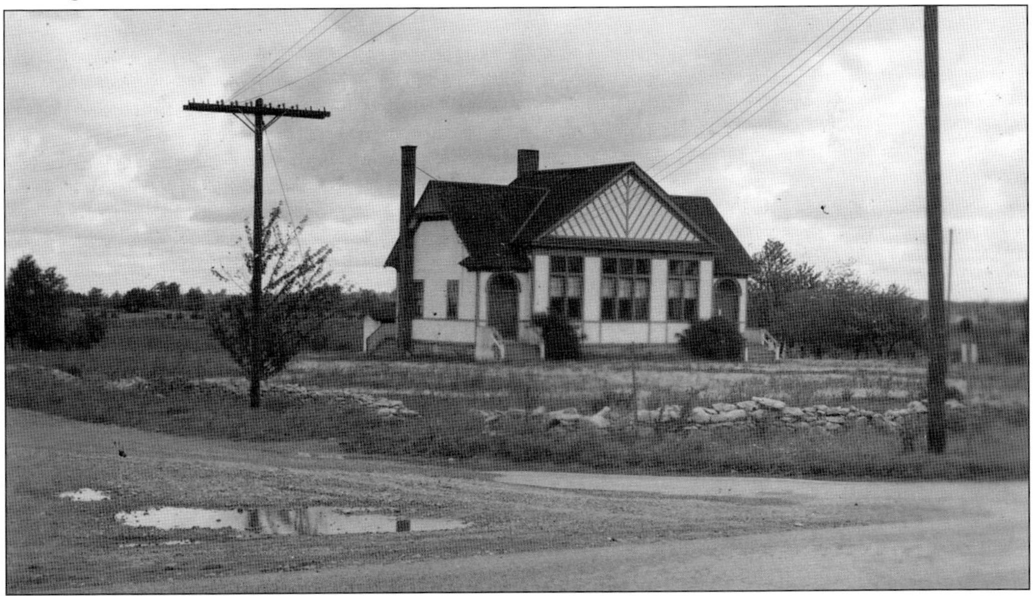

Lime Rock School. The original Lime Rock School was a stone building that is still standing as part of a dwelling. This frame school, built in 1898, was located on the corner of Church Road and Route 5. The Lime Rock School was District No. 21 in 1866 and 1876 but was changed to District No.7 in 1904. This building was razed in the 1950s.

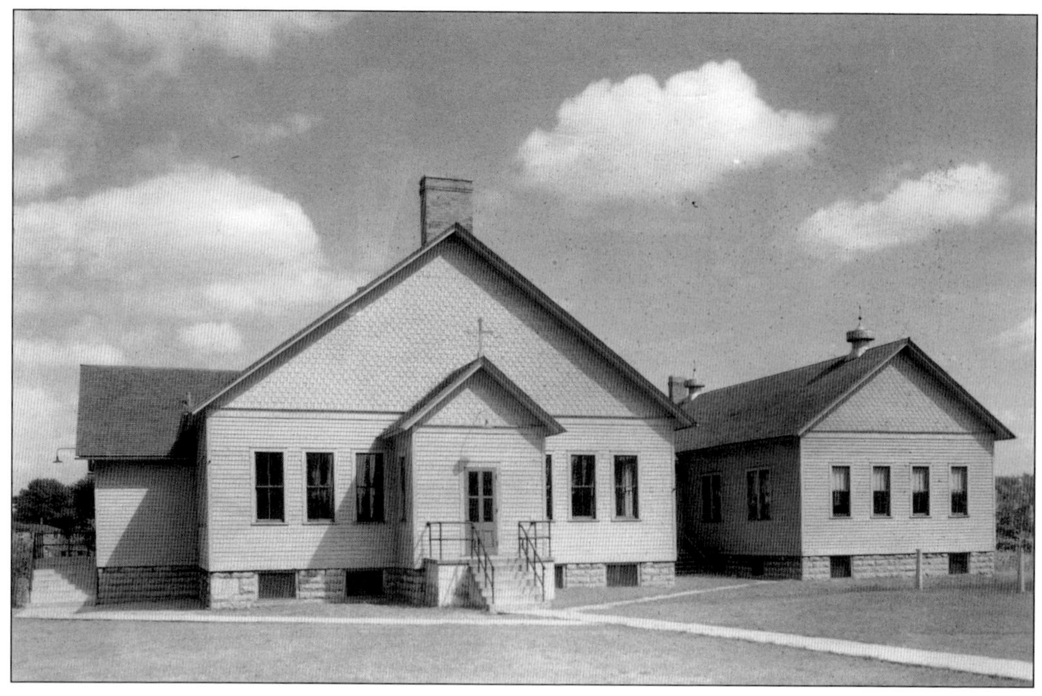

St. Peter's Parochial School. St. Peter's Parochial School was constructed in 1889 and was under the direction of the Sisters of Mercy from Batavia. For the first few years, the Sisters commuted from Batavia daily. The school served the Catholic community until 1955 when Holy Family School was built.

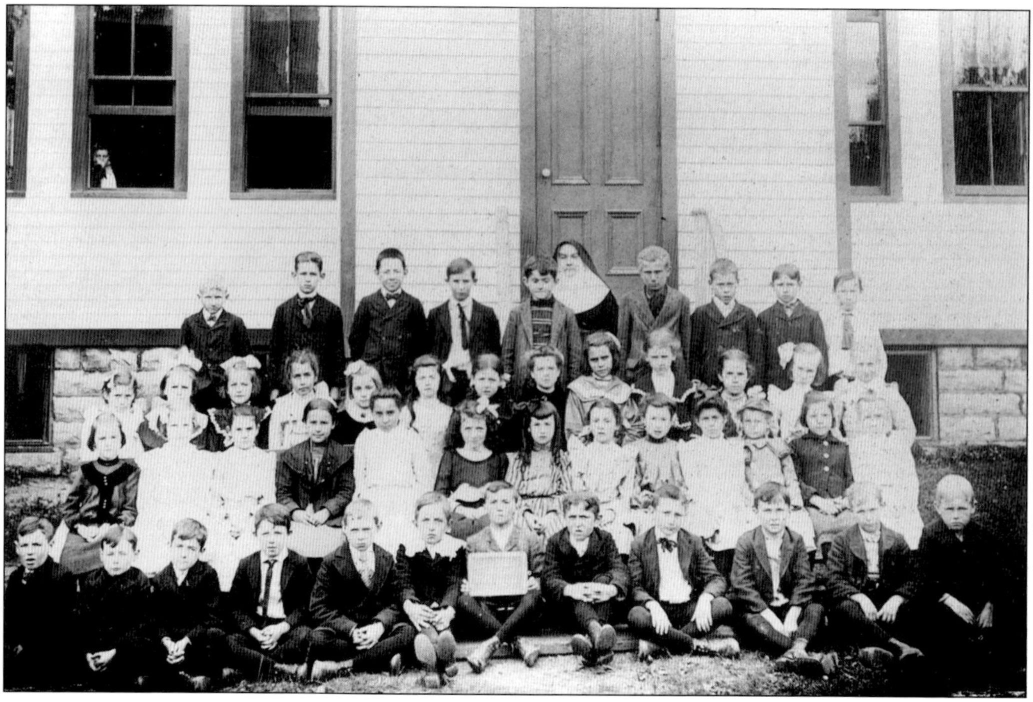

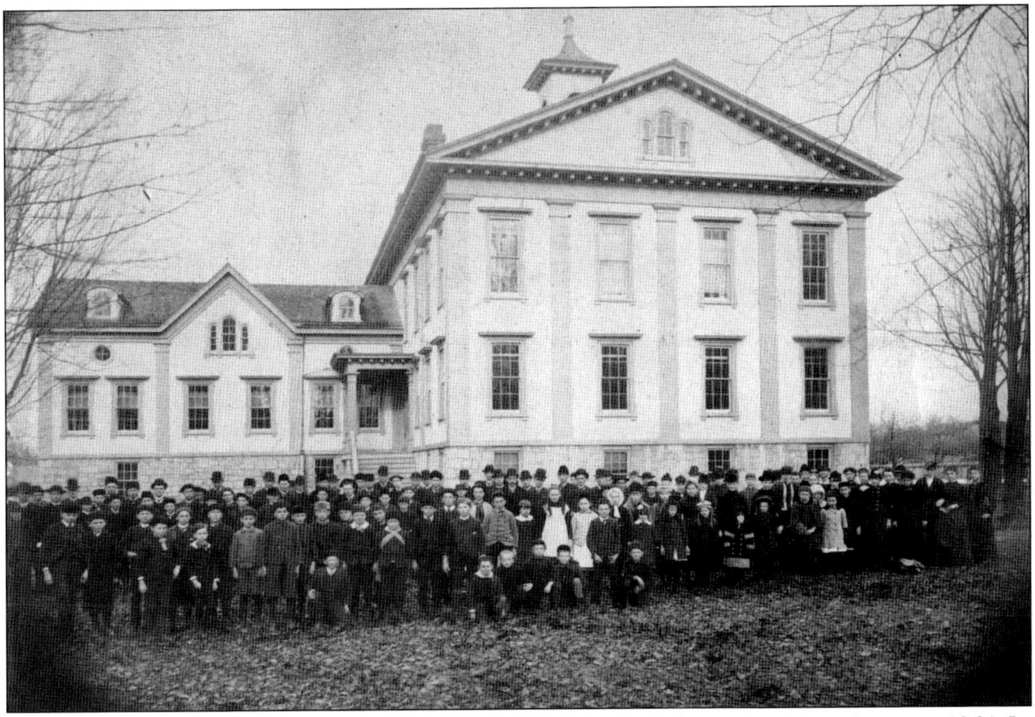

LeRoy Academic Institute, 1890. The institute was founded on West Main Street in 1864. In 1865, it acquired the LeRoy family estate on East Main Street and erected this two-story school. It had an enrollment of 250 students and provided a classical, business, and practical education. LeRoy House served as a boardinghouse for faculty and students. In 1891, the building was sold to the Union Free School for $10,000. The building was razed in the 1950s.

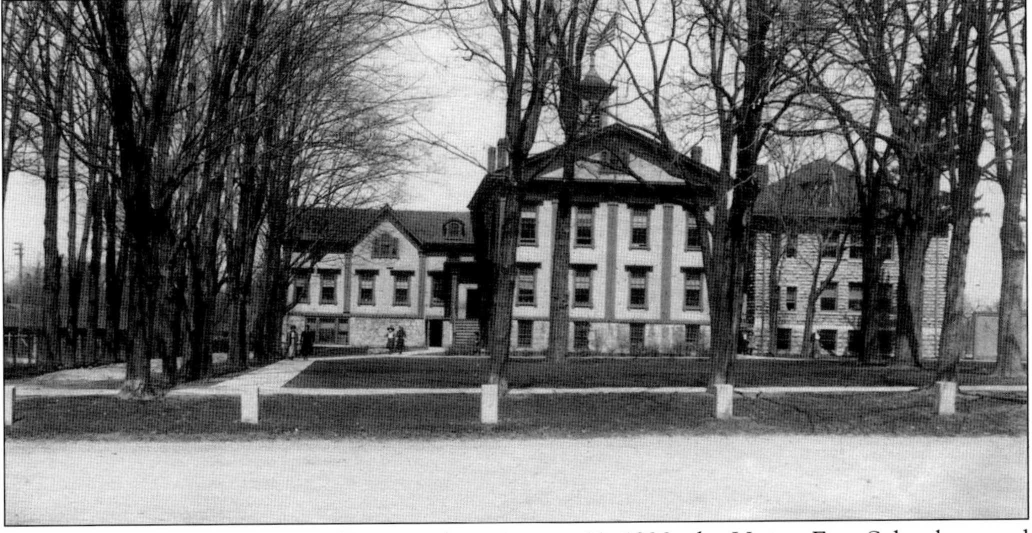

LeRoy Union Free School. Organized on August 21, 1890, the Union Free School merged Districts No. 1, No. 3, No. 4, and No. 10. The two-story limestone building on the right was added in 1898. After the new high school was built on Trigon Park in 1911, this building was sold to Allen Olmsted and it was a factory for patent medicines. The offices of the LeRoy Historical Society and the Jell-O Gallery are located in the 1898 limestone addition.

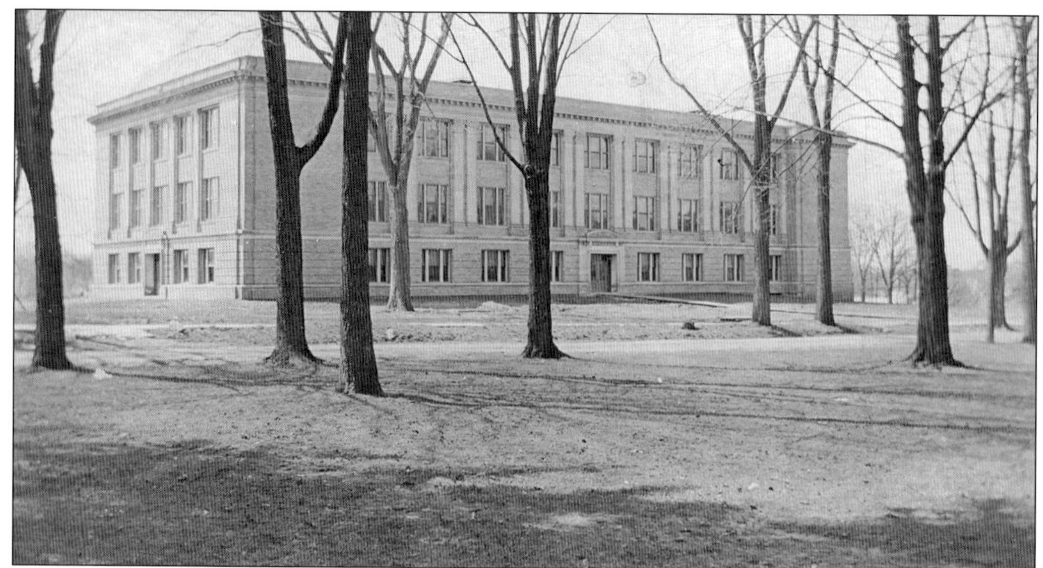

LeRoy High School. Designed by E. E. Joralemon and built for $80,000 in 1911, the school was erected on the old Ingham University campus. An auditorium and gymnasium were added in 1951. Today this building houses the superintendent's office and elementary school classrooms. In 2003, a new high school was built on South Street Road.

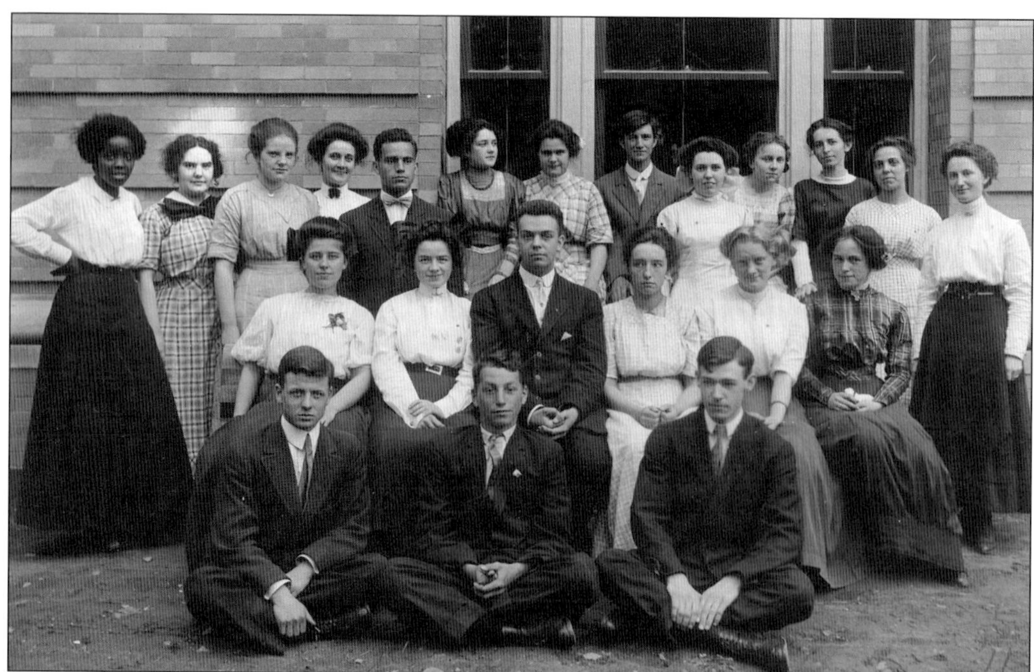

Class of 1911. The first class to graduate from the new school is pictured here. They are, from left to right, as follows: (first row) John Kelly, Irving Wilder, and Francis Kemp; (second row) Martha Shepard, Dorothy Gillett, Reid Marcellus, Ida Radley, Anna Kurtz, and Ethel Lewis; (third row) Esther Steverson, Mary Muller, Elsey Larkin, Julia Connor (teacher), Arthur Selden, Lillian MacDonald, Ruby Artman, Henry Scott, Mary Kemp, Gertrude Wells, Agnes Gleason, Florence Pestle, and Hazel Empie.

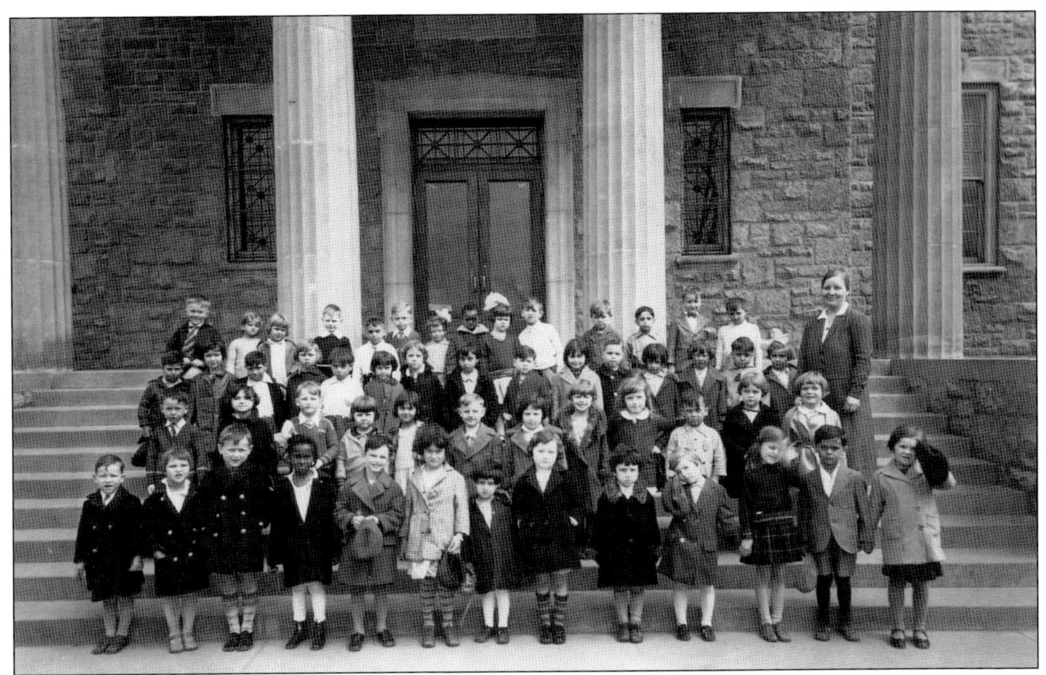

WOLCOTT STREET SCHOOL KINDERGARTEN, 1931. The Wolcott Street Elementary School was built in 1924 on land donated by Ernest Woodward. A public referendum was held to raise $225,000 for the school. The first principal was Adrienne Sanderson.

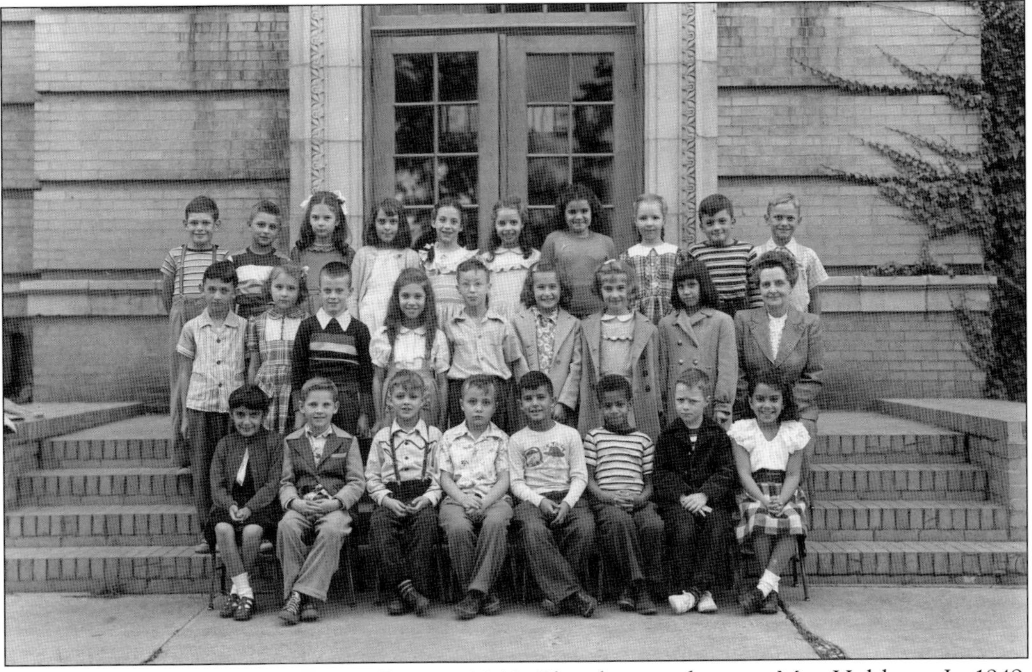

WOLCOTT STREET SCHOOL THIRD GRADE, 1949. The class teacher was Mrs. Holthaus. In 1949, Fort Hill District No. 3, Asbury Road No. 5, Harris Road No. 6, Lime Rock No. 7, West Main Road No. 8, Langworthy No. 10, Jug City No. 11, and Stafford No. 1 voted for consolidation as the LeRoy Central School. Shortly after, the Morganville District joined the LeRoy system.

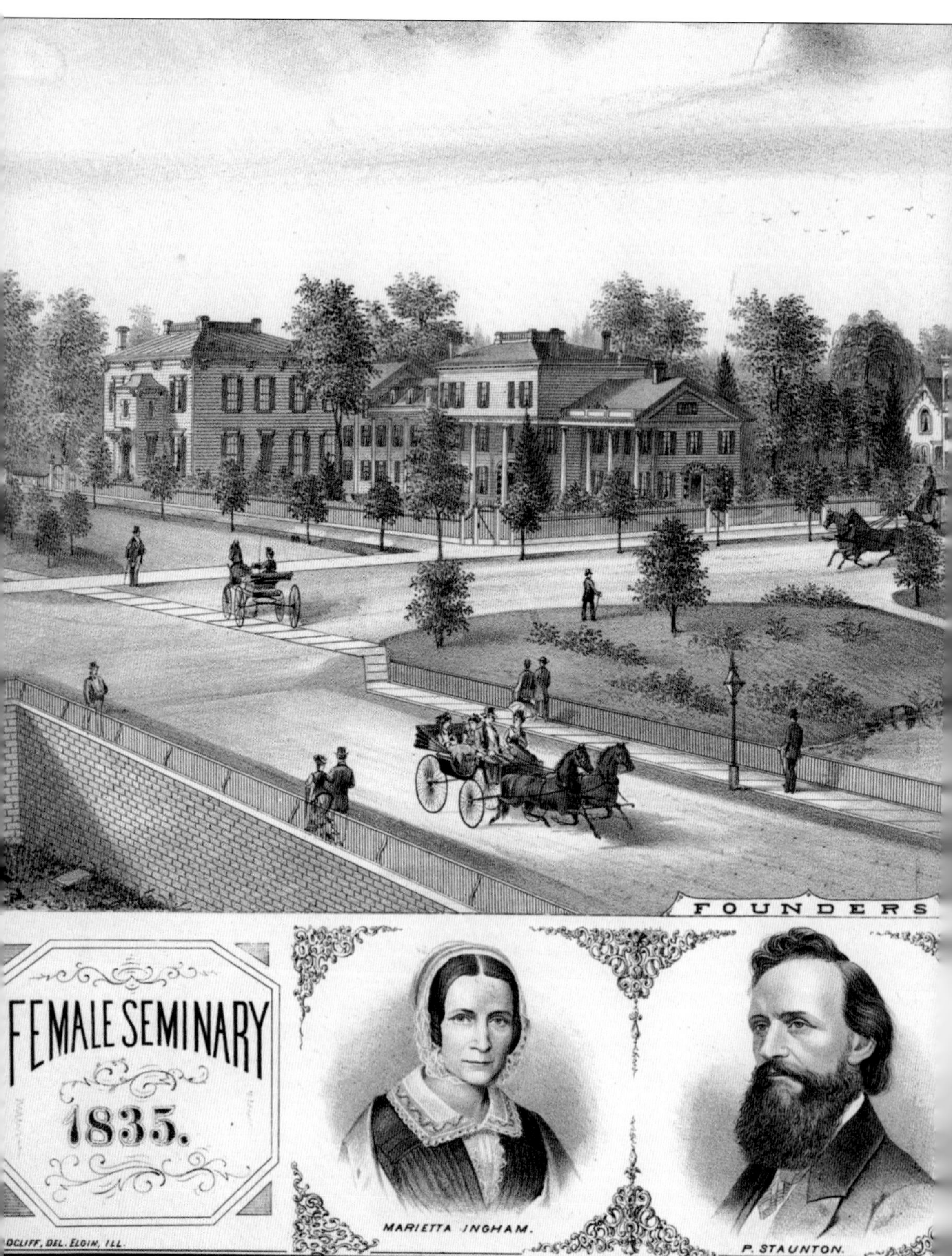
FOUNDERS
FEMALE SEMINARY
1835.
MARIETTA INGHAM.
P. STAUNTON.
DCLIFF, DEL. ELGIN, ILL.

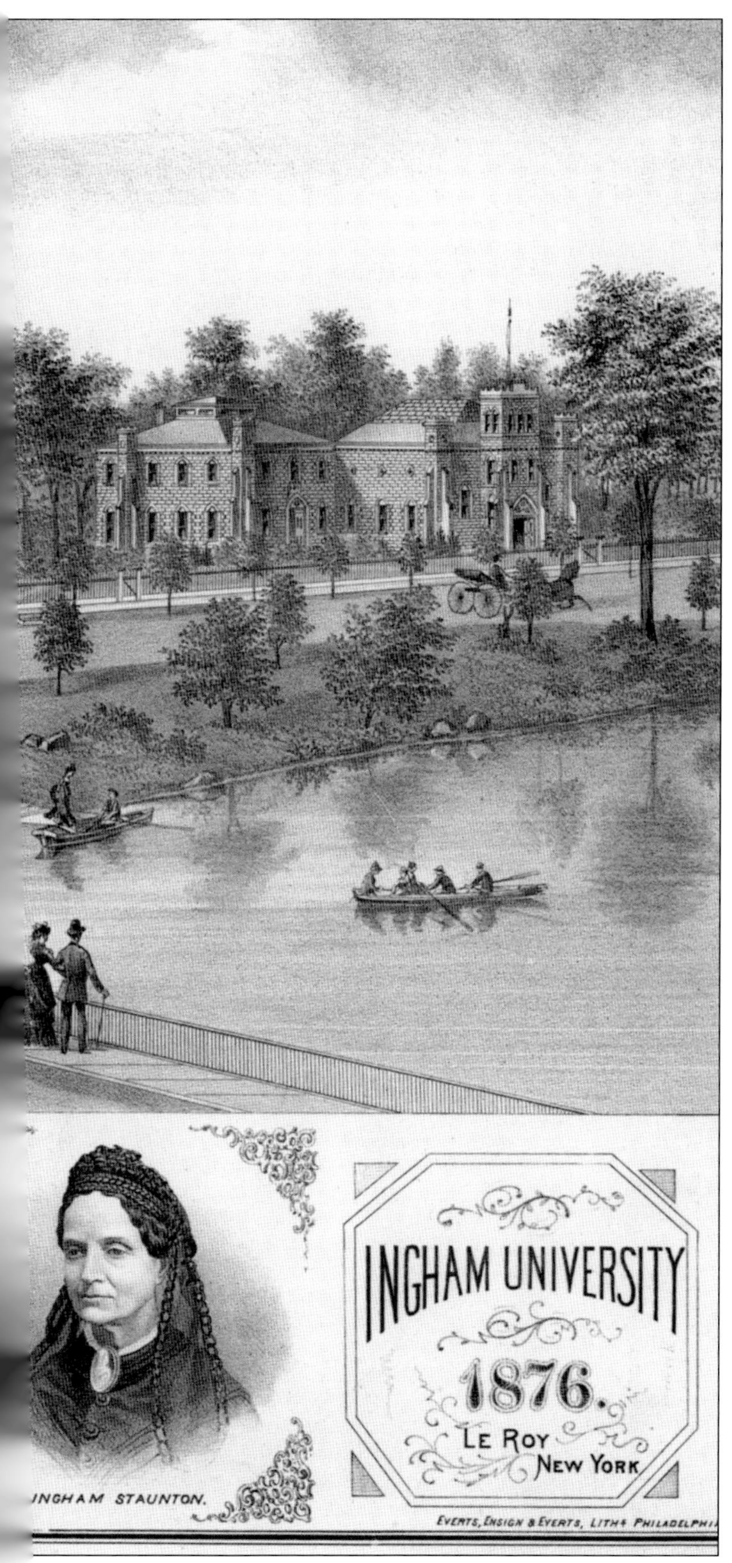

Ingham University. In 1837, Marietta and Emily Ingham from Saybrook, Connecticut, founded the LeRoy Female Seminary in the former Bayard house on the corner of Wolcott Street and Trigon Park. Emily Ingham married artist Phineas Staunton in 1847, and he became instrumental in the advancement of the school. In 1852, New York State granted the school a collegiate charter. Rev. Samuel Cox became the first chancellor of the college in 1852, and on April 28, 1857, the school was granted a university charter. It became the first women's university to grant a degree. According to a national survey conducted in 1876, Ingham University was one of only seven women's schools to offer a curriculum equivalent to male institutions. Ingham University closed in 1892 because of financial difficulties.

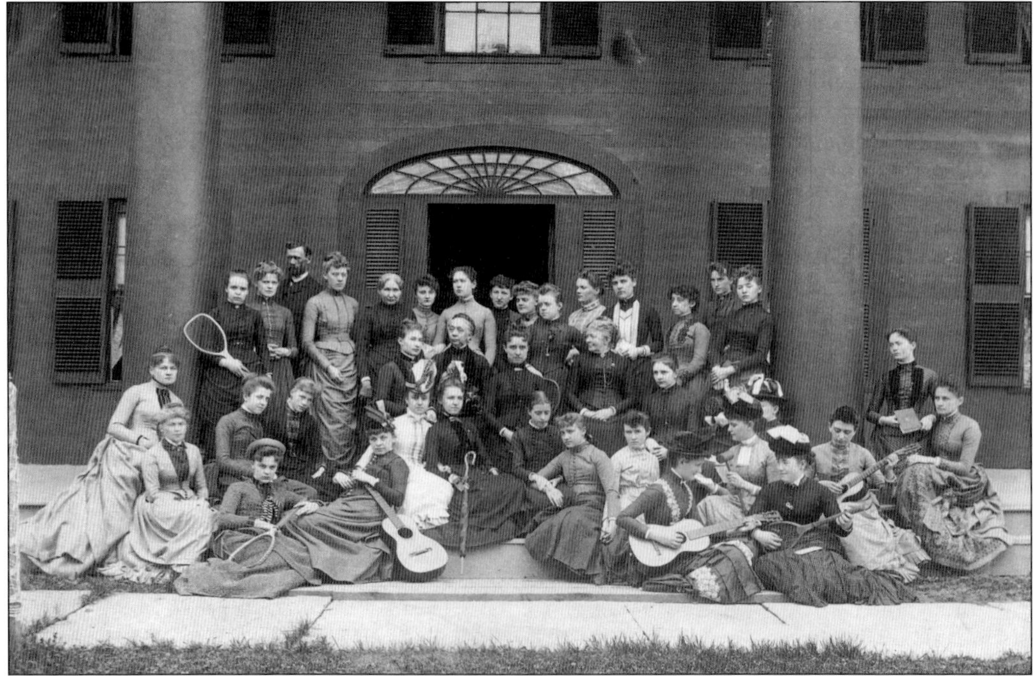

INGHAM STUDENTS AND FACULTY. Students came from across the country to attend Ingham University. It was organized into three colleges: the Literary College, the College of Fine Arts, and the Conservatory of Music. Although most of the students were women, the College of Fine Arts accepted men. Over 8,000 students attended Ingham University between 1837 and 1892.

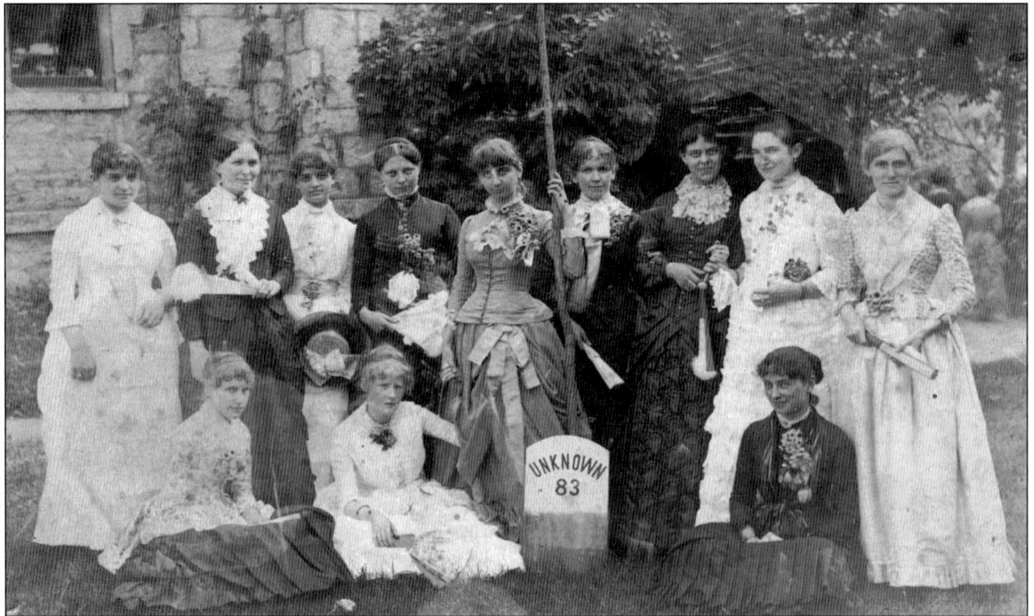

INGHAM CLASS OF 1883. While standing in front of the Staunton Art Conservatory, the class of 1883 poses for a photograph. Katherine Smith, president of the class, stands with the pole. To the right of Katherine is Nellie Harmon. Lizzie Coe stands second from the left. Fandria Crocker is on the extreme left. Stephenia Wentworth is seated on the lower right.

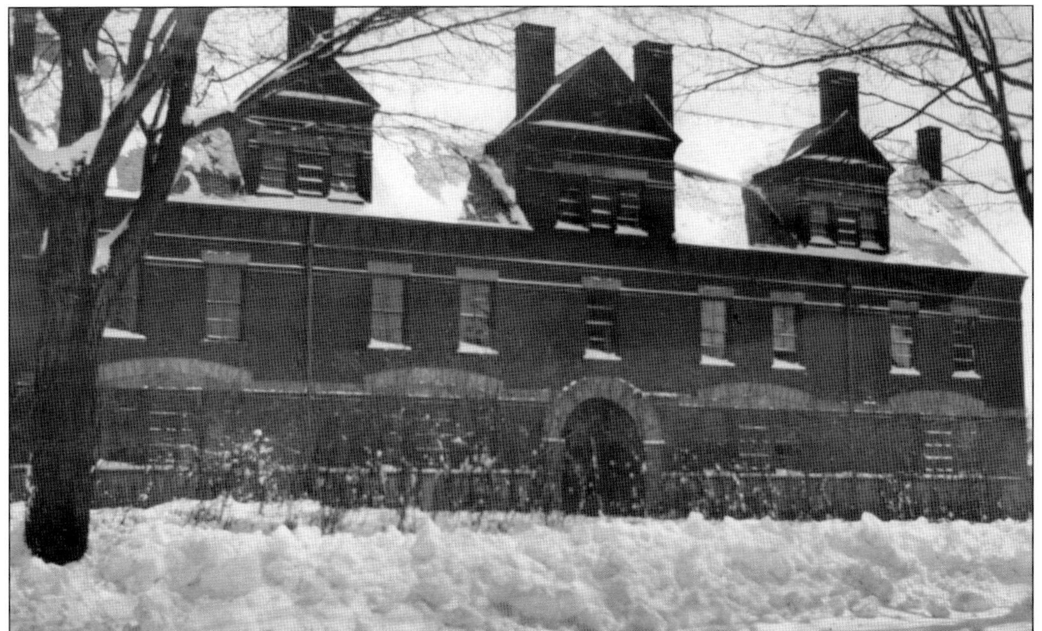

Ingham Dormitory. In 1886, a dormitory was built facing the Oatka Creek. The rooms were heated with steam radiators. A gymnasium was built on the third floor. The building was boarded up in 1892 when the university closed. Although the alumnae hoped to revitalize Ingham University, the building was razed and the bricks were used for fill on the west end of the new Main Street bridge in 1909.

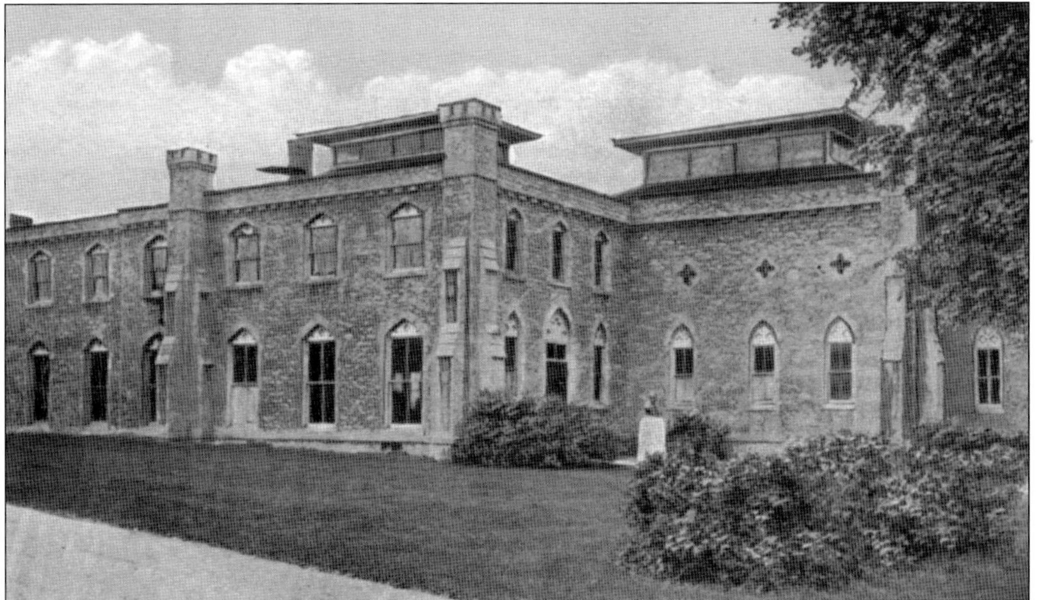

Staunton Art Conservatory. Phineas Staunton died in 1867 on a Smithsonian expedition to South America. His wife, Emily, raised funds to build the conservatory, which was erected in 1870. The main floor included exhibit cases filled with specimens collected on the Smithsonian expedition. The upper gallery was filled with Staunton's art. In 1929, the building was razed and the stone was used to build the Woodward Memorial Library.

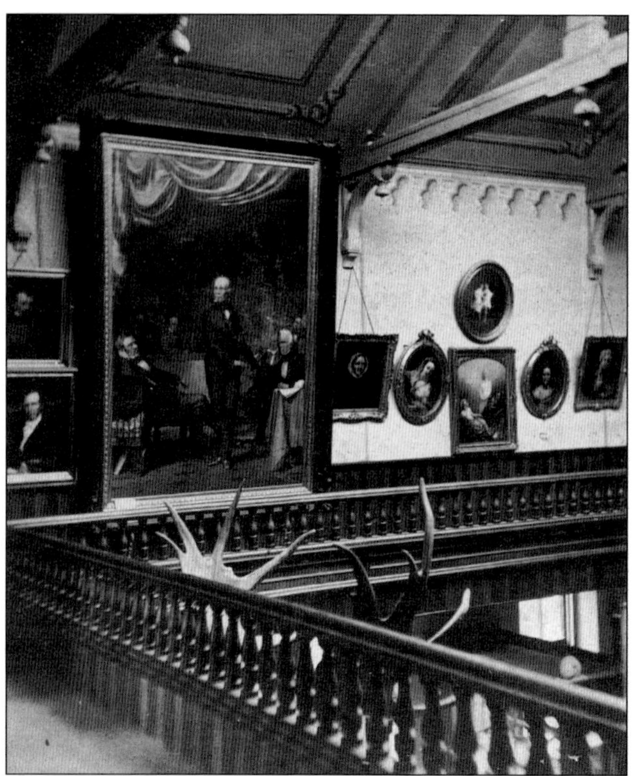

Portrait of Henry Clay. The second floor gallery of the Staunton Art Conservatory featured art by Phineas Staunton, including *Henry Clay on the Floor of the Senate*. This portrait was entered into a contest in Kentucky in 1865 but was rejected and returned to the university. It was given to the LeRoy Historical Society in 1955. In 2006, it was donated to the United States Senate and it hangs in the Capitol building.

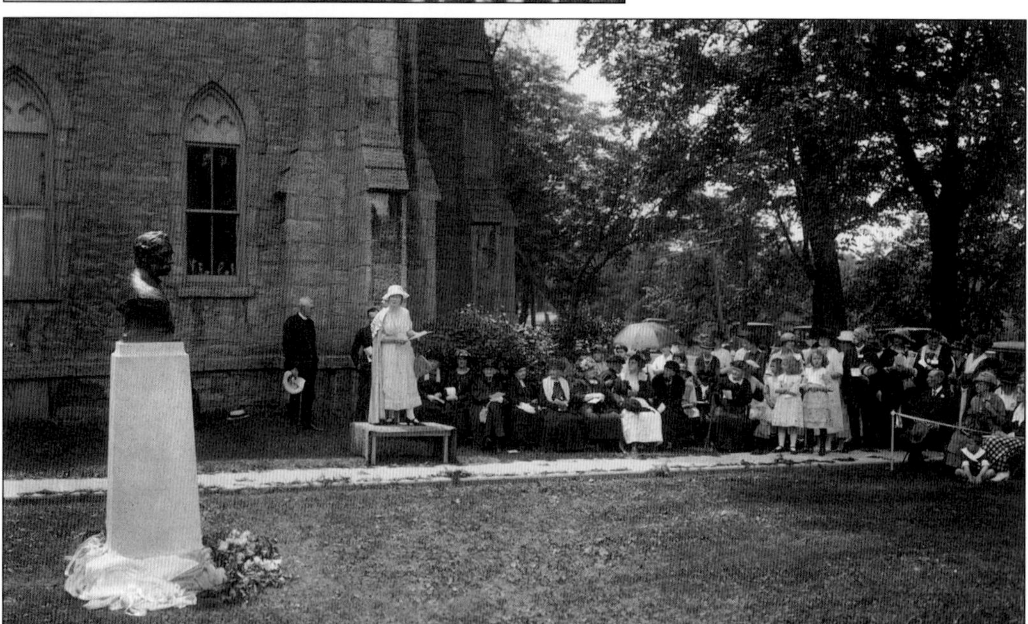

Lemuel Wiles Dedication. After the death of Phineas Staunton, his widow, Emily, hired noted artist Lemuel Wiles to become the head of the Ingham University art school. Wiles soon became the students' favorite instructor. After a disagreement with the trustees over studio fees, Wiles left the university in 1888. In 1922, his former students erected a bust of Wiles in front of the Staunton Art Conservatory. It now stands in front of the Woodward Memorial Library.

Four

Agriculture and Industry

Fertile land and an abundant source of waterpower enabled the early settlers to grow wheat and grain, which was ground into flour at the LeRoy mills and shipped east to Albany and New York City. Dairies, orchards, poultry farms, beans, potatoes, cabbage, hay, and other agricultural products would become part of the legacy of LeRoy. Calvin Keeney introduced the stringless bean, and together with his father, the Keeneys amassed a fortune on agricultural commodities. Today agriculture continues to be the largest industry in Genesee County and a major part of LeRoy's economy.

LeRoy's largest natural resource has been the huge deposits of limestone, which have supplied building material for churches, schools, homes, railroad bridges, and even the Genesee County Courthouse in Batavia. LeRoy limestone was pulverized in what was described as the largest stone crusher in the world and was used for ballast in railroad beds, highways, the New York State Thruway, and the Mount Morris Dam. Today gravel trucks continue to haul gravel from the LeRoy quarries.

For nearly 50 years, salt was a viable industry in LeRoy. Both evaporated brine and mined salt was processed into a variety of products. LeRoy also became known for a burgeoning patent medicine industry, which offered a wide variety of cures for ills and complaints. The larger companies included the Shiloh Company, O. F. Woodward Medicine Company, Kemp and Lane, and Allen's Foot-ease Company.

Other LeRoy industries included the Bacon Stove Foundry, Empire and Union Explosives, Haxton Canning Company, Lapp Insulator, Rogerson Cold Storage, the Malt Company, Belmont Salt Block, LeRoy Cotton Mills, Bay State Mill, LeRoy Machine Company, Rib-Stone Cement Company, Baudry Organ Company, Fluxo bathroom cleaner, Rough On Rats, Union Steel Chest, LeRoy Plow Company, LeRoy Canning Company, the Upham (railroad) Car Shop, Hirshman Pohle ventilators, and the White Airplane Company. Only Lapp Insulator and the limestone quarries remain in business today.

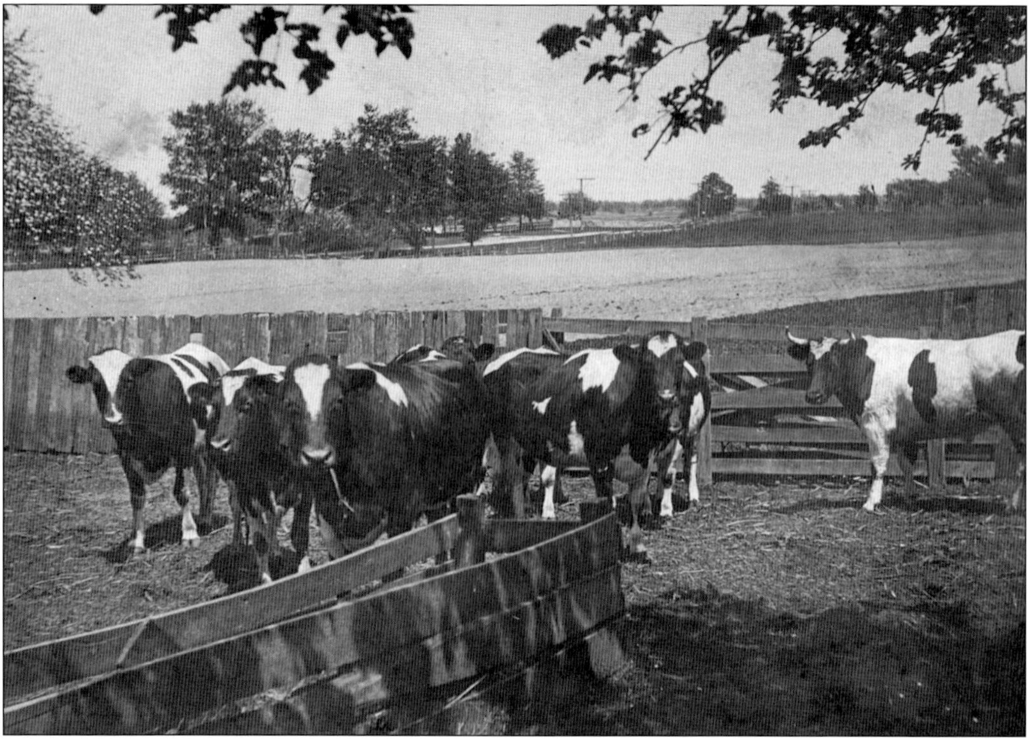

COWS ON THE STRIPP FARM, 1900. The Stripp photograph collection includes many images of the Stripp farm east of the village on the south side of Route 5. In 1850, there were 2,524 farms in Genesee County. In 1900, there were 3,286 farms. By 1996, the number had dropped to 516 farms. Although no longer in business, the Elm Dairy and Stowell's Dairy processed milk in LeRoy.

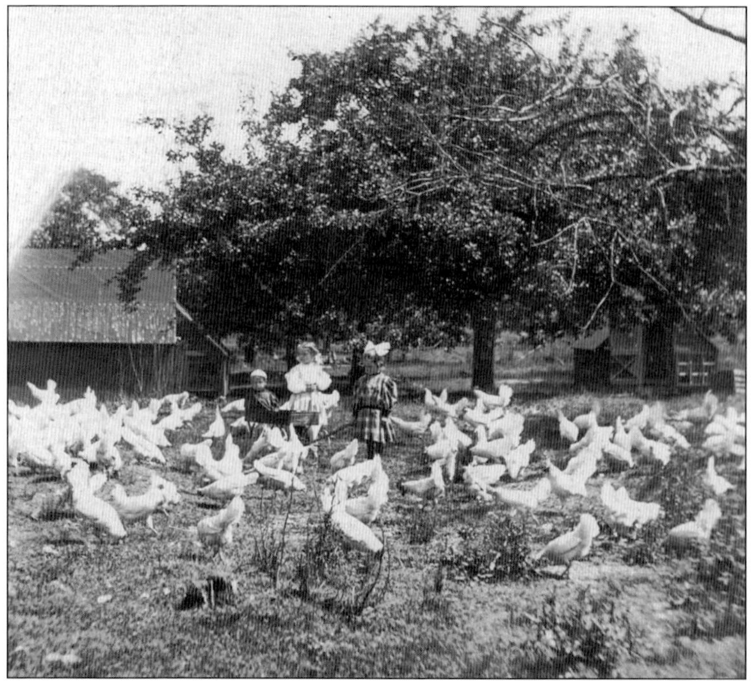

POULTRY CITY. Frank Edson owned Poultry City and raised single-comb white leghorns. He also ran a truck farm at his home at 101 Wolcott Street.

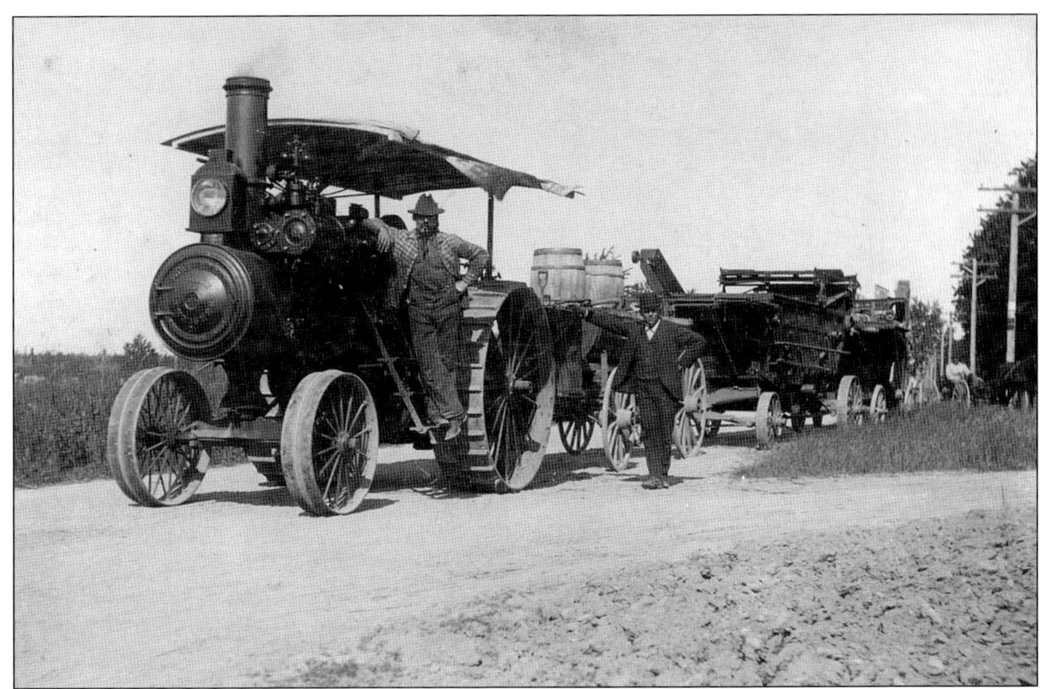

Threshers. This photograph was taken at the Stripp farm in the late 1800s. It shows a threshing team with a stationary Port Huron steam engine, a water wagon, and two threshing machines. Teams of threshers traveled from farm to farm threshing wheat for farmers.

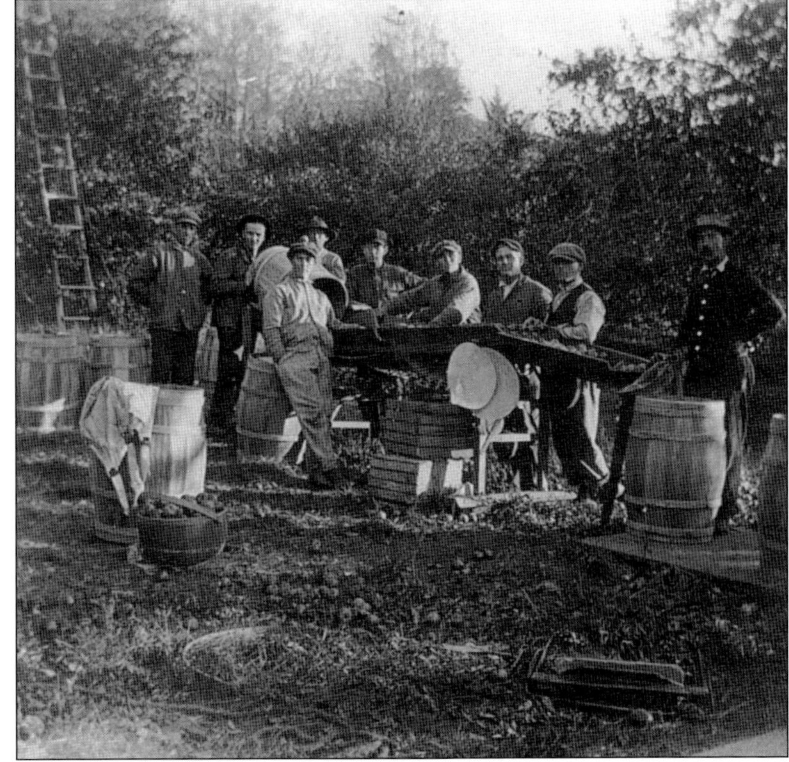

Packing Apples on the McPherson Farm. This photograph was taken in 1908 on the McPherson farm on Oatka Trail. This farm has been in the same family since 1801. Roy McPherson served as president of the New York State Horticultural Society. He also was the first president of the LeRoy Historical Society in 1940. Today the farm continues to harvest apples, press cider, and grow pumpkins and Christmas trees.

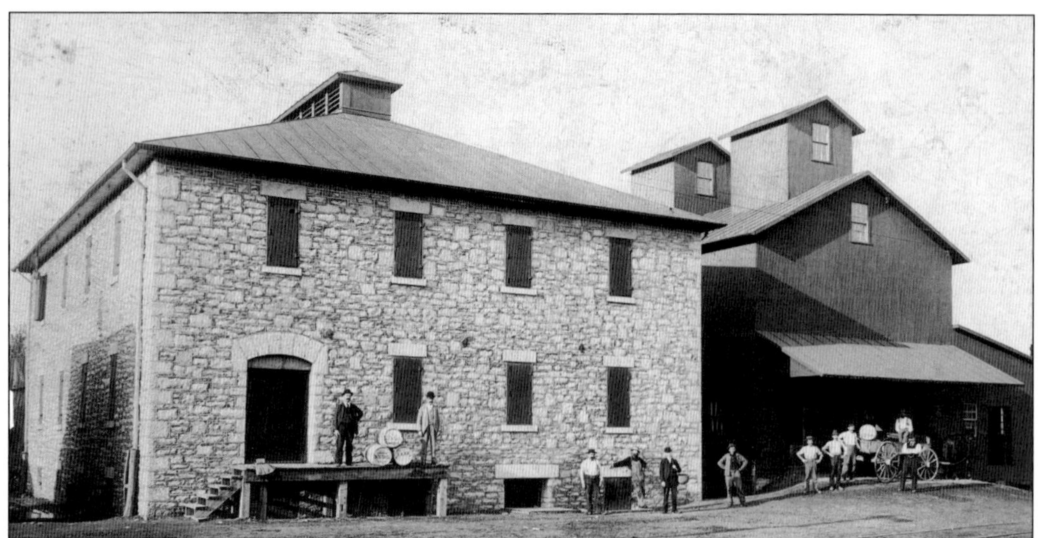

Gleason Cold Storage. Located on Lake Street, the Gleason warehouse was considered the largest in the state and was devoted to apples and pears exclusively. Patrick Gleason was known as the "apple king" because of his extensive storage operations and marketing of fruit. The Gleason Cold Storage facility was serviced by five different railroads. Gleason also handled 250,000 bushels of beans annually.

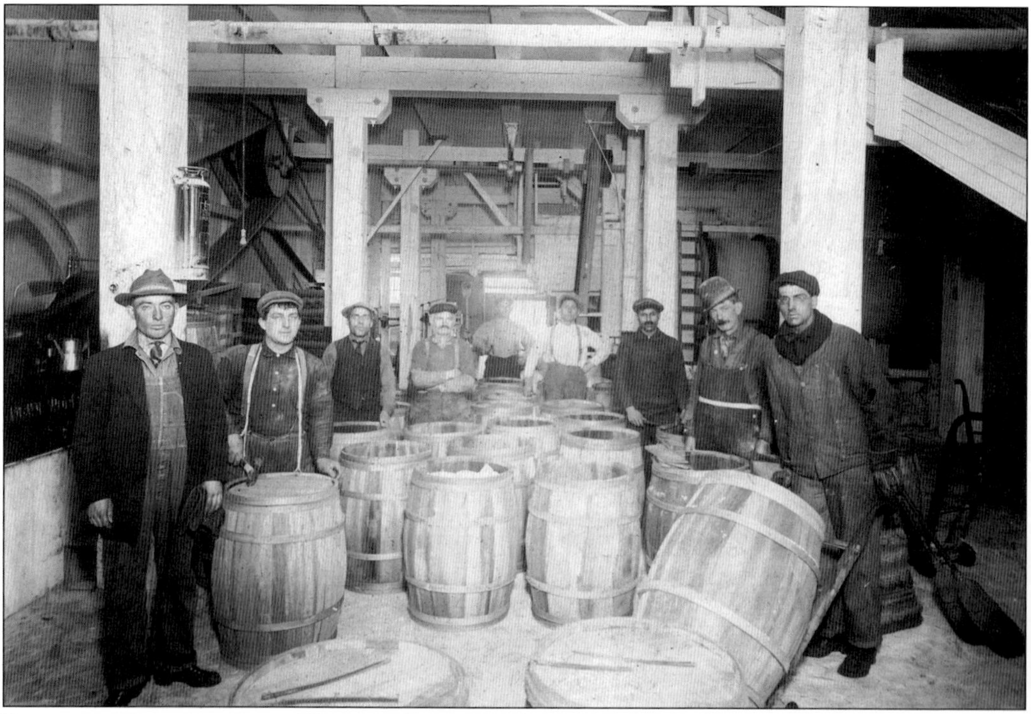

Rogerson Cold Storage. This warehouse was located on Church Street in the old malt plant. The men included in this photograph are James Powers, Charles Hillman, James Joy, Robert Henry, Joseph O'Melia, Sam Vinci, Sam Valone, John Kelty, and Clarence Blood. The building was converted to an ice making plant for the Crystal Ice Company.

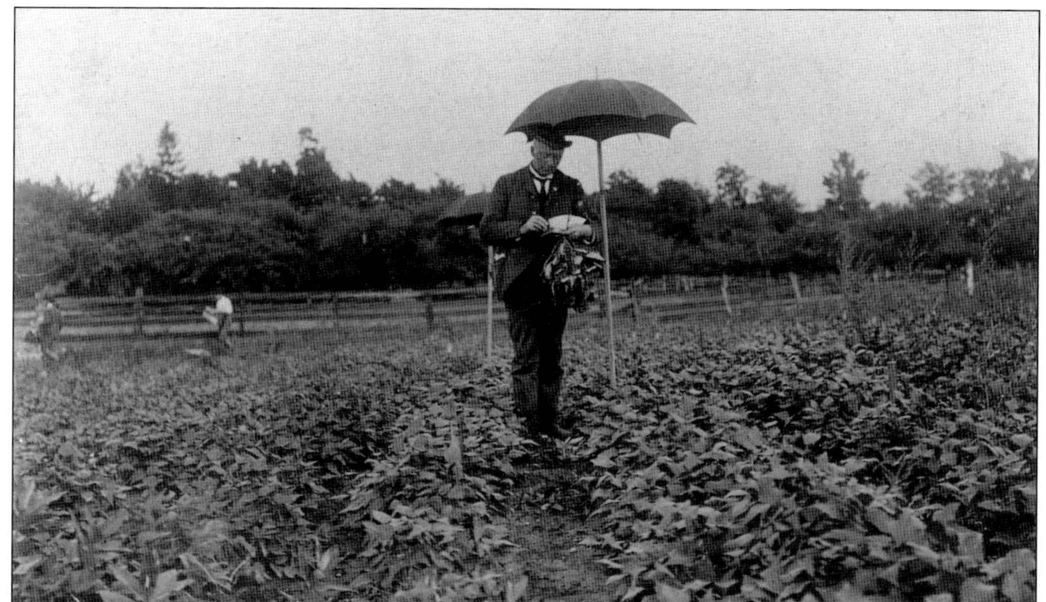

Calvin Keeney. Born in 1849, Calvin Keeney developed the first stringless bean, the Black-eyed Wax, in 1887. Disaster struck when fire destroyed most of his trial seeds and he had to begin again. By 1928, he had developed 17 different varieties, which were distributed by Burpee Seed Company.

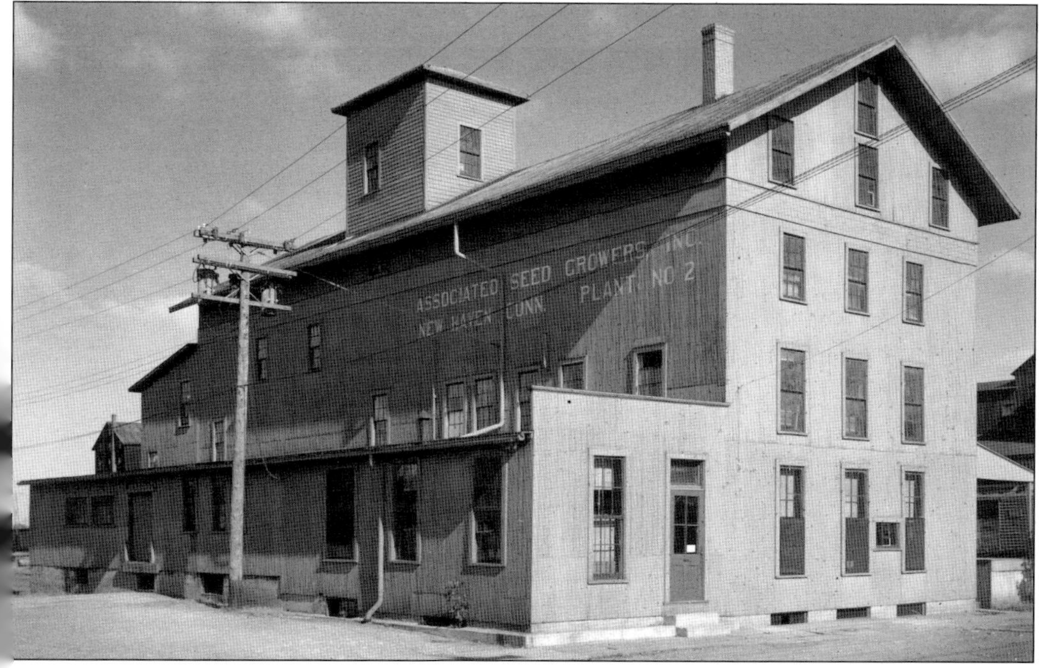

Associated Seed Growers. Nicholas Keeney and his son Calvin Keeney founded their partnership in 1872, establishing a worldwide reputation as wholesale growers for the canning industry and the retail seed trade. In 1928, the company merged with the Associated Seed Growers of Connecticut, known as Asgrow. The LeRoy facility closed in 1950. This warehouse on Lake Street was destroyed by fire.

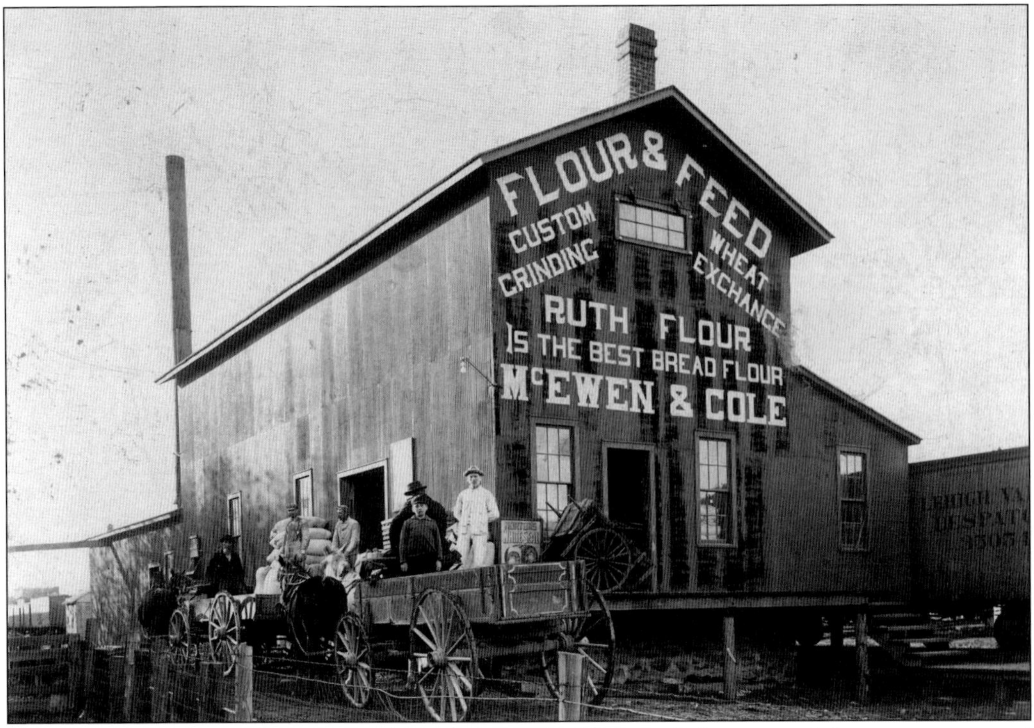

Lake Street Mill. William Winfield Cole Sr. and J. William Cole operated this steam-powered feed and flour mill on the west side of Lake Street between the railroad tracks. In 1910, the mill was bought by Herbert F. Morris, who advertised LeRoy's Cornell Laying Mash for chickens and high quality flour.

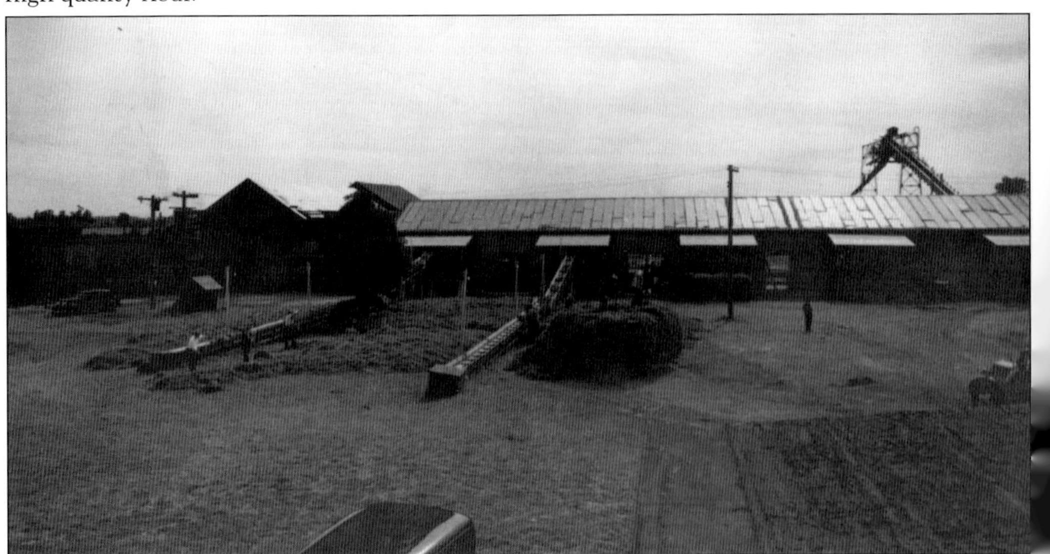

Haxton Canning Factory. Located on North Avenue, the facility was originally founded as the LeRoy Canning Company in 1909, and it continued until 1939 when it became the Haxton Canning Company. It processed vegetables under a variety of labels, including Royal Castle, LeRoy, Genesee, Primo, KaKo, Diploma, Queen Quality, and Korn Kream. During World War II, German and Italian prisoners of war worked at the factory.

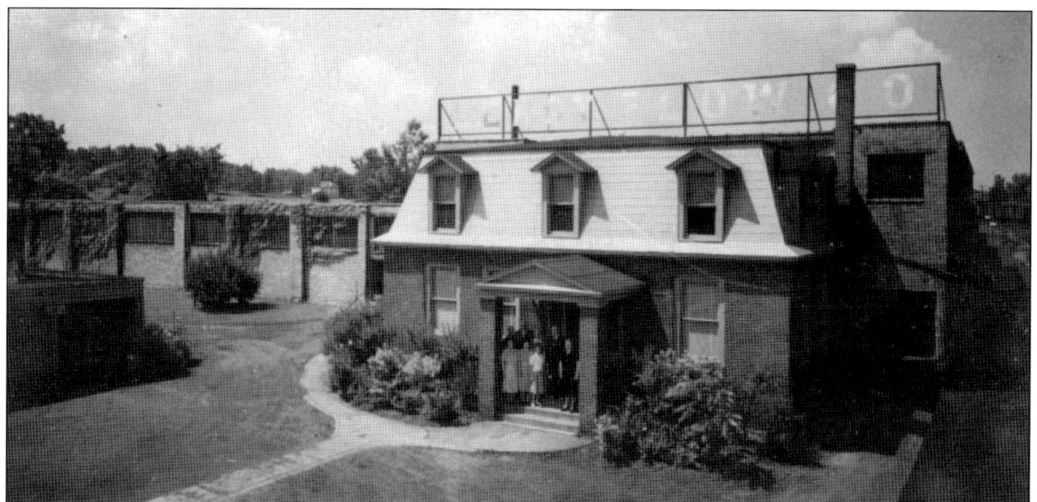

LeRoy Plow Company. Organized in 1899, the LeRoy Plow Company manufactured the Boss Potato Digger and the Miller Bean Harvesters, as well as cultipackers, buzz saws, manure spreaders, wood and steel beam plows, and riding plows. It burned to the ground in 1903 but was rebuilt and remained in business until the early 1950s. Later the factory was used by Dusing and Hunt for the manufacture of steel fire doors.

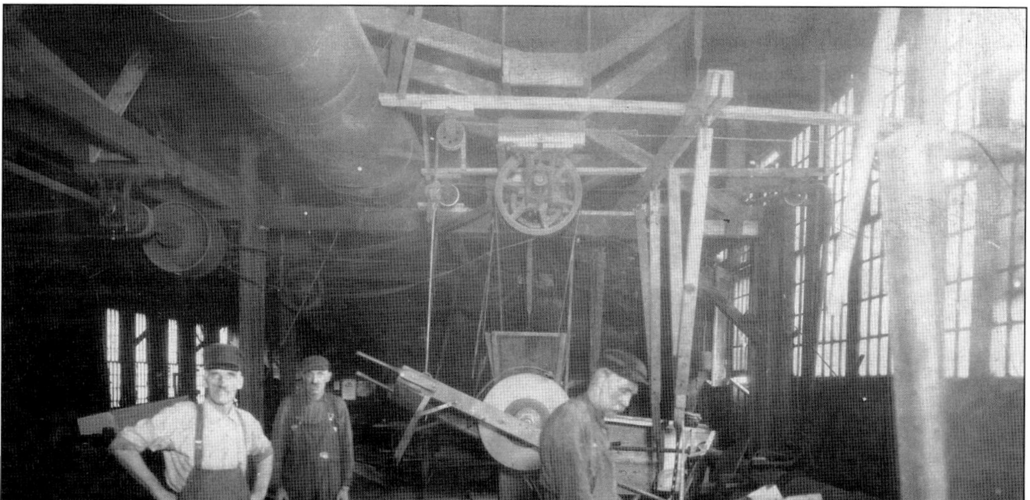

Blacksmith Shop at LeRoy Plow Company. The large emery wheel was used to polish the plow moldboards. The man on the right is "Buzzsaw" Stevens, who received his nickname because he talked constantly. In 1915, the company manufactured 25,000 plows.

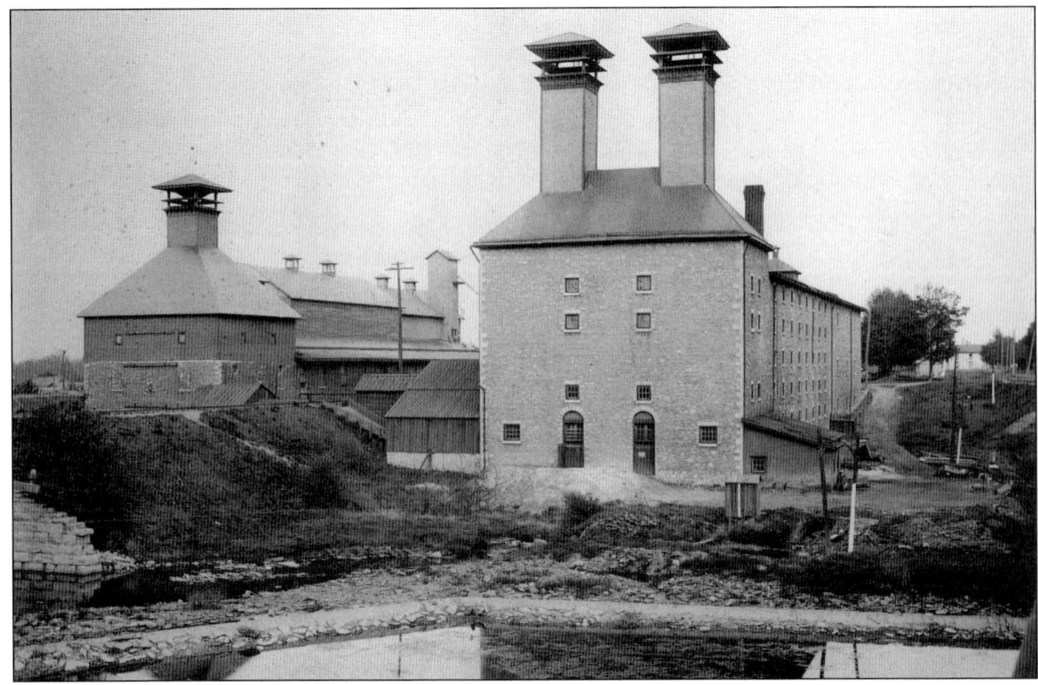

W. D. Matthews Malting Company. The malt company was started by Hugel and Company in the old stone railroad car shops on Church Street. The barley was shipped by railroad from Canada. In 1878, W. D. Matthews bought the plant and it was considered to be the largest malt house in the United States. The kiln produced 800,000 bushels of malt annually. In 1897, it became part of the American Malting Company.

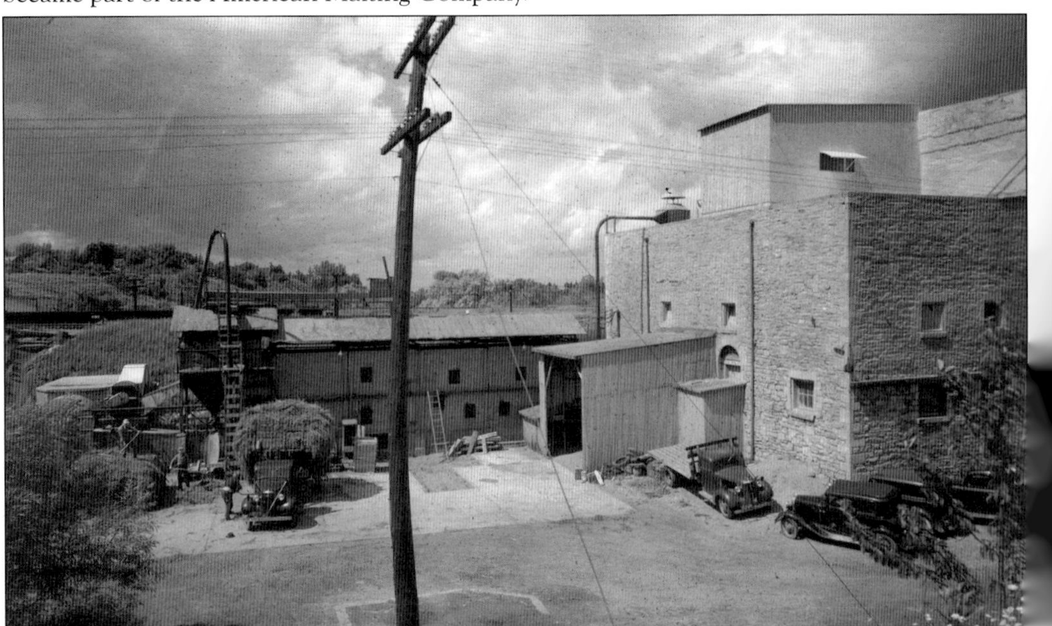

Alfalfa Plant. Established in 1938, it was located at 53 Church Street in the old malt factory buildings. Jesse Moulton was the superintendent. Hay was dehydrated and ground into fine meal with a high vitamin A content that was used for poultry feed.

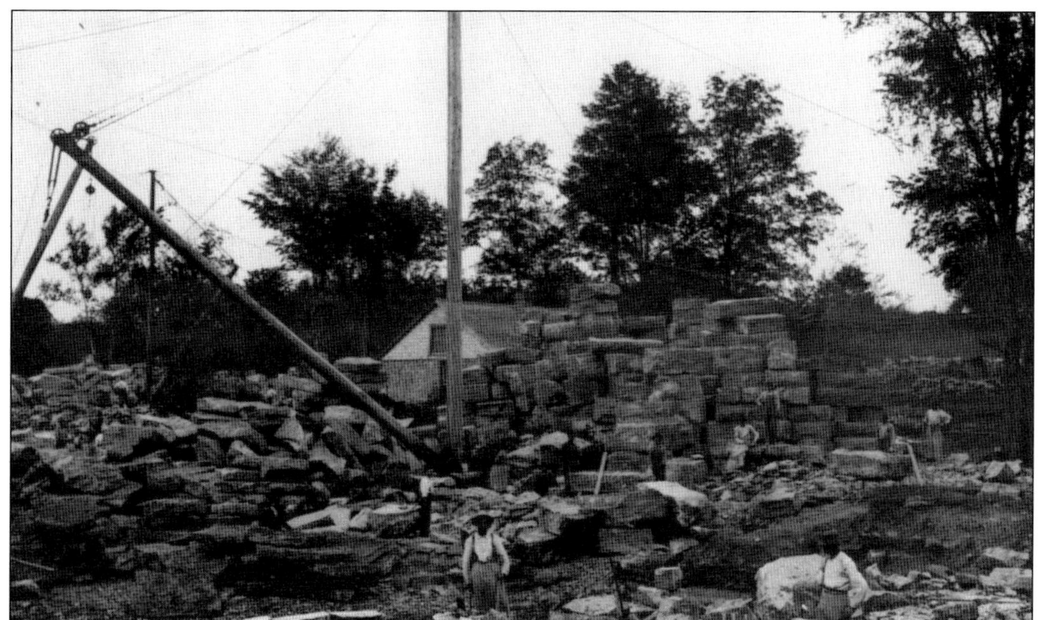

KEENEY QUARRY, 1896. Located on Oatka Creek behind Machpelah Cemetery, the quarry was originally known as the Morris and Strobel quarry and employed between 50 and 60 men. The powder building was located on the west side of the creek and was eventually donated to the Girl Scouts to be used as a clubhouse (See page 121).

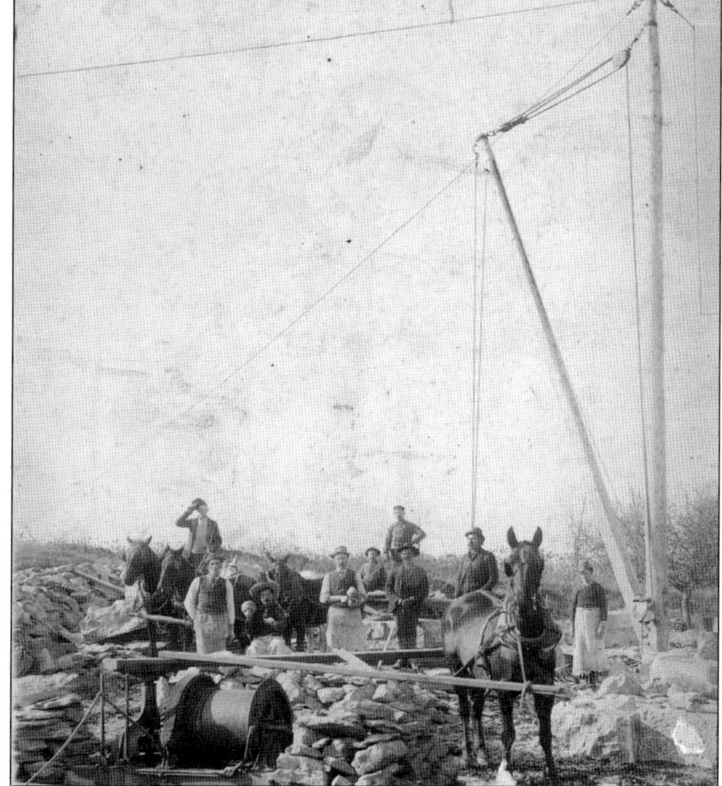

LIME ROCK QUARRY. This photograph was taken about 1887 at the quarry located on York Road. The early quarries produced architectural stone that was used for buildings and railroad culverts, as well as flux for the Bessemer steel plants in Buffalo and Pennsylvania. A different quality of limestone was burned in the nearby limekilns.

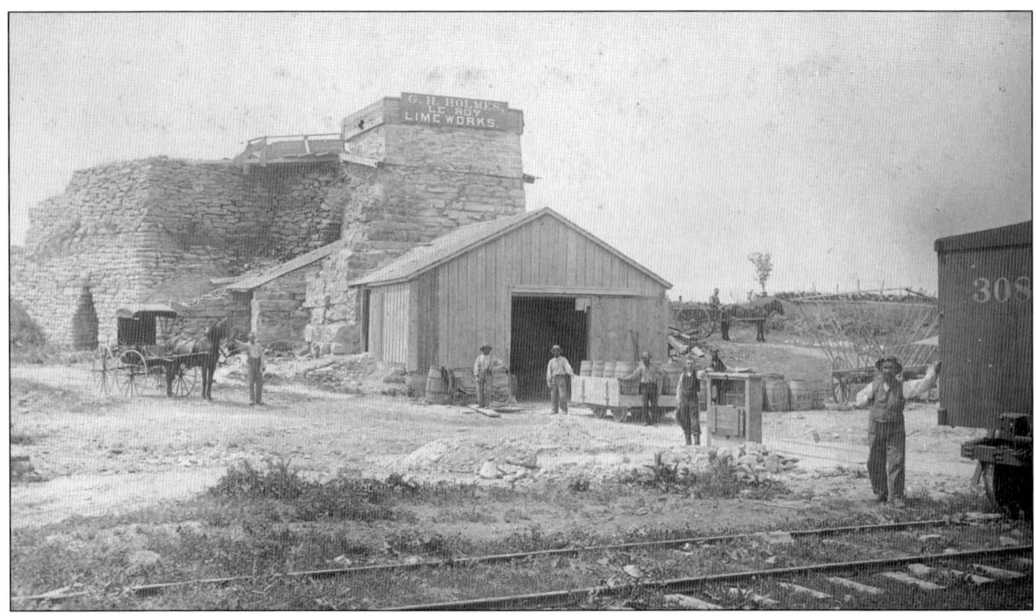

Holmes's Limekiln. There were several limekilns in the Lime Rock area. The limestone was burned to produce quick lime that was soaked with water to make slaked lime and then mixed with sand for mortar. Some of the kilns produced 700 bushels of lime a day. Pictured in this 1883 photograph are George Holmes (by the boxcar), Parley Holmes (by the packer), and Fido. The Holmes's kilns were bought and operated by John Heimlich.

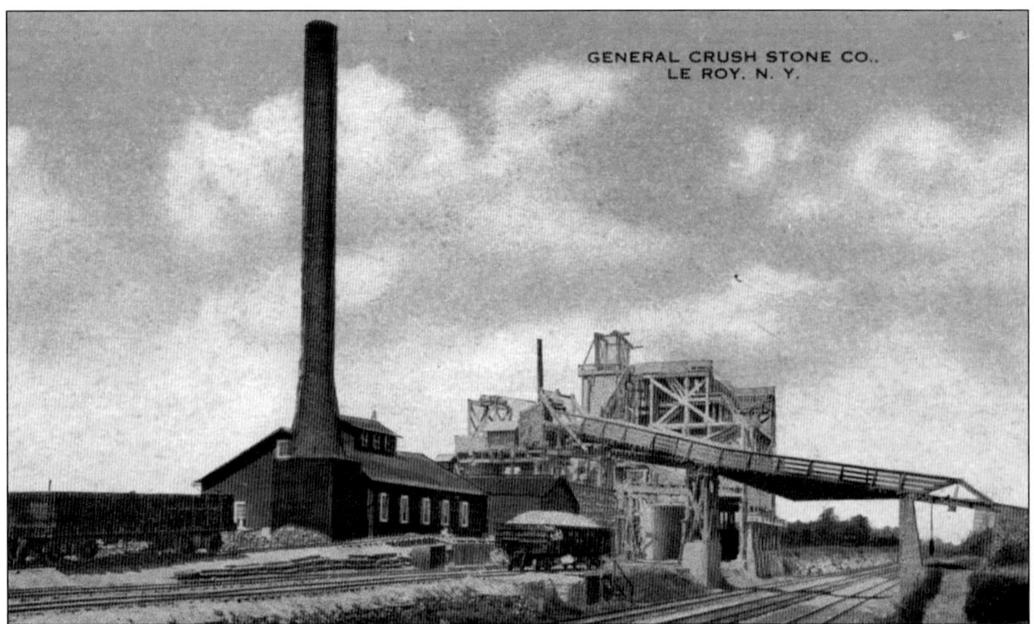

General Crushed Stone Company. In 1906, General Crushed Stone Company in LeRoy boasted that it had the largest stone crusher in the world. Driven by the demand for crushed stone for railroad ballast and new roads, the company continued its operation and provided all the crushed stone for the Mount Morris Dam between 1949 and 1951. It also supplied gravel for the New York State Thruway.

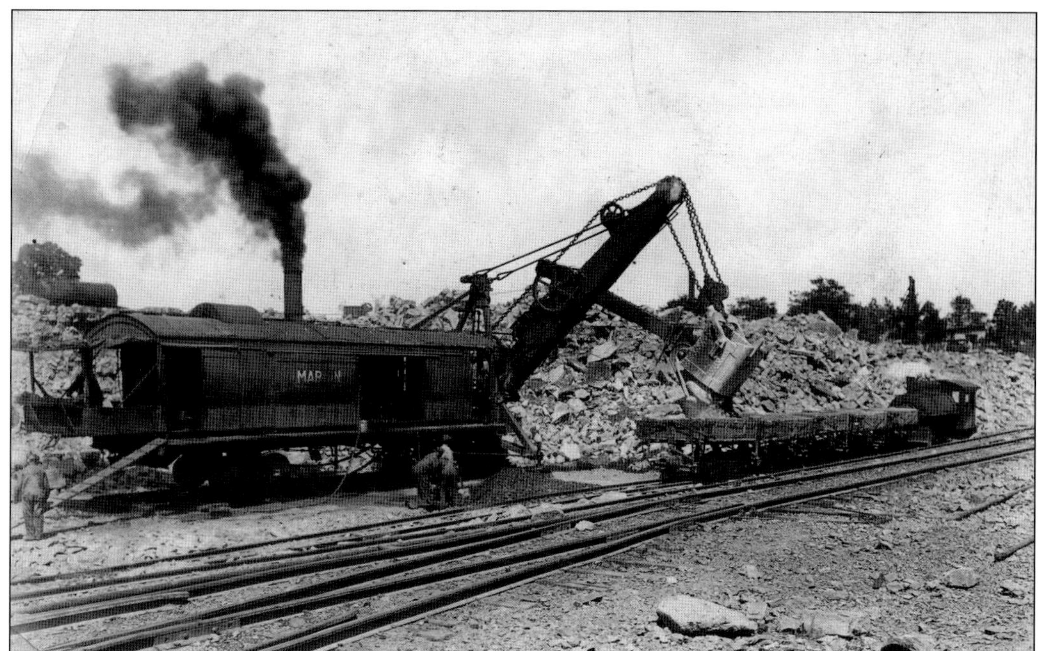

Steam Shovel. In 1906, General Crushed Stone Company bought a 100-ton Model No. 91 Marion steam shovel. The partial-swing shovel kept the huge stone crushers in operation. It ran on railroad tracks laid on the floor of the quarry. By 1924, it was fitted with caterpillar tracks. The shovel was driven out of the quarry in 1949. In 2008, it was placed on the National Register of Historic Places.

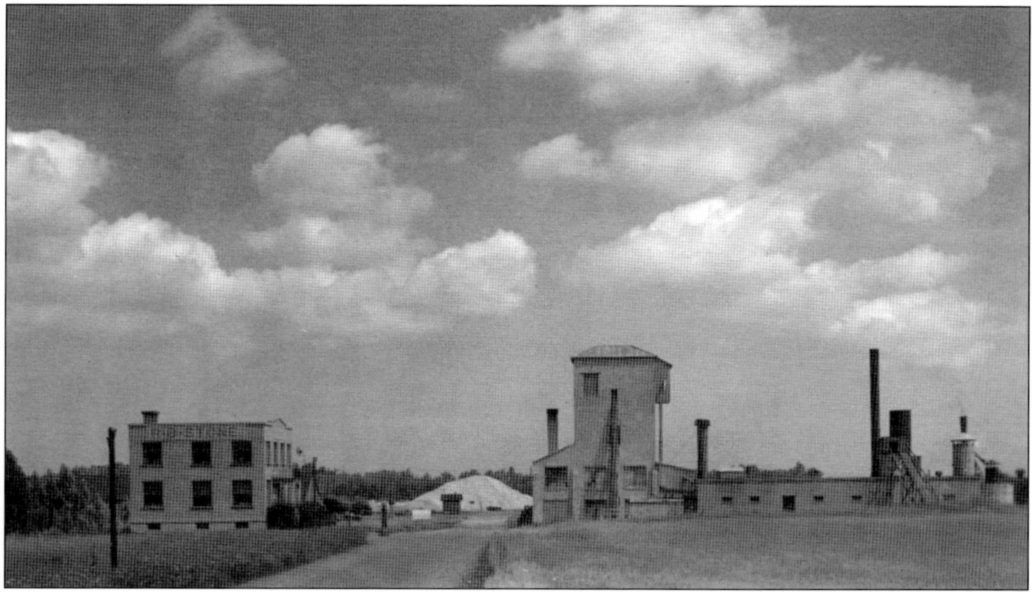

Ribstone Concrete Company. The company was organized in Alexander in 1919. In 1923, Donald Woodward became involved with the company and it became part of the LeRoy Lime and Crushed Stone Corporation. The company manufactured cement tile silos as well as wooden staved silos. Woodward constructed the Tower, a five-story house on Asbury Road, from the cement tiles (see page 80).

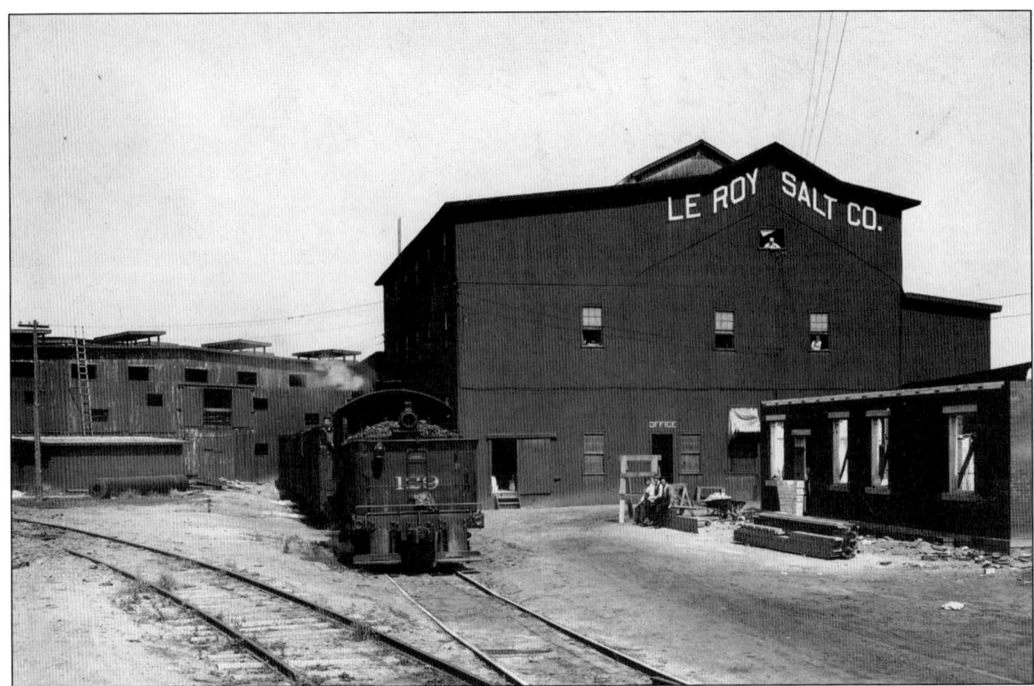

LeRoy Salt Company, 1914. Incorporated in 1883, the LeRoy Salt Company pumped brine to the surface and the water was evaporated in huge vats. Salt was also mined south of LeRoy by the Lehigh Salt Mining Company at Beaver Meadow. In 1891, the company sunk a shaft 802 feet deep, but three years later, the mine closed because the salt ore contained too much iron.

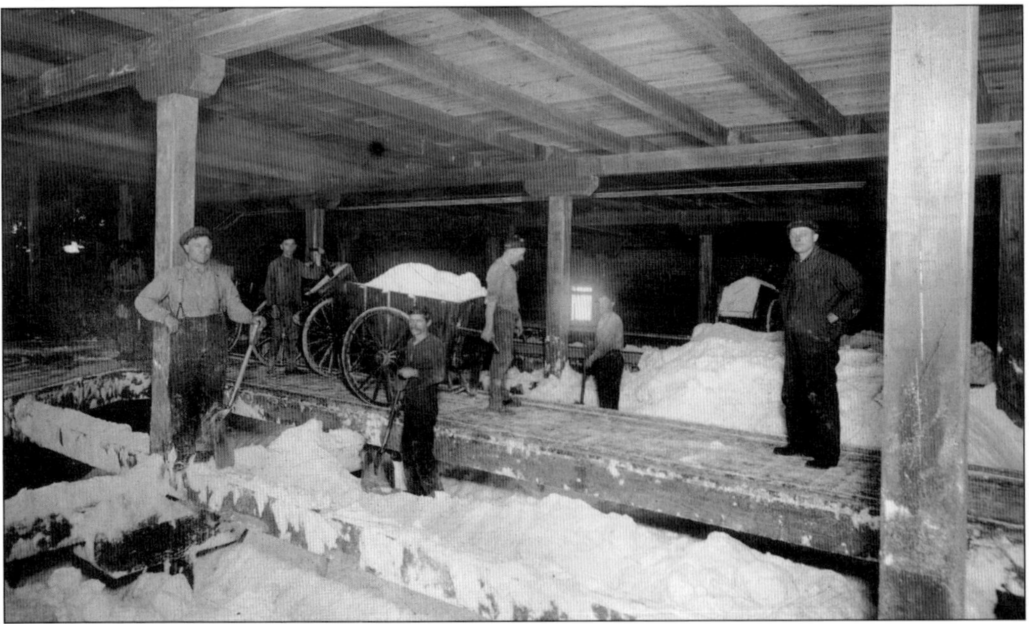

Salt Workers. Work at the LeRoy Salt Company was dangerous. Accidents were common and some men were scalded by the hot brine. A devastating fire swept though the salt plant in 1915, but the plant was quickly rebuilt. The company was bought by the Watkins Salt Company in 1928 and the factory was closed. The landmark smokestacks were demolished in the 1960s.

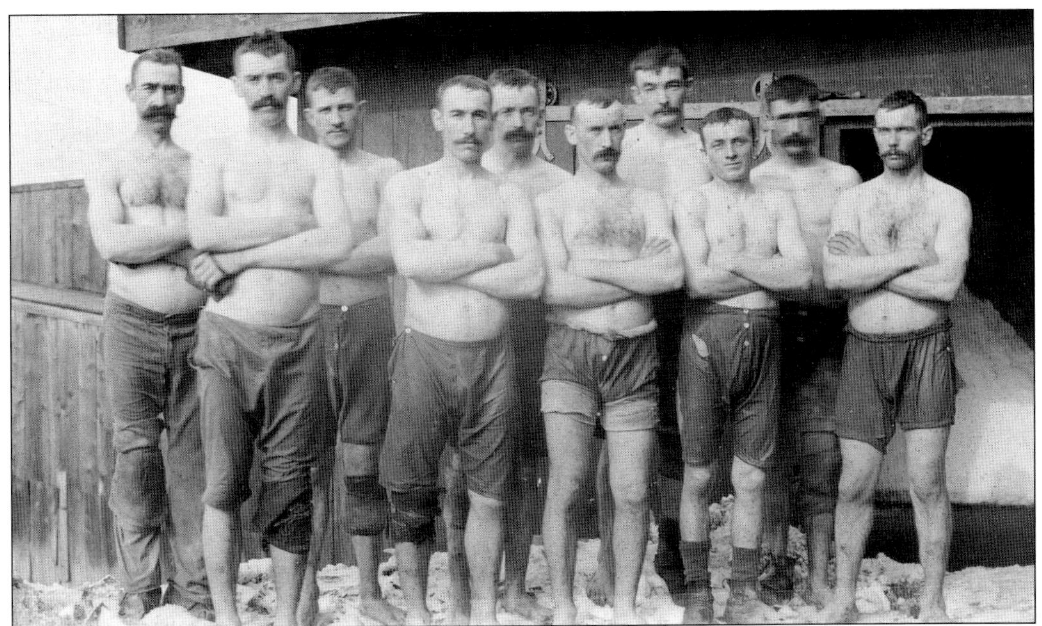

Workers at the Belmont Salt Block Company. The Belmont Company manufactured salt blocks and salt block holders for livestock. The work was hot, as evidenced by the men's clothes and lack of shoes.

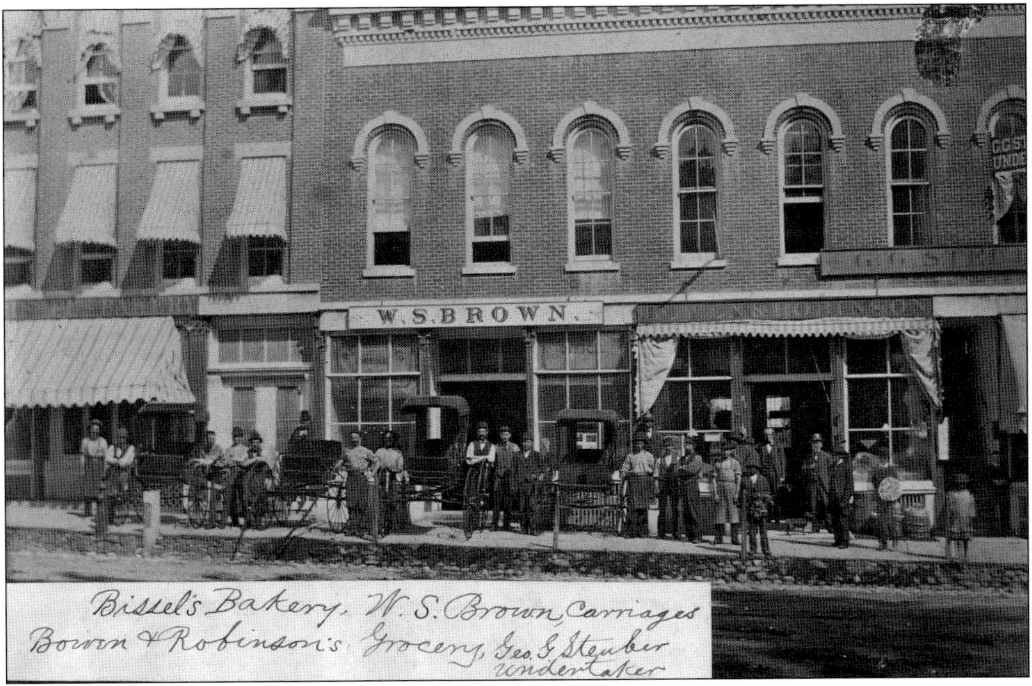

Brown Carriage Company. Established in 1857, the William S. Brown Carriage Company manufactured all kinds of wagons, carriages, and sleighs. Brown was a dealer in lime and stone in the area, handling over 85,000 bushels of lime each year. He employed about 15 men in the carriage business. In 1869, fire destroyed the building, but Brown rebuilt his factory and continued business.

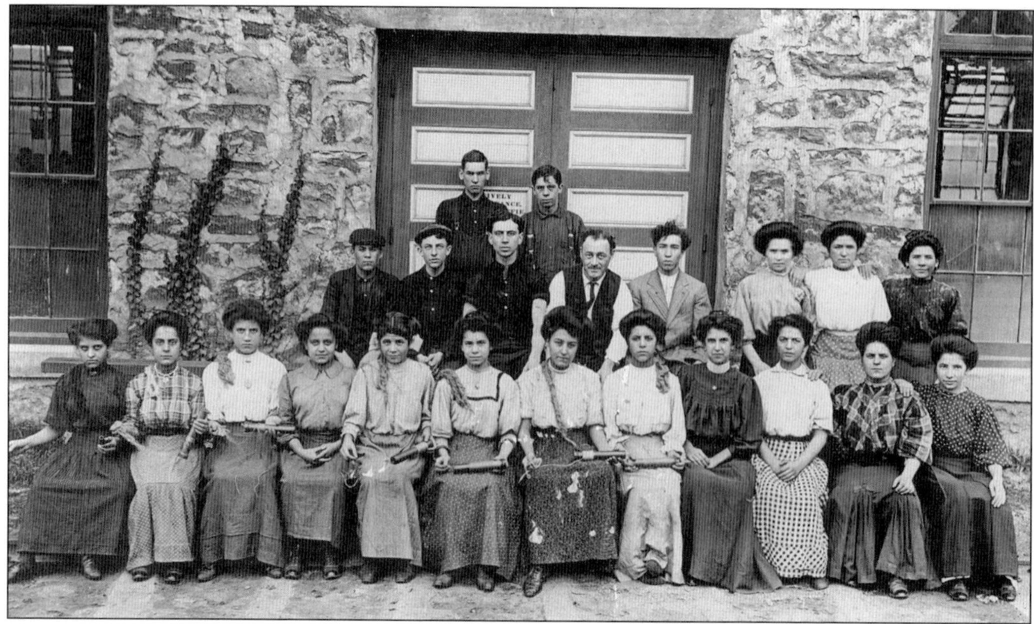

COTTON MILL WORKERS. LeRoy Cotton Company manufactured cotton yarn. Many of the workers were young Italian women and boys. Standing in the third row are Raymond Roblee (left) and Louis Mandrell. The women in the first row are (from left to right) Mary Pastrella, Santa Miserentino Ogeen, two unidentified women, Rose Shinta, three unidentified women, Mary Leone, Josephine Mancuso Baglio (who was ten when she started working at the mill), Mary Cacamise, and unidentified. The second row is unidentified.

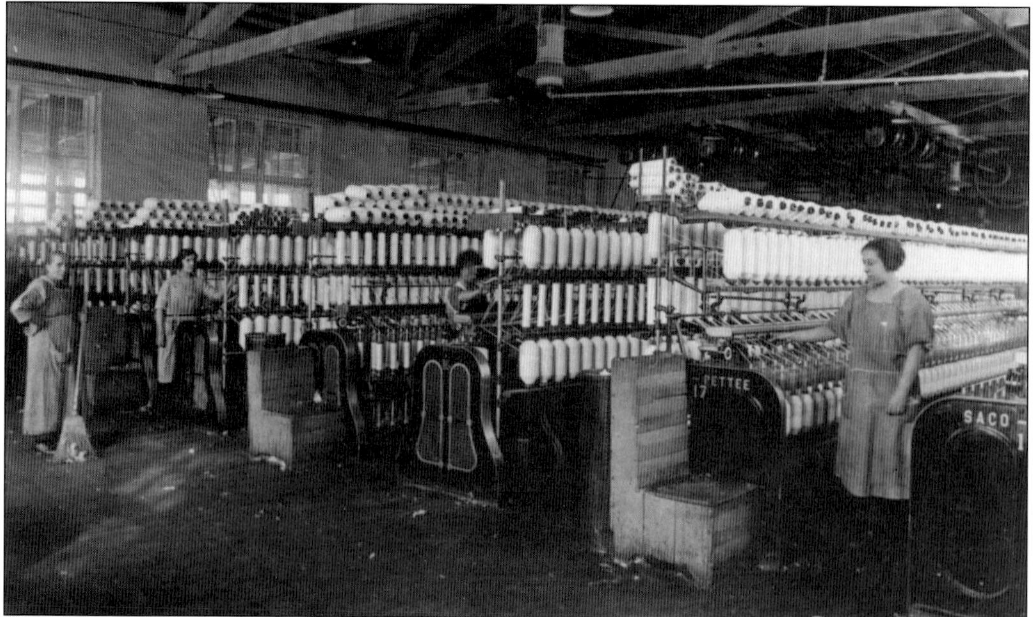

BAY STATE COTTON MILL. The LeRoy Cotton Company was succeeded by the Bay State Cotton Mill in 1906. The mill not only produced cotton thread but also manufactured cotton mailbags. Standing from left to right are Mrs. Chimino, Josephine Mancuso, unidentified, and Mary Ange Battaglia.

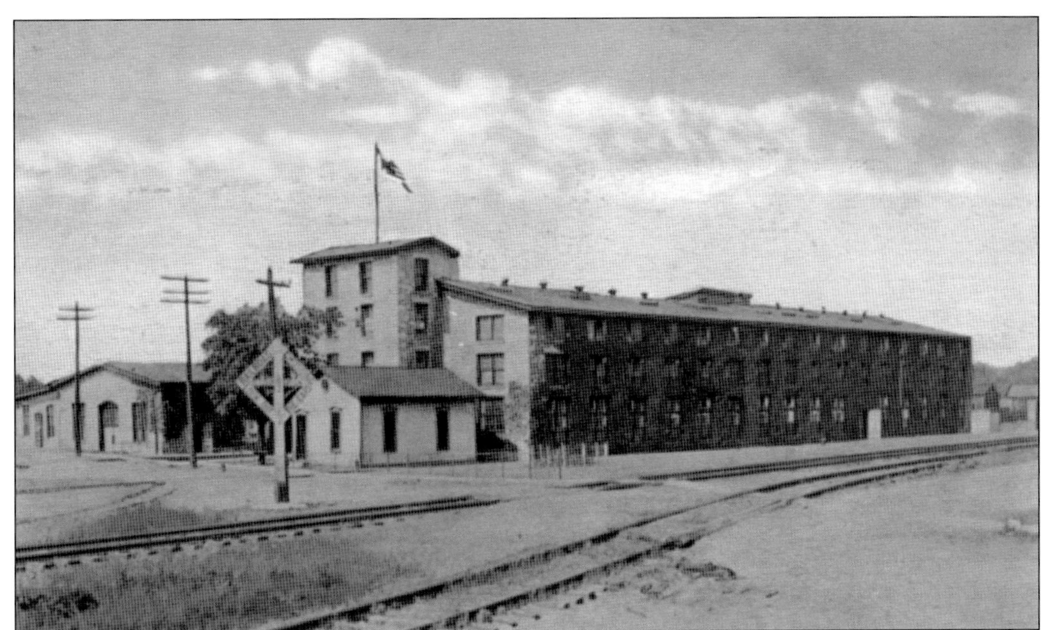

Bay State Cotton Building. In 1906, the malt company buildings on the east side of Church Street were renovated by the LeRoy Cotton Company. This structure was built before the Civil War as a factory for carriages and railroad cars. During the Civil War, it housed soldiers. In 1932, the building was used by the Union Steel Chest Company. It was destroyed by a massive fire on March 15, 1949.

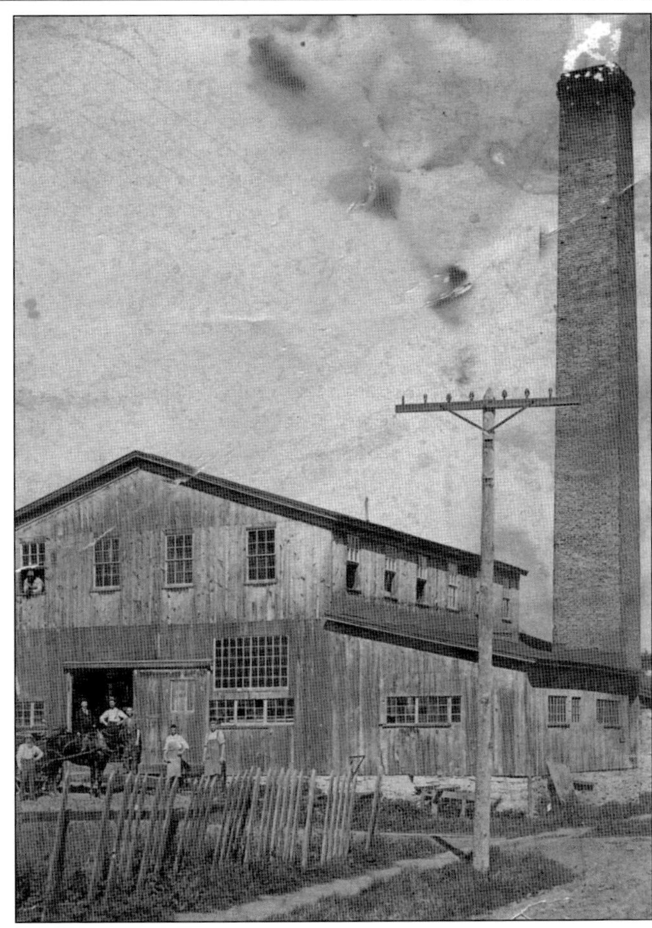

Lapp Lumber, c. 1903. In 1852, Chauncey Olmsted established a planing mill on Mill Street. In 1898, Joseph Lapp began the Lapp Lumber Company after buying out his partner, George Kroner. Joseph's sons took over the business in 1930. The third generation, Richard and Joseph Lapp, continued the business until their deaths when the company was sold.

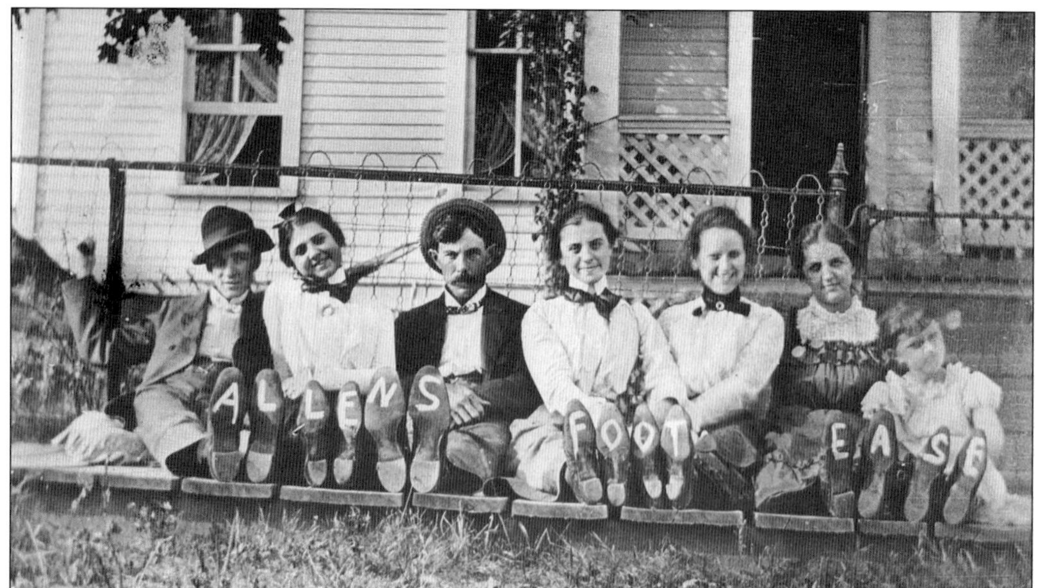

ALLEN'S FOOT-EASE. Founded in the early 1900s by Allen S. Olmsted, the company produced Foot-Ease Medicated Soap, Knock-A-Cold, Allen's Discovery for Piles, and Allen's Sanitary Tooth-Ease. The company also distributed Pope's Blood and Liver Medicine and Mother Grey's Sweet Worm Powder. In 1911, the factory was located in the Academic Institute building behind LeRoy House. In 1942, the company was sold to the Foster Milburn Company in Buffalo.

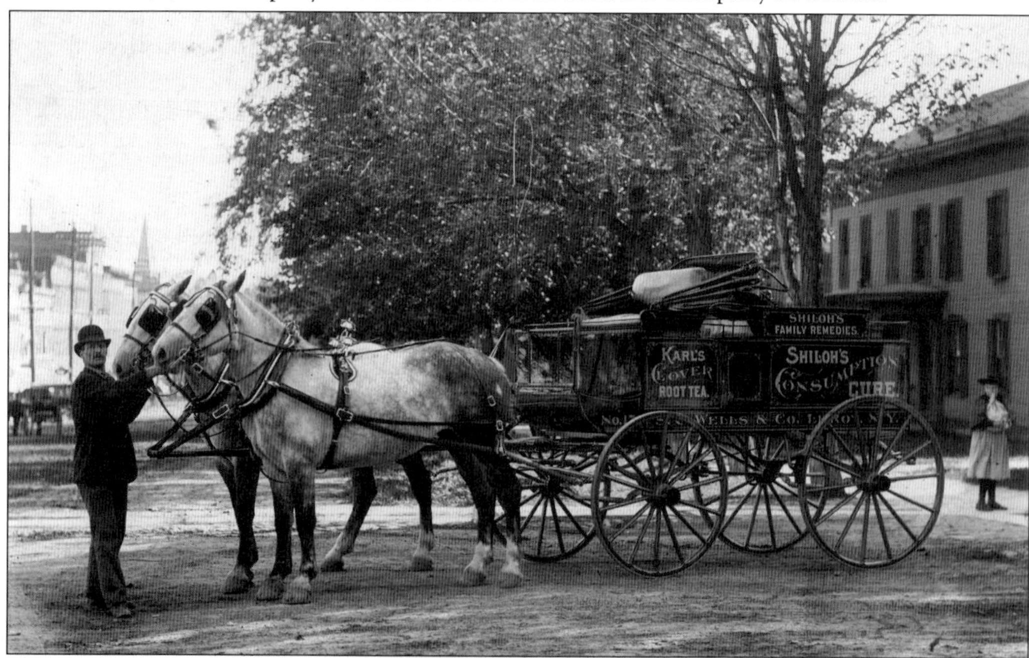

SHILOH MEDICINE COMPANY. In 1873, Schuyler C. Wells developed a variety of proprietary medicines. He built the Shiloh building on Church Street in 1877. After his death in 1897, his son, Carl, took over the business. This wagon was photographed in front of the First Presbyterian Church. Later known as the Brown Manufacturing Company, it purchased the Rough-On product line, including Rough-On-Rats poison. The annual Brownie Calendar is still distributed today.

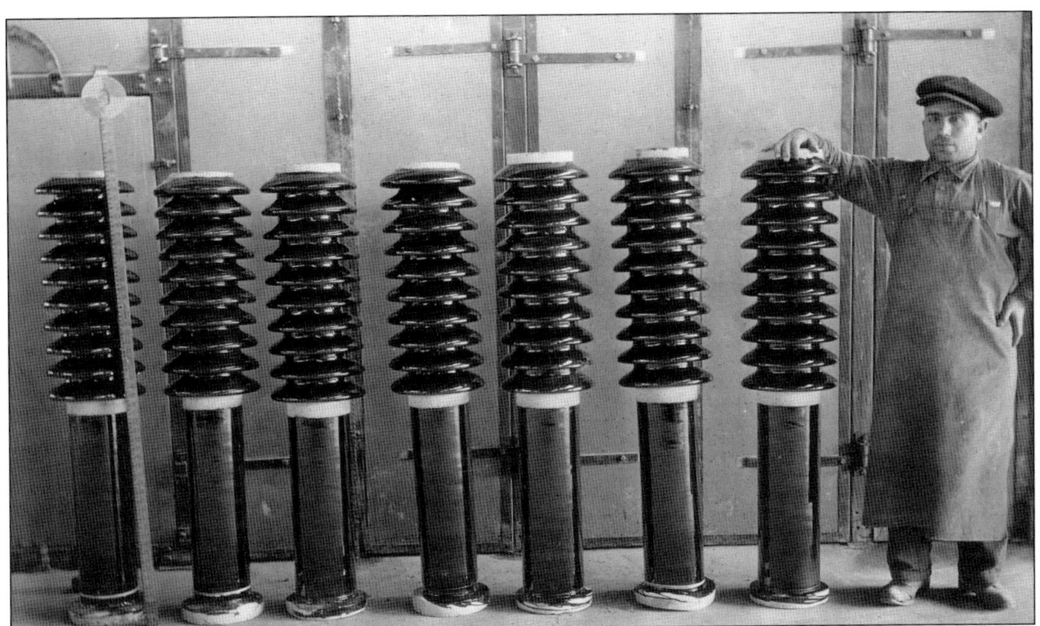

Lapp Insulator Company. John S. Lapp founded the company in 1916, and with his brother, Grover, he developed a line of commercial insulators and special porcelain for the electrical utility and allied industries. In 1969, the company became part of the Interpace Corporation, which was purchased by the Clevepak Corporation in 1983. It is now an independently owned company.

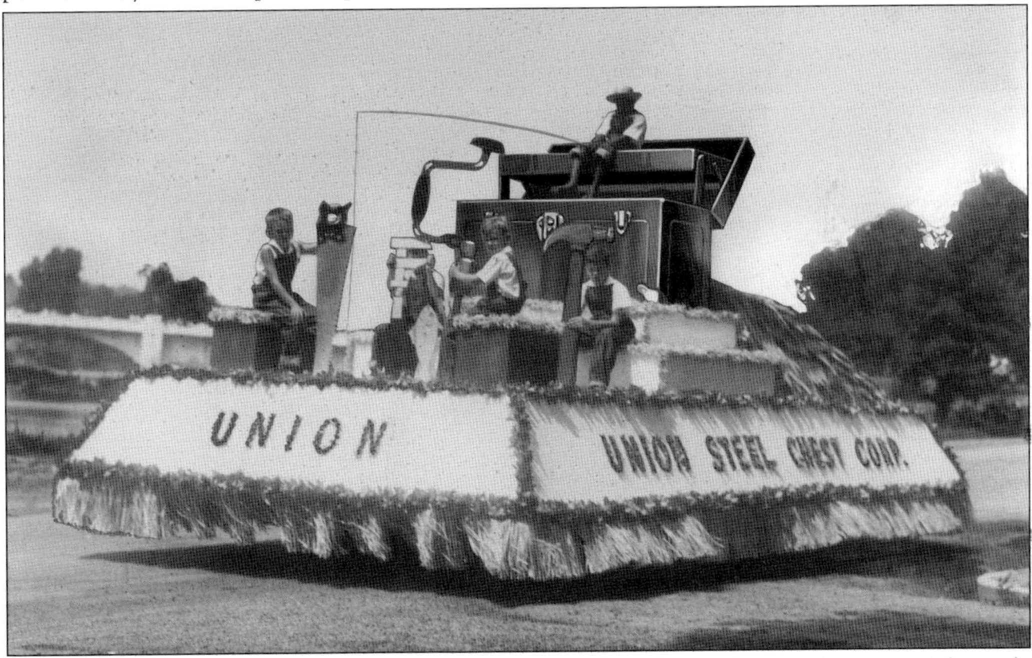

Union Steel Chest Company. This photograph was taken during the town's centennial parade in 1934. The Union Steel Chest Company was founded in Rochester in 1893. It manufactured machinists' chests, tool boxes, and fishing tackle boxes. In 1932, the company moved production to LeRoy, into the former malt house on Church Street. In 1972, the company moved to Chandler, Arizona.

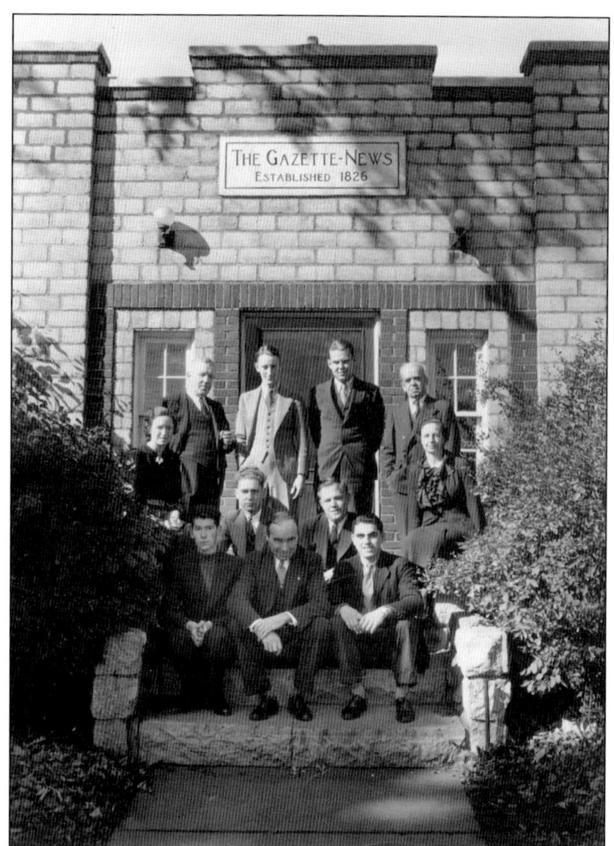

THE GAZETTE NEWS, 1940. The LeRoy *Gazette-News* was established in 1826. It was in continuous production until the 1980s. In 1912, it merged with the *LeRoy News*. Pictured from left to right are (first row) Benjamin Donnelly, David Paganin, and J. Francis Blood; (second row) Helen Chiler, Corrin Chiler, Walter Butts, and Amelia Pfeiffer; (third row) Frank Wade, Ellsworth Baldwin, Avery Perkins, and Edward Perkins.

LEROY TIMES. The *LeRoy Times* was established in LeRoy in June 1881 and merged with the *LeRoy Gazette* in 1894. There were several other newspapers in LeRoy, including the *Genesee Courier*, the *Genesee Daily Herald*, the *Genesee Herald*, the *Genesee Republic and Advocate for Liberty*, the *Genesee Republican and Herald of Reform*, the *LeRoy Advertiser*, the *LeRoy Courier*, the *LeRoy Democrat*, the *LeRoy News*, the *LeRoy Times*, and the *Republican Advocate*.

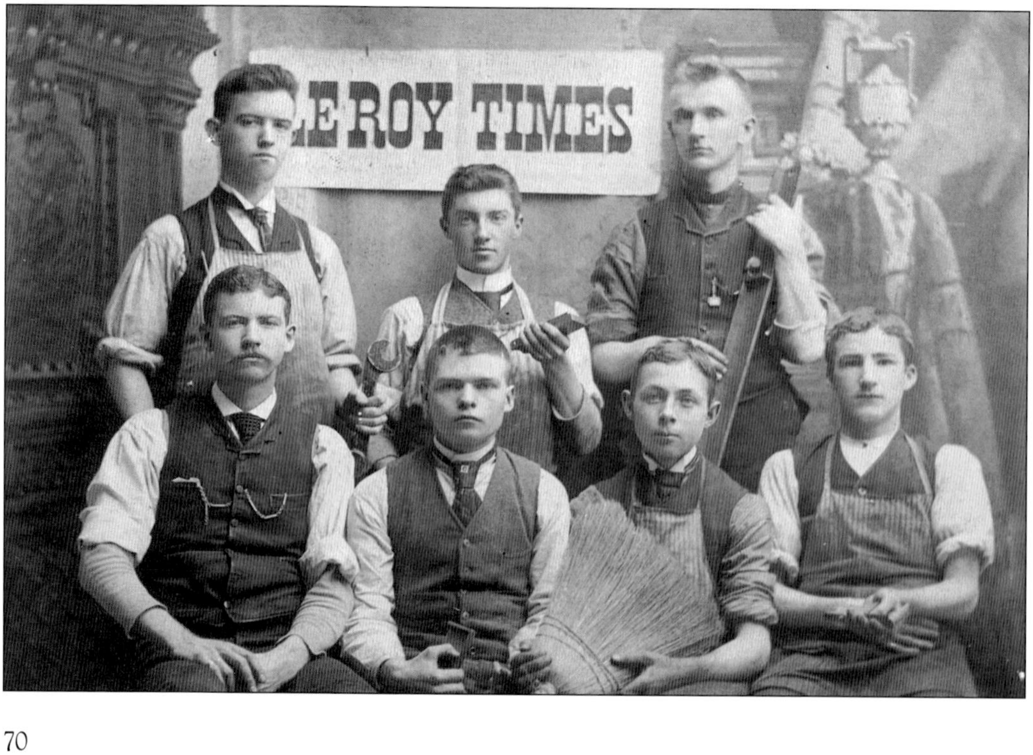

Five

THE JELL-O STORY

In 1897, Pearle Wait, a carpenter in LeRoy, introduced a new brand of gelatin dessert. His wife, May, named it Jell-O. He registered Jell-O as a trademark in 1897. The first four flavors of the gelatin dessert were orange, lemon, strawberry, and raspberry. Two years later, he sold the rights to Jell-O to a prosperous LeRoy businessman, Orator Woodward, for $450. Pearle Wait would continue to build houses and dabble with patent medicines, but he would never reap fortunes from Jell-O. In the meantime, Orator Woodward, a self-made businessman and owner of the O. F. Woodward Medicine Company and the Genesee Pure Food Company, invested time and money into perfecting the gelatin product. In 1902, he launched a nationwide advertising campaign in the *Ladies Home Journal*. Two years later, he introduced the Jell-O Girl and sent horse-drawn wagons to rural communities to promote the new product. Woodward died in 1906, and within a year, Jell-O was grossing $1 million a year. A few years later, Orator's eldest son, Ernest, became president of the company. He negotiated the sale of the company to Postum in 1925 by an exchange of stock that brought the Woodward family over $65 million. Jell-O and Postum became the first two subsidiaries of General Foods. In 1964, General Foods closed the factory in LeRoy, and production was moved to Dover, Delaware. Today Jell-O is owned by Kraft Foods.

The story of Jell-O and LeRoy is not complete without the story of the Woodward family. Their lifestyles and philanthropic contributions to the community left an indelible mark on LeRoy. Today there are no descendents of the Woodward family living in LeRoy, yet Pearle Wait's granddaughter, a retired schoolteacher, has lived in LeRoy all her life.

To commemorate the 100th anniversary of Jell-O, the LeRoy Historical Society established the Jell-O Gallery in 1997 to exhibit the story of "America's Most Famous Dessert."

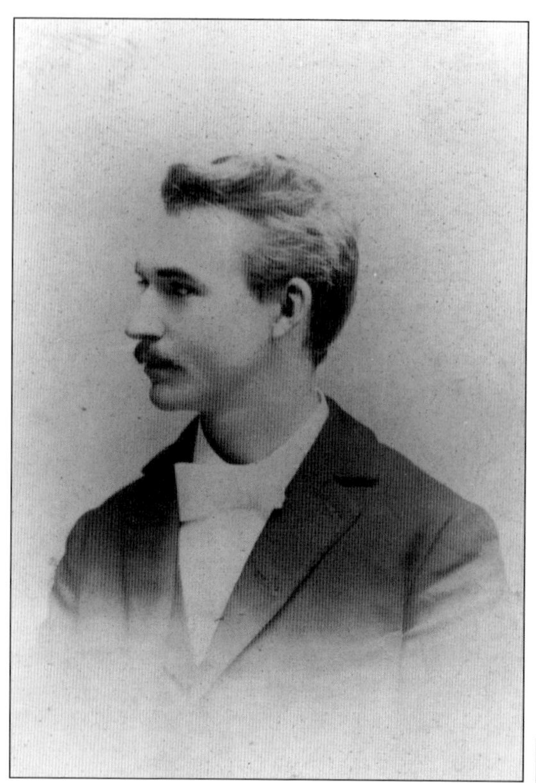

Pearle Wait (1871–1915). Pearle Wait developed Jell-O in 1897 and registered the Jell-O trademark in March. It is believed that his wife, May, coined the name. In 1899, he purchased a small building on Lake Street for a factory, but shortly after, he sold Jell-O for $450 to the Genesee Pure Food Company, owned by Orator Woodward. Wait lived long enough to see the Woodward family make millions from Jell-O.

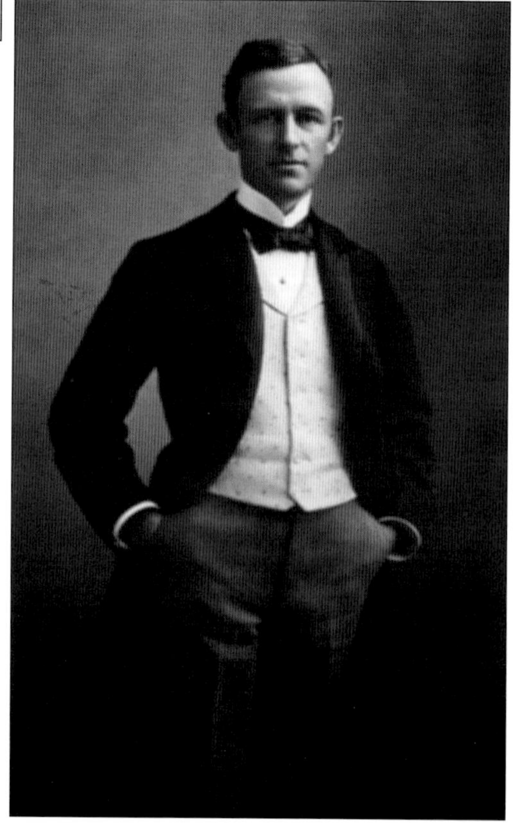

Orator Woodward, (1856–1906). Born in Bergen, his father died in the Civil War and the family moved to LeRoy. He first manufactured plaster of paris skeet targets. Then he manufactured medicated nest eggs that killed lice on chickens. The O. F Woodward Medicine Company was very successful. He also manufactured Grain-O, a roasted-grain coffee substitute, and founded the Genesee Pure Food Company. In 1899, he bought the rights to Jell-O.

The Jell-O Girl. Like many other companies, the Jell-O Company chose a child to be the spokesperson for its products. The Jell-O Girl was four-year-old Elizabeth King from New York City. Her image appeared on the box into the 1940s. Jell-O began national advertising in the *Ladies Home Journal* in 1902. Noted illustrators Norman Rockwell, Rose O'Neill, and Maxfield Parrish designed Jell-O advertising and recipe books.

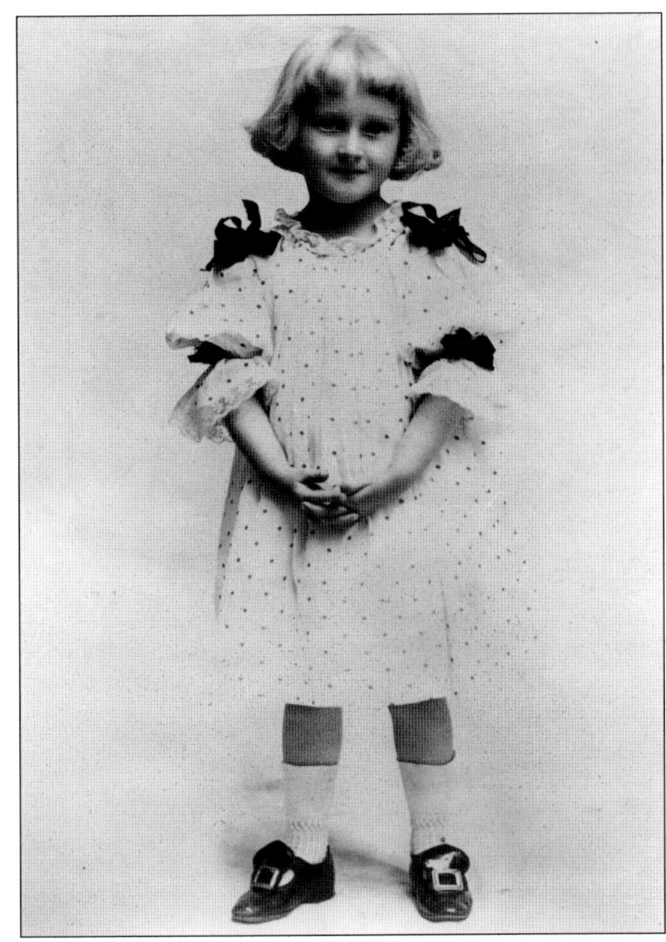

Jell-O Wagon. The Jell-O Company sent salesmen throughout the country to promote its products. The salesmen did not sell Jell-O door-to-door because it would have necessitated the purchase of a salesmen's license, so they gave out recipe books and tacked up posters. They filled store orders and decorated store windows. The horse-drawn wagons were phased out around 1915 and replaced with trucks.

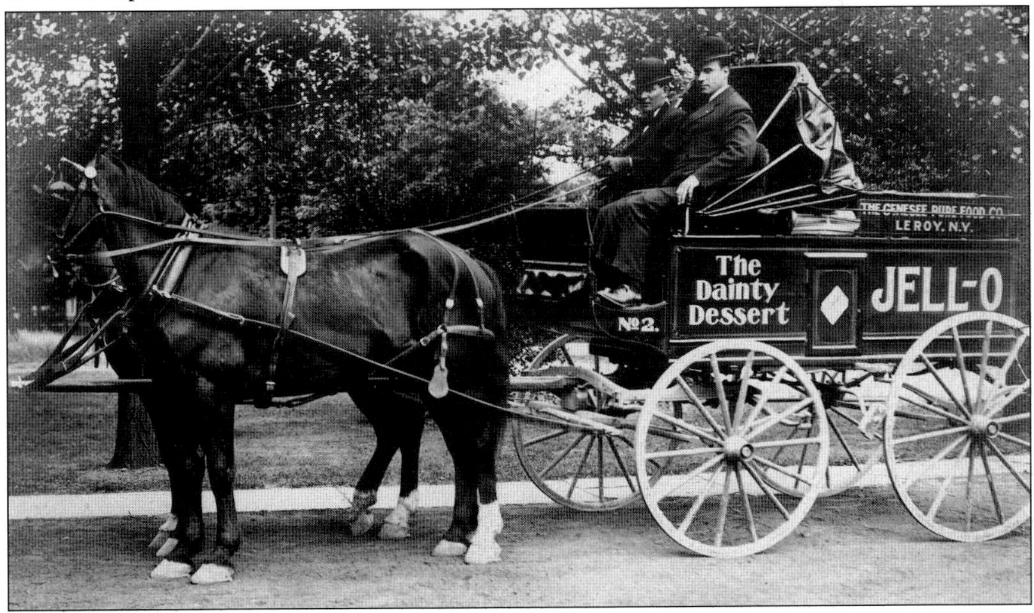

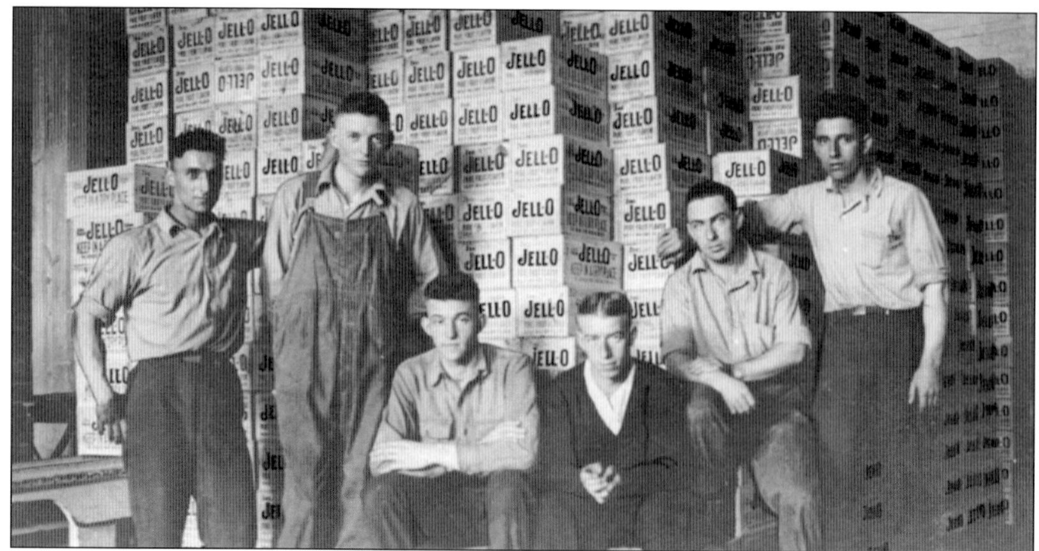

SHIPPING DEPARTMENT, 1918. These men served in the 108th Infantry Regiment, 27th Division during World War I. The photograph appeared in the *American Legion Weekly*, which noted that they "had returned to work tossing boxes of Dainty Dessert after their experiences throwing hand grenades in the Hindenburg Line." The men are (from left to right) Joseph Fox, Leo Mooney, John Vescovi, Carl Lee, Gordon Hoffman, and James Spillane.

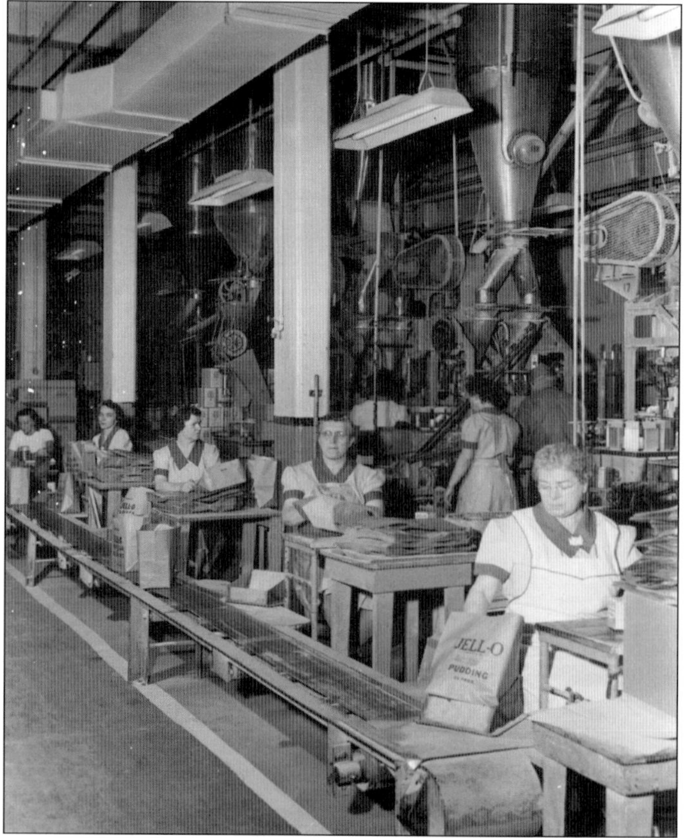

FACTORY WORKERS. Jell-O employed about 350 people, most of them women. At first, the boxes were packed by hand, but the invention of an automatic packaging machine in 1914 enabled Jell-O to be packaged in a seamless wax paper bag. During the peak season, there were three shifts at the factory. After the factory closed, some of the employees moved to the new factory in Dover, Delaware.

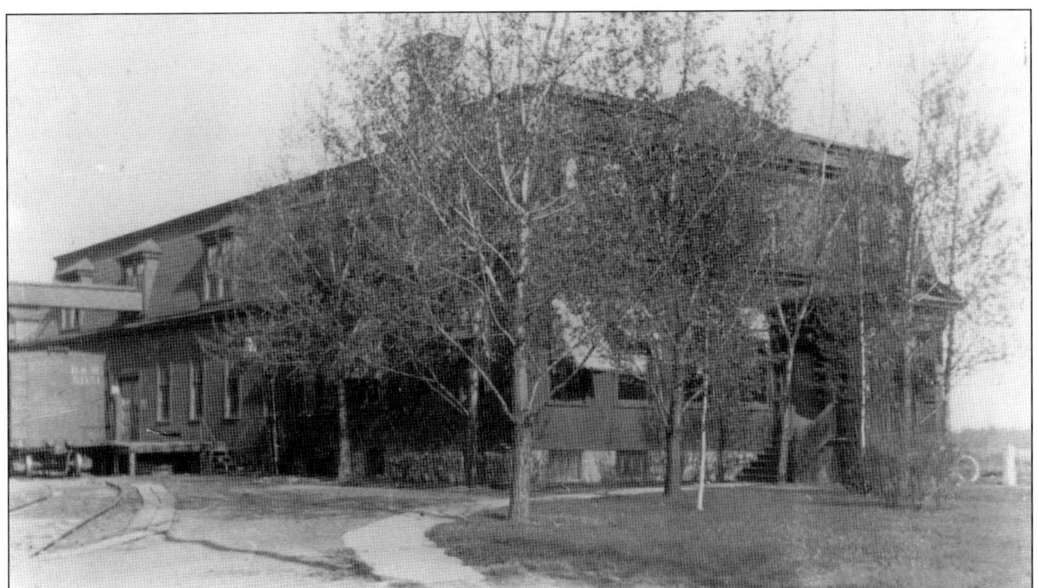

Factory. Orator Woodward built a factory on North Street for the production of Grain-O in 1897. After the acquisition of Jell-O, the factory was enlarged several times. Bordered on one side by the railroad tracks and on the north by the cemetery, it eventually became outdated and General Foods decided to build a new facility in Dover, Delaware. The LeRoy factory closed in 1964.

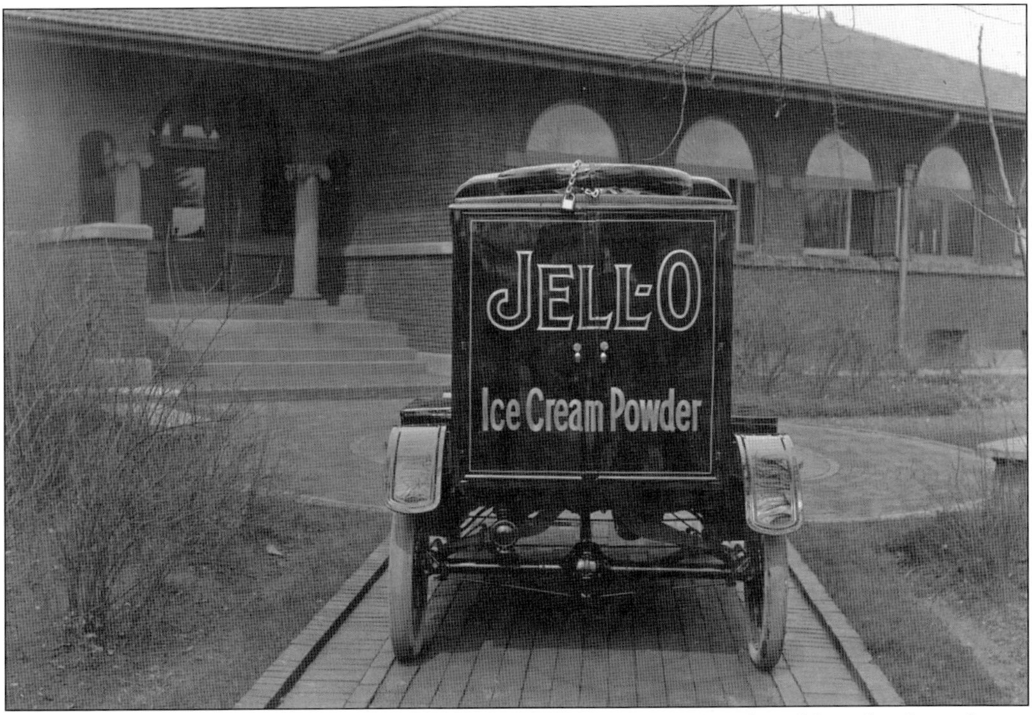

Jell-O Truck in Front of Jell-O Office. Soon after Orator Woodward bought the rights to Jell-O, he introduced a product that could be mixed with milk to make ice cream. Jell-O Ice Cream powder was sold for many years. In 1930, Jell-O introduced Jell-O pudding, and a few years later, Jell-O instant pudding. Today the Jell-O name is on 50 different products.

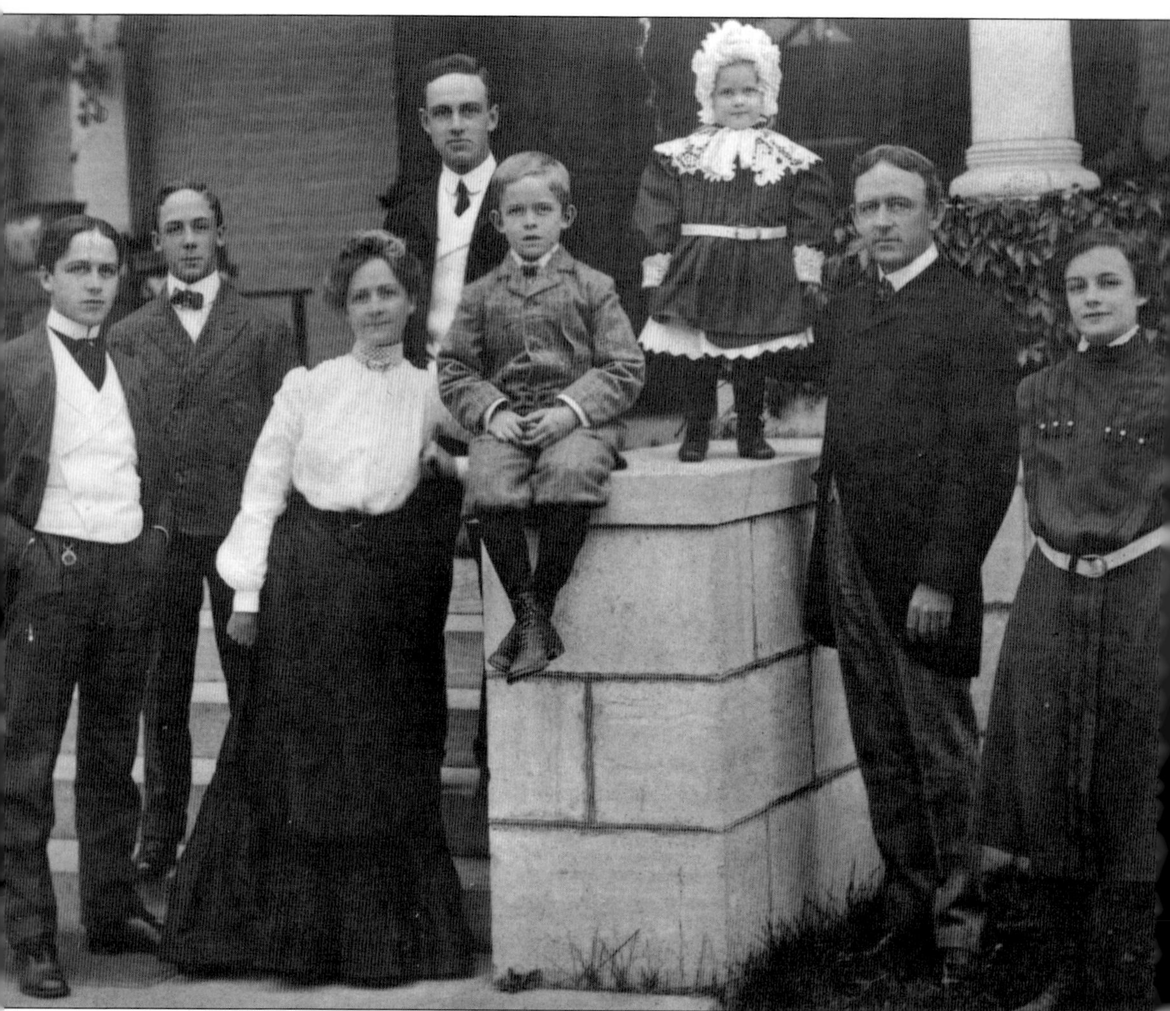

Woodward Family. Pictured here from left to right are Ernest (1882–1948), who became president of the Jell-O Company and negotiated the sale of the company in 1925 for over $65 million; Paul (1886–1910), who died young; Mrs. Cora Woodward (1860–1923), who became president of the company upon the death of her husband; Orator Frank (1884–1952), who was known as the playboy of the family; Donald (1893–1958), the youngest son, who took over the O. F. Woodward Medicine Company; Helen (1899–1965), who married several times and donated millions of dollars to a variety of organizations, including Strong Memorial Hospital; Orator Woodward (1856–1906), who bought Jell-O for $450; and Eleanor (1889–1938), who married Dr. John Vietor of New York City, a noted heart surgeon. In 1930, the Woodward children donated the Woodward Memorial Library to the LeRoy School District in memory of their parents.

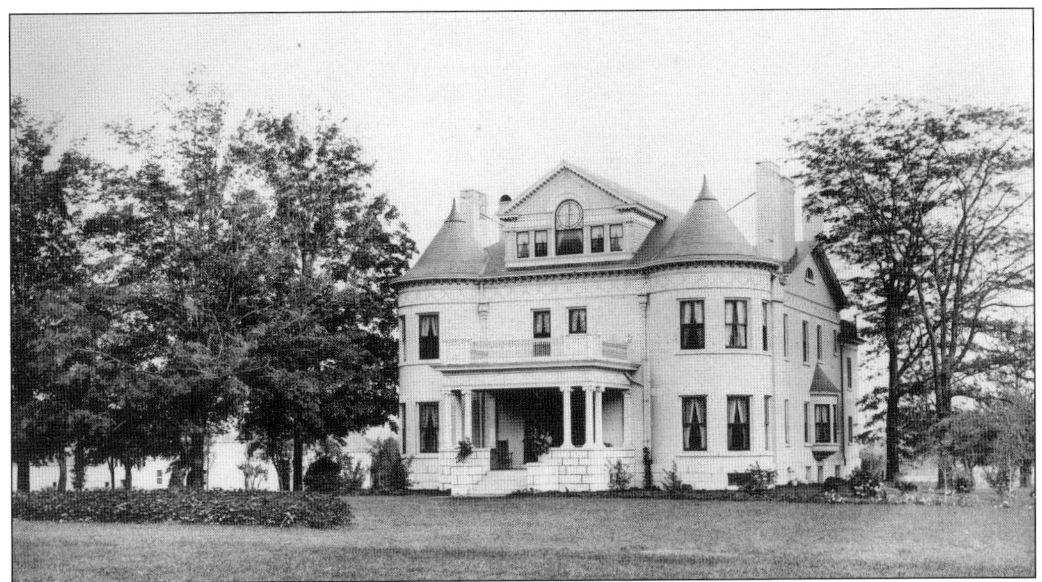

Hill Bar. This was the home of Orator Woodward and his family. He purchased a large brick Colonial-style home on the south side of East Main Street and added large circular towers on each end of the house (which some of the locals called silos) and created a French chateau for his family. He spent over $40,000 on the renovations and gardens.

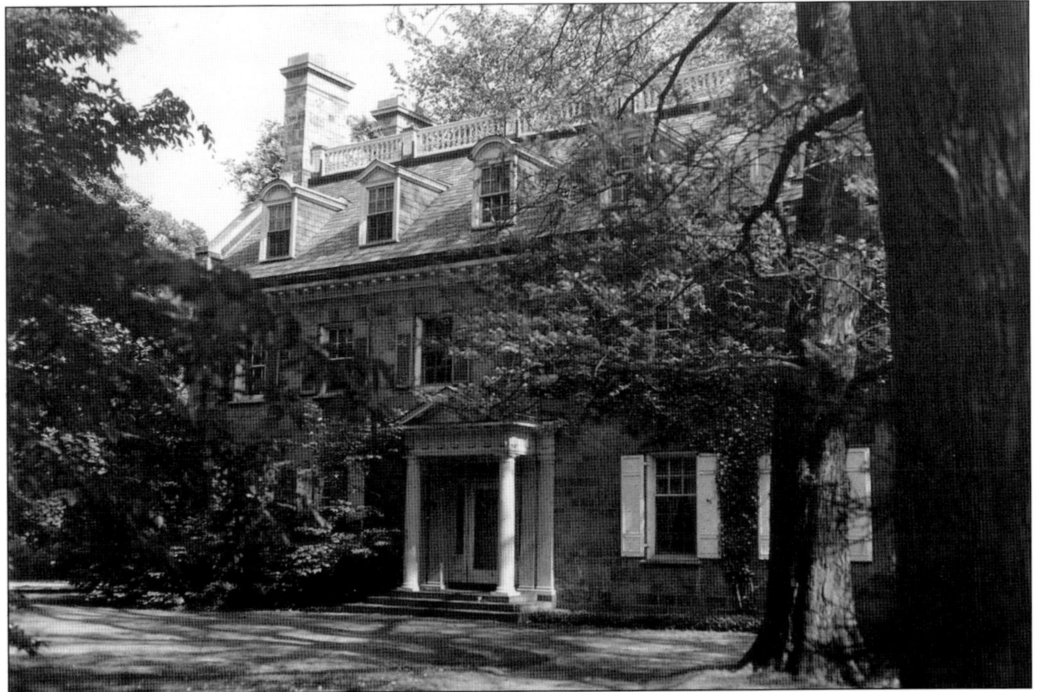

Poplar Lane. Ernest Woodward razed his father's house and completed Poplar Lane in 1921. The Georgian-style mansion built of Quincy granite featured wood paneled formal rooms and doorknobs of Tiffany silver. After Ernest and his wife died, the property was given to the University of Rochester. It was torn down in 1960, under the provision that it be razed if the university did not want it.

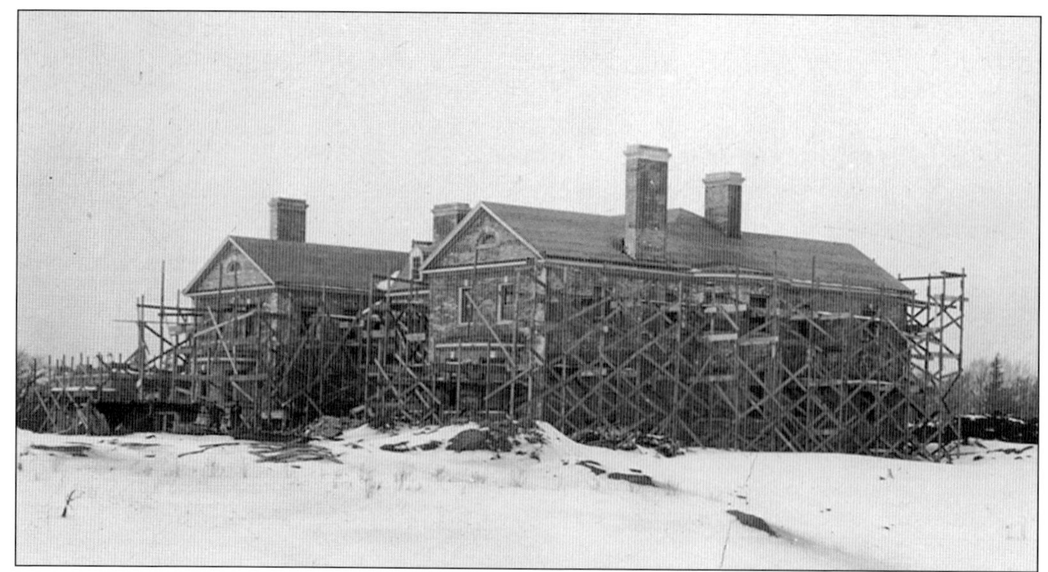

Mercygrove. Completed in 1928 for Donald Woodward, the mansion included an indoor pool, a walk-in vault for fur coats, and a dining room with silver fixtures and Birchfield wallpaper. The 56-acre estate included formal gardens, natural plantings, cabins, and greenhouses. The house was purchased by Donald's brother Ernest, and it became the Edith Hartwell Clinic for children. It is now owned by the Mercedarian Fathers.

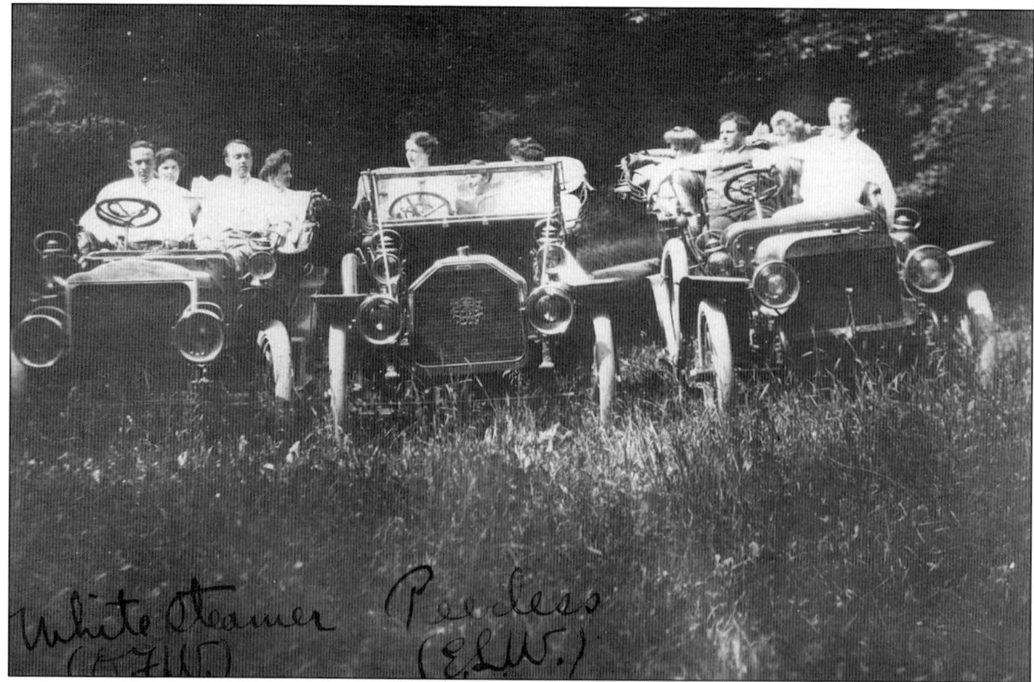

The Woodward Machines. Cora Woodward referred to the family's automobiles as the "machines." In this photograph is a White steamer (on left) driven by Orator (Jr.), and in the center is a Peerless owned by Ernest. The Woodwards also owned Stanley steamers, Popes, Packards, Cadillacs, Reos, and a Rolls Royce. Although they hired chauffeurs to drive and maintain their vehicles, the Woodwards also enjoyed getting behind the wheel.

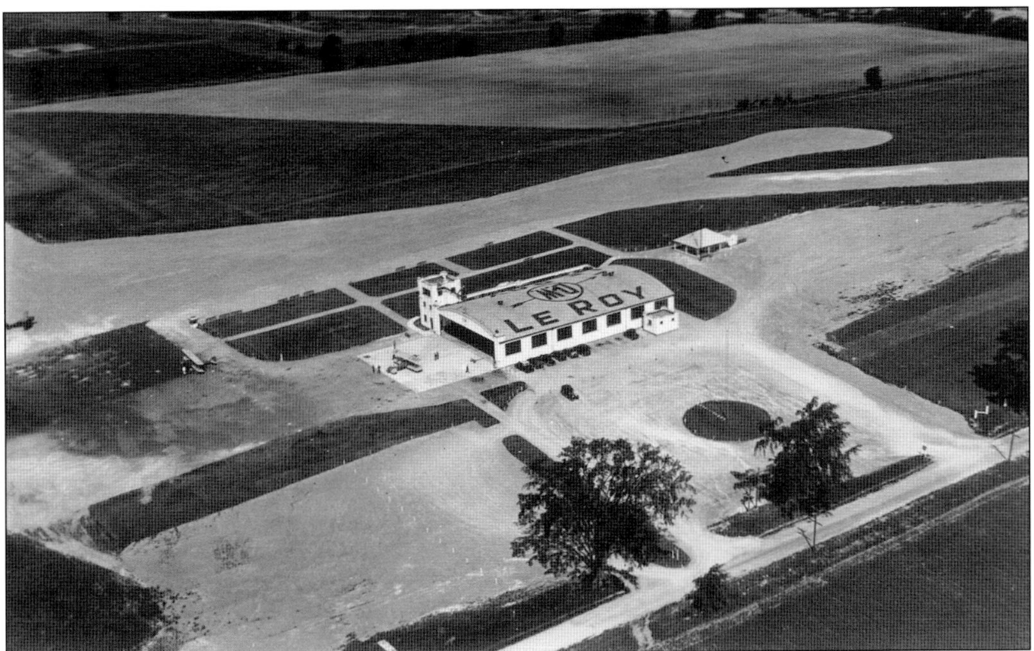

The DW Airport. Donald Woodward hired pioneer aviator Russell Holderman to coordinate the airport's design and construction. On opening day, October 12, 1928, an estimated crowd of 60,000 people arrived in LeRoy to see one of the finest private airports in America. It was one of the earliest government-approved flying schools. During World War II, the Wilkinson School trained army and navy pilots. The airport closed after the war.

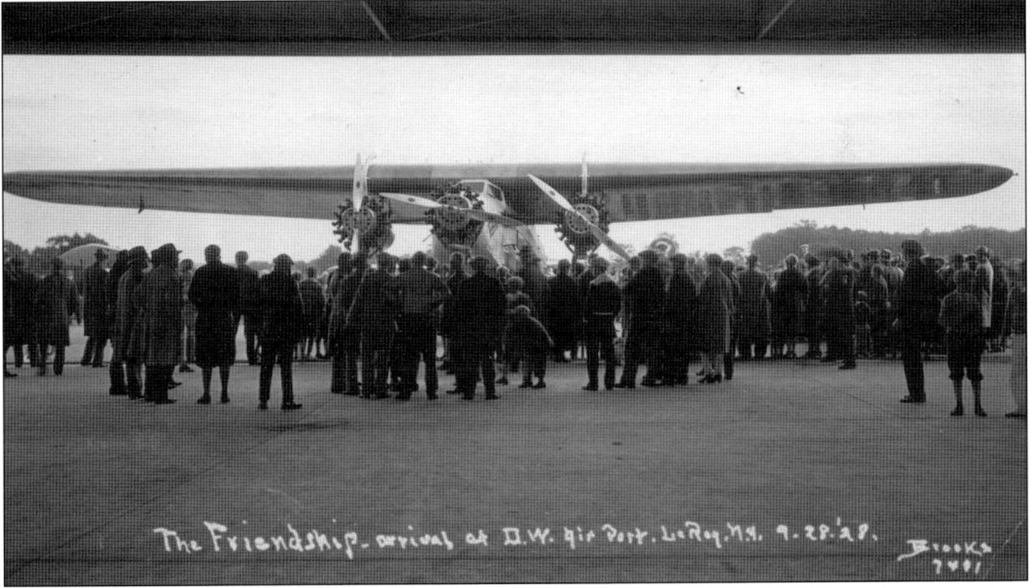

The *Friendship*. On June 17, 1928, Amelia Earhart became the first woman to fly across the Atlantic Ocean. She flew in the *Friendship*, a trimotor Fokker that was piloted by Wilmer Stultz with copilot Louis Gordon. Donald Woodward bought the *Friendship*, which became the flagship of his fleet of airplanes in LeRoy. It was refitted with observation windows and seats but was sold in 1929.

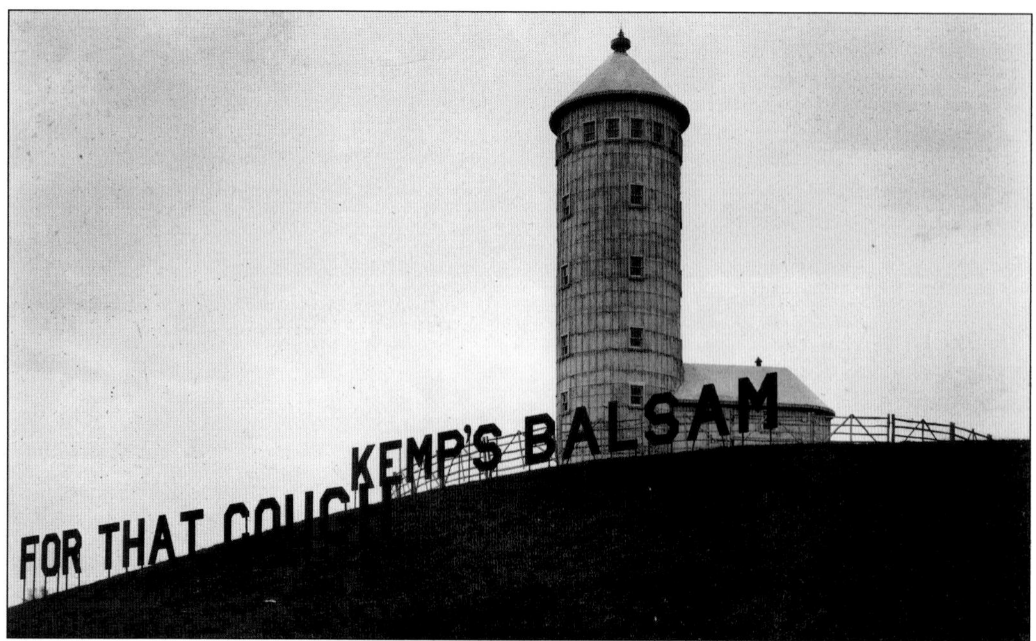

THE TOWER. Donald Woodward built this five-story tower south of LeRoy on Asbury Road. Constructed of cement tiles manufactured at Woodward's Ribstone Cement Company, the tower was a party house with an observation room on the top floor. It was often used as a pylon during the air shows at the DW Airport. It is now privately owned and unoccupied.

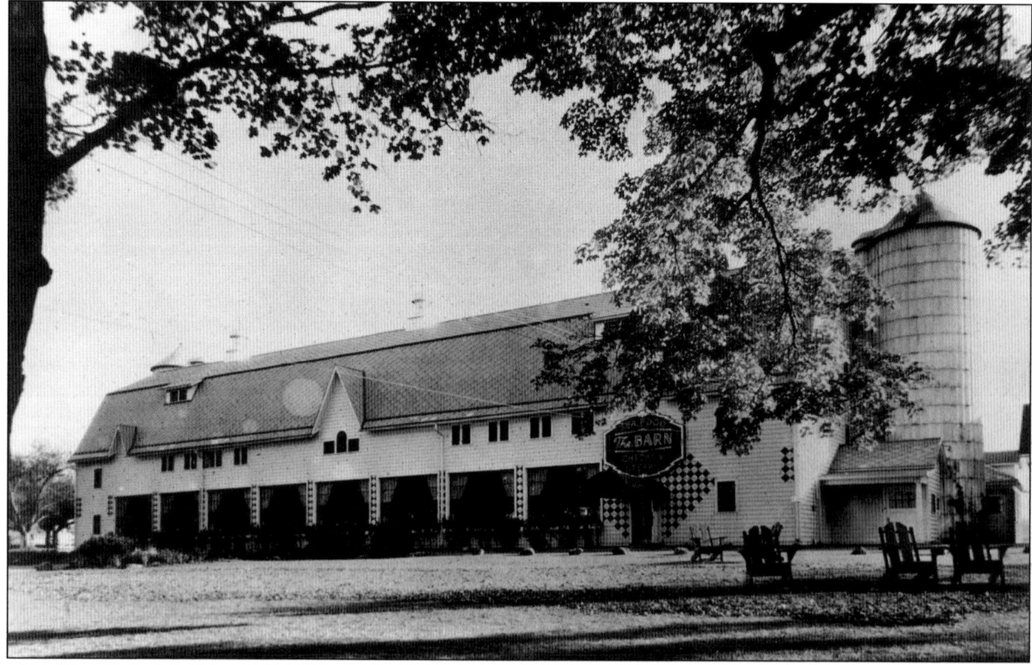

THE BARN. Located on the corner of Asbury Road and East Main Road, the barn was originally built for Donald Woodward's prizewinning shorthorn cattle. In 1930, it was converted into a restaurant and indoor miniature golf course and became part of Woodward's recreation facilities, which included the airport, golf course, and ball fields. It closed in 1936 and was razed.

Six

All Around the Town

Communities are defined in history by people and events. LeRoy is no exception. For nearly 200 years, LeRoy has witnessed and participated in historical events in Western New York. But without the camera, many events were not recorded. Yet it would be an omission not to mention these events and people in the history of LeRoy. In 1813, men from LeRoy marched to the Niagara frontier and participated in the Battle of Black Rock. Some were captured and imprisoned in Canada. Some were killed. Many returned to LeRoy. The terror on the frontier continued until the war ended. Later, in 1826, LeRoy found itself in the middle of political turmoil. William Morgan, who had connections with the Masonic Lodge in LeRoy and Batavia, disappeared, and the resulting investigation created an Anti-Masonic fervor throughout the country. The local lodge surrendered its charter in 1827 and did not resume meetings until 1847. In the years before the Civil War, Daniel MacDonald arrived in town and settled on the west side of town near the Keeney Cemetery. No one knew that he was helping slaves escape to Canada on the Underground Railroad except for young Elijah Huftelen, who much later would write two booklets about the role LeRoy played in this epic history of the United States. There are no photographs, but the stories remain and need to be remembered. For the history that was captured with the camera, it should be known that for every photograph included in this book, there are 50 more that were not included. An entire book could be devoted to sports teams and sports events. Another book could be devoted entirely to the fires that have swept through LeRoy. So this chapter can only give a brief glance of LeRoy's unique history.

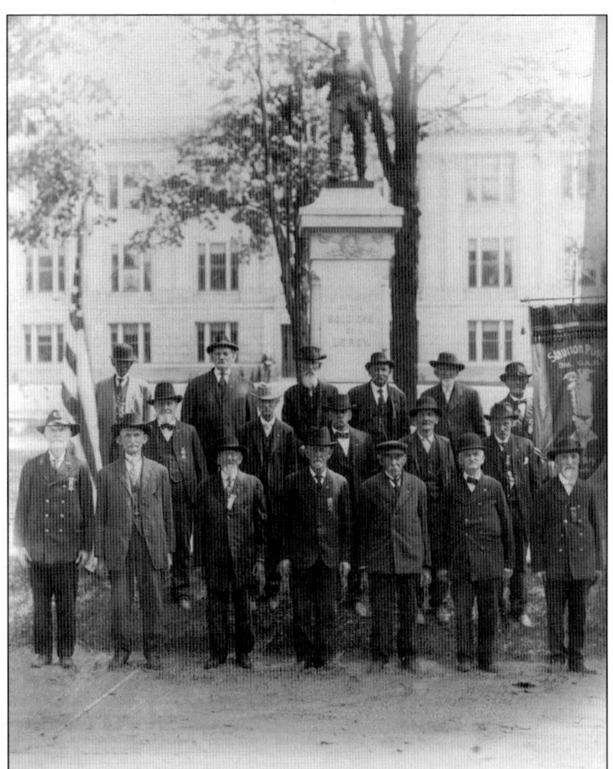

GRAND ARMY OF THE REPUBLIC (GAR). The Staunton Post 386 of the GAR was formed on September 6, 1883, in memory of Col. Phineas Staunton, artist and vice chancellor of Ingham University. The photograph was taken on Trigon Park in front of the Soldier's Monument on dedication day, May 30, 1906. The last Civil War veteran in LeRoy, Richard Geer (on the extreme right), died in 1928.

REUNION OF THE 151ST VOLUNTEER INFANTRY. During the Civil War, men from LeRoy enlisted in the Union army. Many were members of the 100th New York Volunteers mustered out of Buffalo. Others joined the 105th New York Volunteers. Some served in the 151st Volunteer Infantry mustered out of Lockport. The 151st held a reunion in LeRoy in 1917. The reunion was organized by LeRoy veteran Patrick McCarrick.

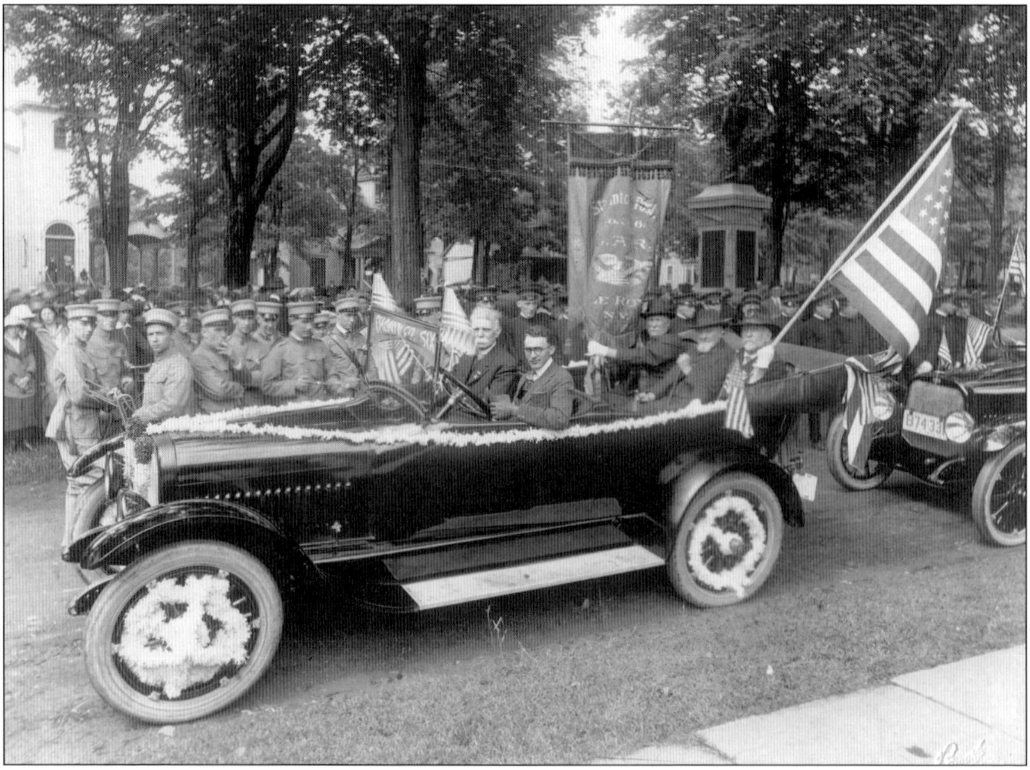

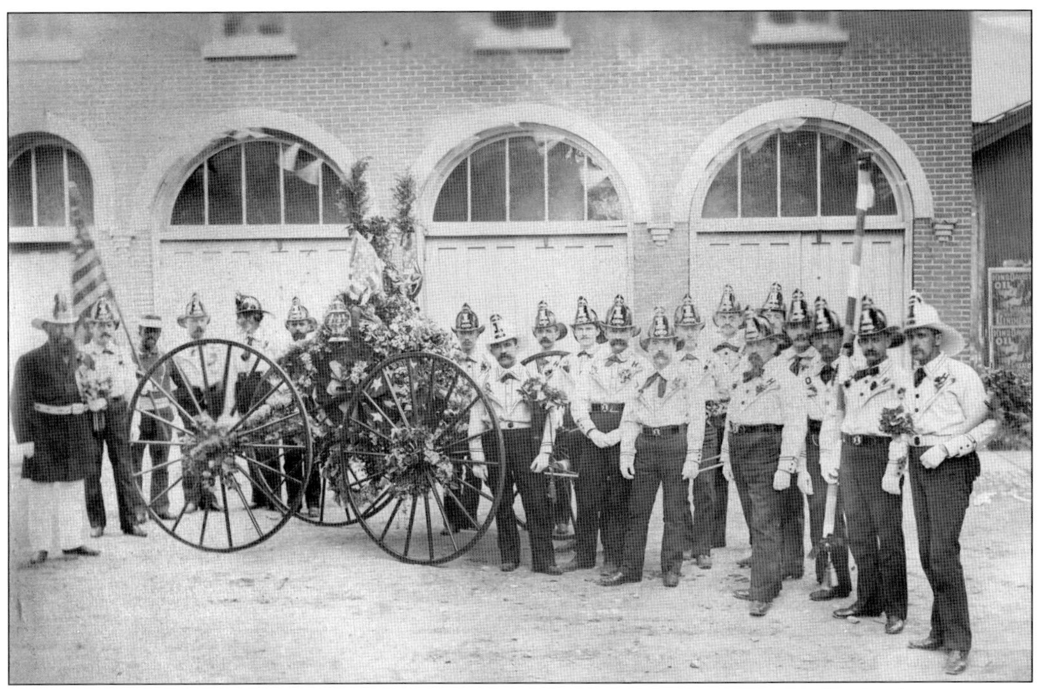

Oatka Hose Company. Originally known as Hydrant Hose Company, it changed its name to the Oatka Hose Company in 1875. The men are standing in front of the old town hall and fire house on Bank Street, which had a tower equipped with pulleys to hoist the canvas hose to the top to allow the hose to dry. The building burned in May 1911.

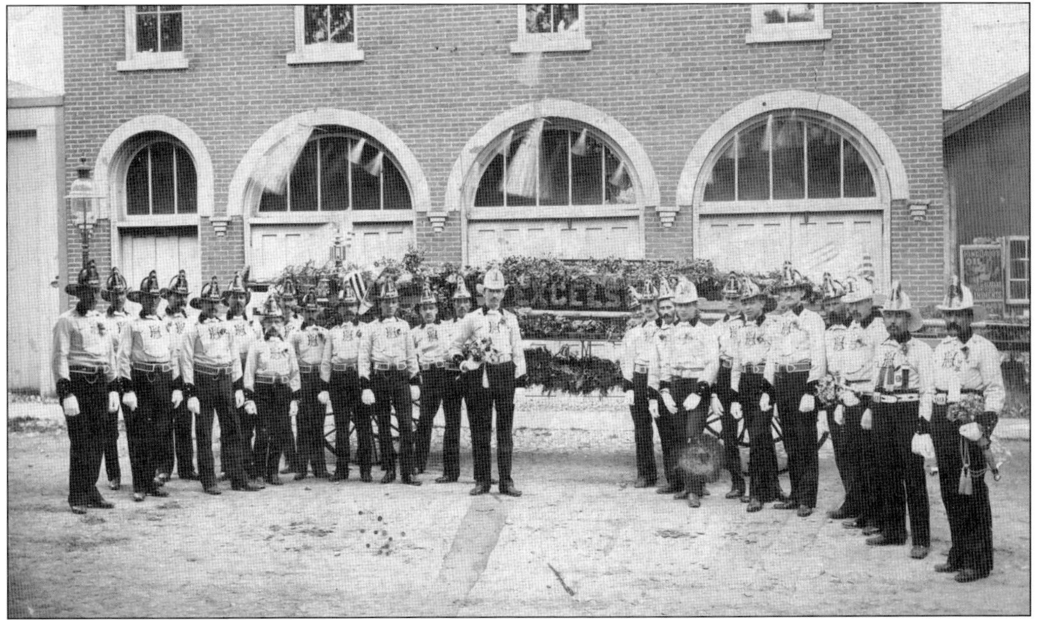

Excelsior Hook and Ladder Company. Founded in 1857, this is the oldest fire company in LeRoy. The 1834 Village Charter included provisions for a fire department and established a fire code. At one time, there were five fire companies in LeRoy. Each one was responsible for a different piece of equipment. The "Hooks" still have the hook and ladder wagon shown in the photograph.

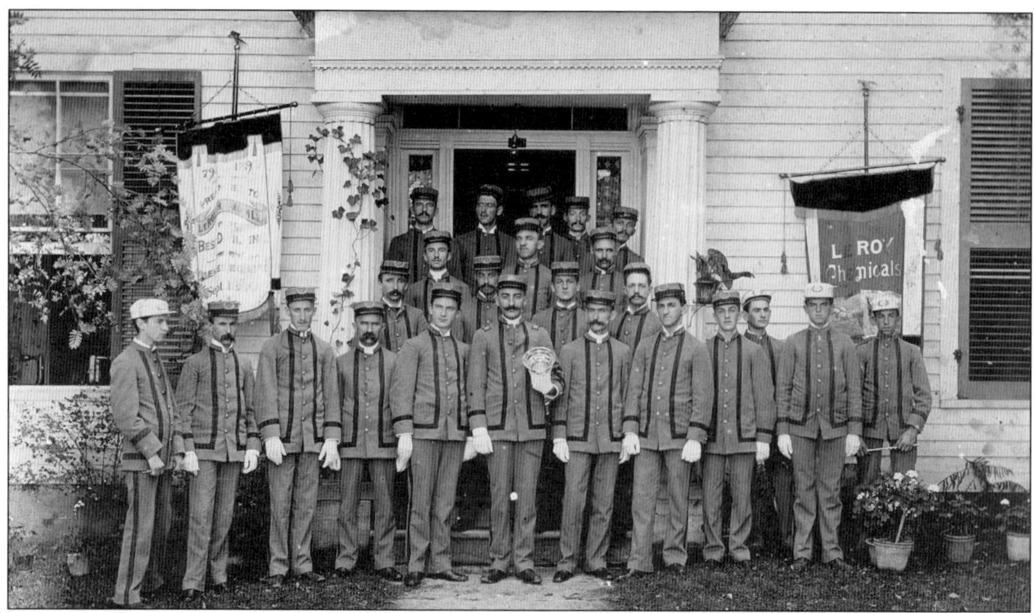

Chemical Hose Company. In 1885, the village purchased a chemical wagon and gave its operation to the "Protectives." They did not want to operate such a heavy piece of equipment, so they disbanded. Several members of the Hook and Ladder Company asked to be recognized as the Chemical Hose Company, and they took charge of the chemical wagon. For many years, the "Chemicals" were known for their marching drill team.

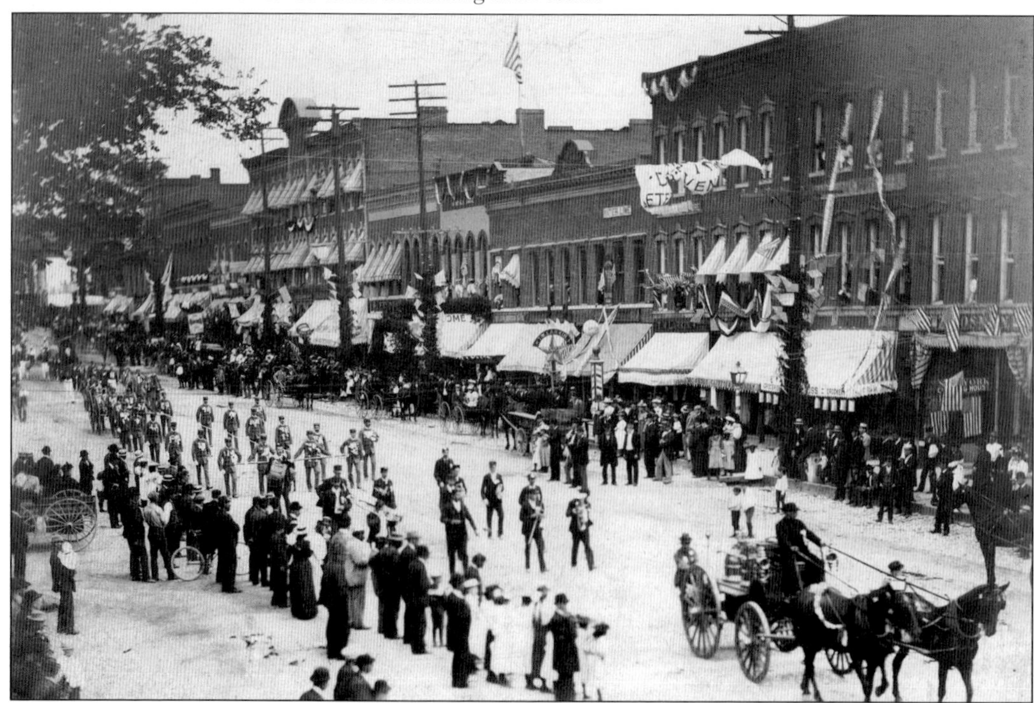

Parade on Main Street. The horse-drawn chemical fire wagon is in the foreground, followed by the Oatka Hose Company pulling the hose reel. The large building on the right is the Washington Block, with the profile of George Washington above each window.

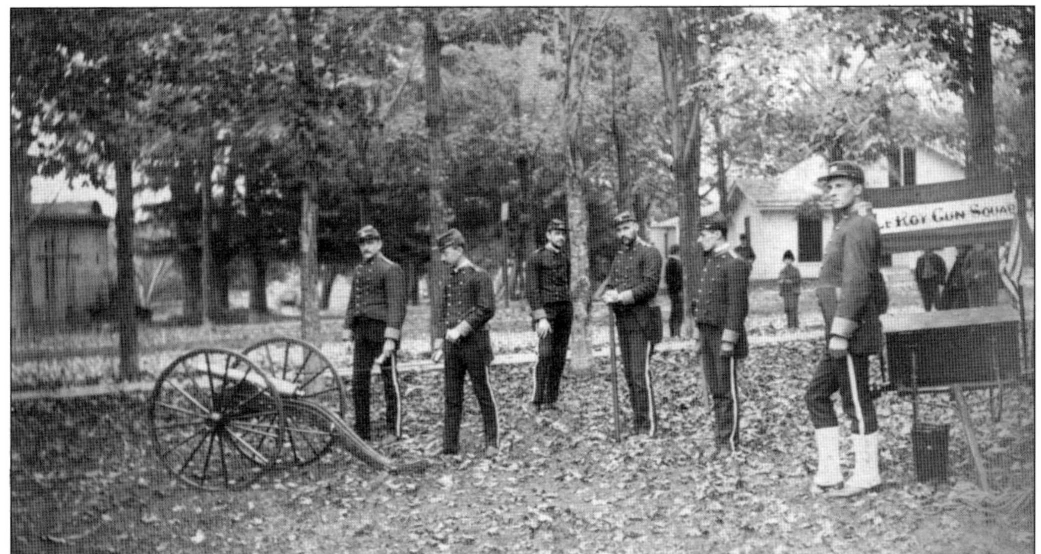

LeRoy Gun Squad. In 1868, during the presidential election of Ulysses Grant, James Annin purchased the brass gun for $150. The carriage and caisson were built by Charles Carlton. The ironwork was done by Edward Hawkins. Lucius Bangs and Hiram Hascall bought the canon for the Republican Party. It was last used to start the races on the creek during the Creekside Regatta. It is now owned by the LeRoy Historical Society.

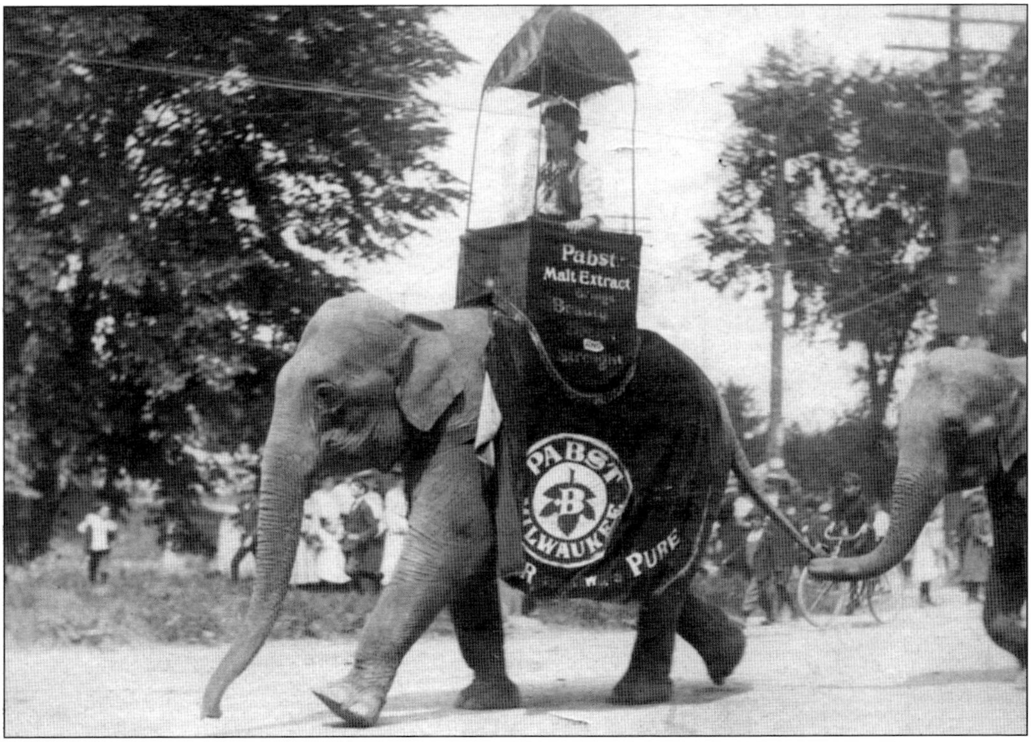

Circus Elephant. This photograph was taken by Roy Shores near the Summit Street tennis court. A note on the back indicates that this was probably the Ringling Circus "because the Scanlons (family) were employed by them."

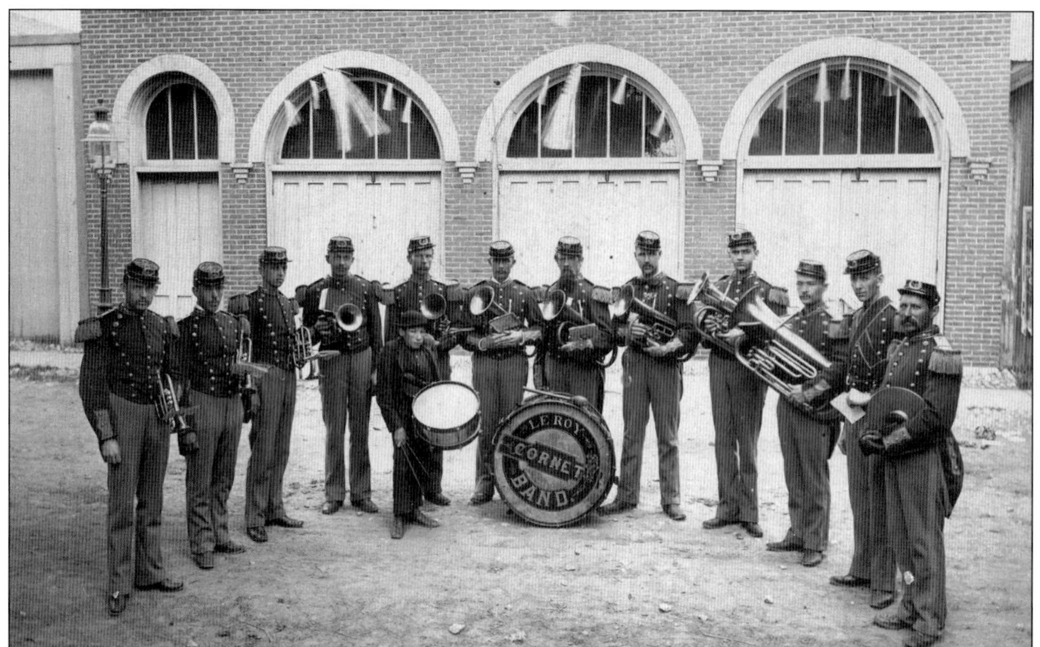

LeRoy Cornet Band. The band formed before the Civil War. The Cornets, as they were known, played concerts, dances, and parades. They performed at the opening of the Lampson House and won a gold medal at the Genesee County Fair.

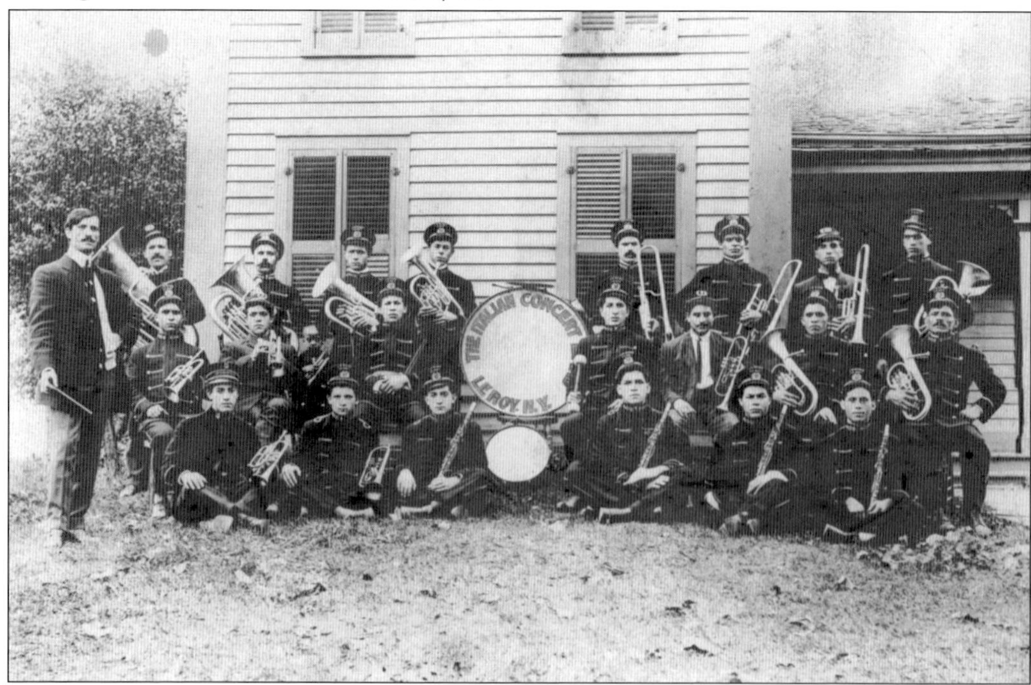

Italian Concert Band. The band was organized on September 11, 1907. The chairman was A. F. Barone, with Charles Panepento as the secretary, and Joseph Miserentino as the treasurer. In 1910, the band planned to be hired as a circus band. The conductor collected money from the members to go to New York City to make contact with the circus but was never seen again.

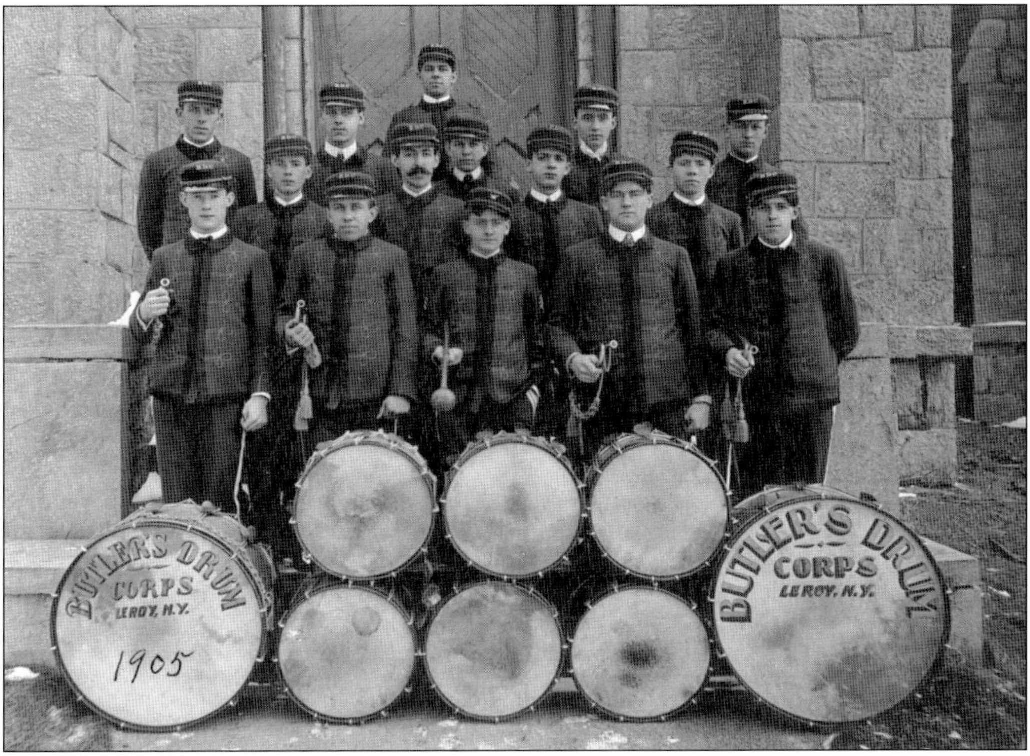

Butler Drum Corps. Joseph Miller, who worked for the Butler family, organized the Butler Drum Corps in 1905. The original band consisted of 10 members, but later the band increased in size. It was a popular musical group at local parades and events for many years.

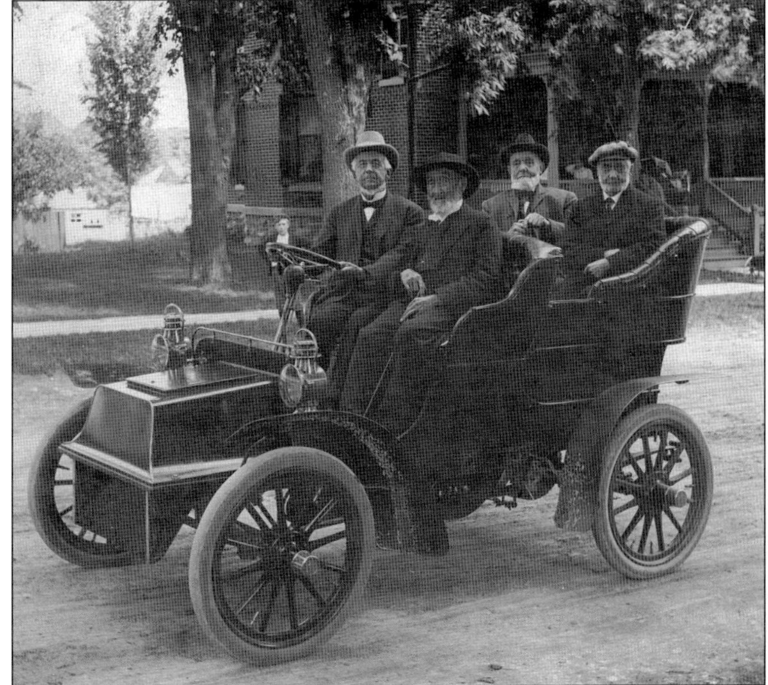

Behind the Wheel, 1905. Nicholas Keeney is at the wheel with Dr. Edmund Taylor on his left. In the back seat are Mr. Robert Clements (left) and Dr. Galen Edson. In 1915, there were 50 automobiles registered in the village: 15 Cadillacs; 6 Pierces; 5 Maxwells; 4 Lamberts; 3 Fords; 2 each of Buicks, Franklins, Oldsmobiles, Reos, and Holsmans; and 1 each of Locomobile, Glide, E.M.F., International, Allan-Kingston, Winton, and White Steamer.

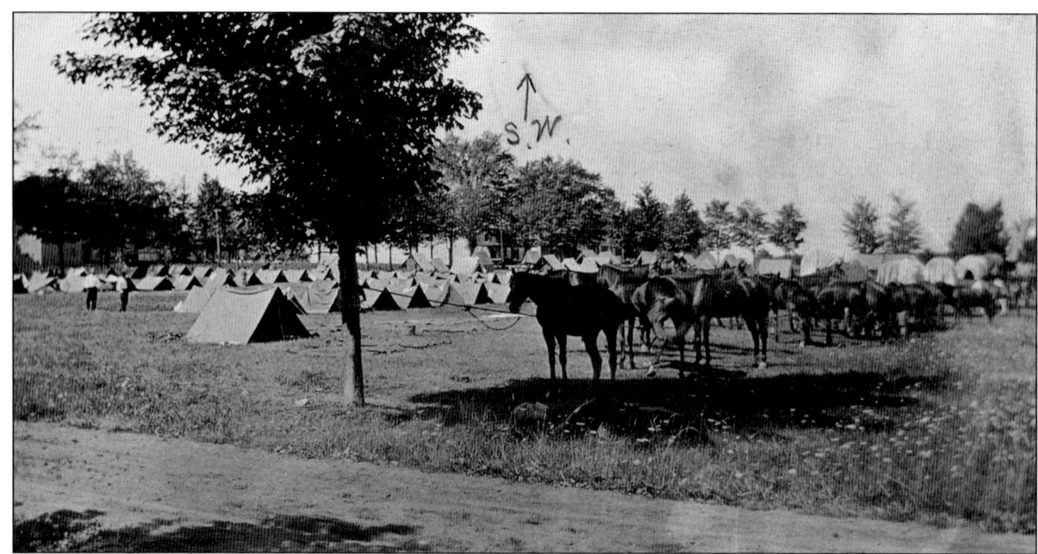

1911 Encampment. Soldiers from the First Battalion, 29th Infantry from Fort Porter in Buffalo stopped in LeRoy on a 139-mile, 12-day march. They set up camp in a field near Summit and Exchange Streets where visitors could observe their daily activities and training. They engaged in a mock skirmish near the railroad tracks and then struck camp and marched back to Buffalo.

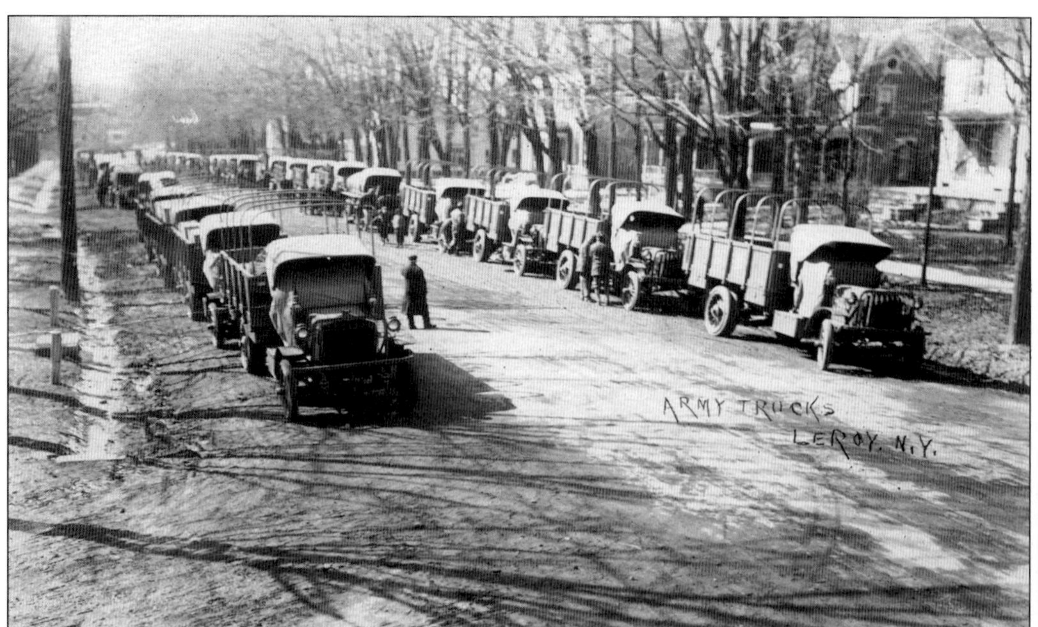

Army Trucks, around 1918. It was not unusual to see convoys of military trucks passing through LeRoy on Route 5. They often stopped at Lally's Diner on Main Street. This photograph was taken on East Main Street looking west with Trigon Park on the left. Military convoys began using the New York State Thruway in 1956.

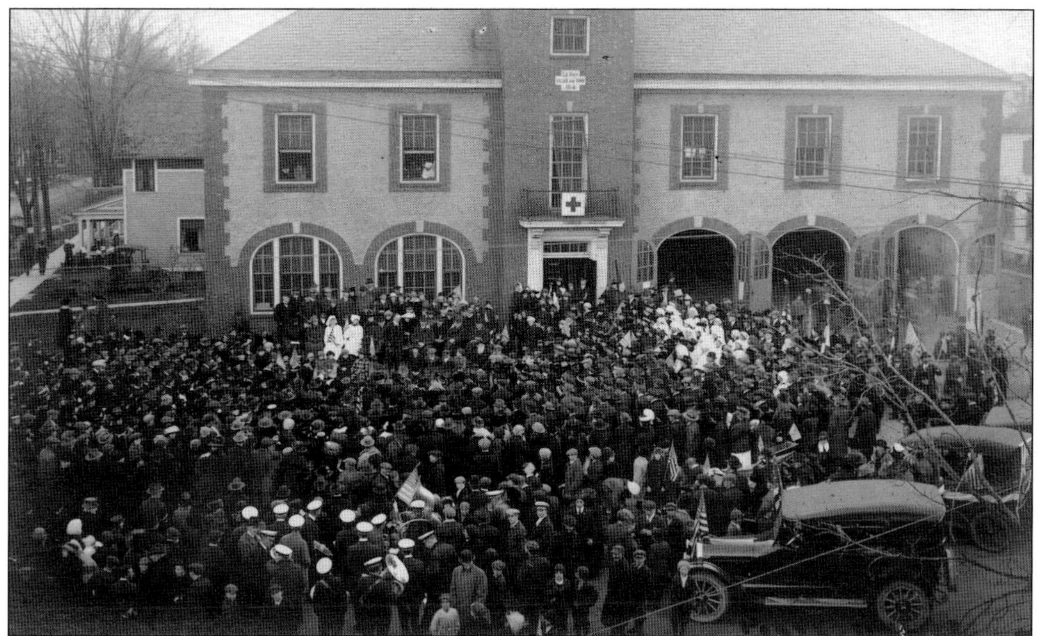

World War I Armistice Parade. Across the country, at the eleventh hour of the eleventh day of the eleventh month in 1918, people gathered to celebrate the end of the First World War. In LeRoy, on a wet, rainy day, community organizations marched to the Municipal Building. The American Legion Botts-Fiorito Post 576 was chartered in 1919. Veterans of Foreign War Post 355 was chartered in 1939 and Post 9590 in 1949.

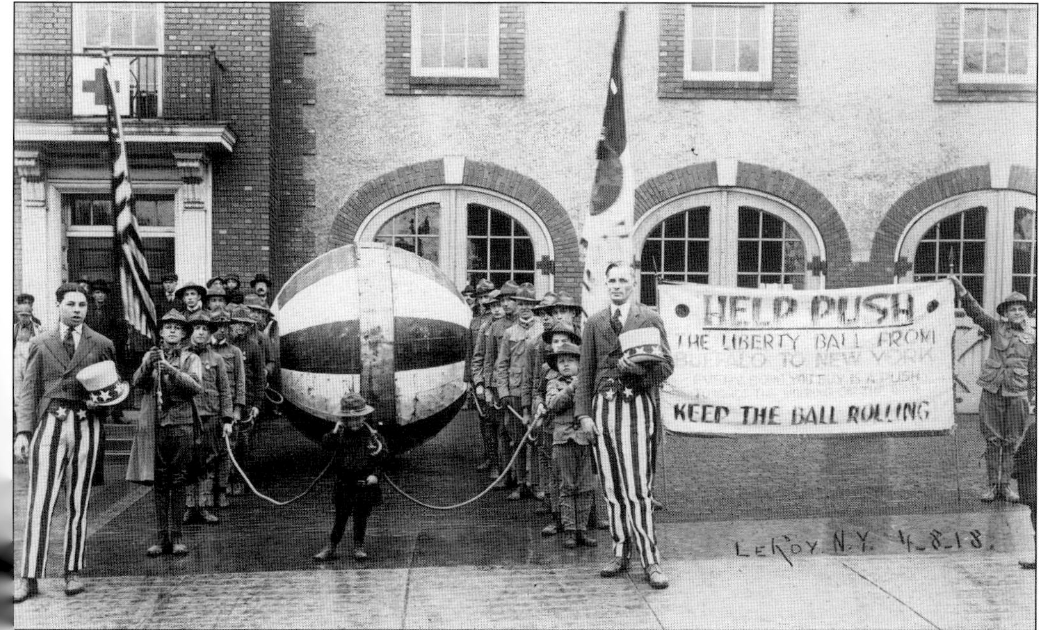

Liberty Loan Drive. On April 8, 1918, the 350-pound Liberty Loan Ball was pulled into LeRoy by 8 local Boy Scouts. The seven-foot ball was being rolled from Buffalo to New York City to raise money for the war effort. The boys were presented with medals for their efforts. The next stop was Caledonia. The ball reached New York City on May 4th.

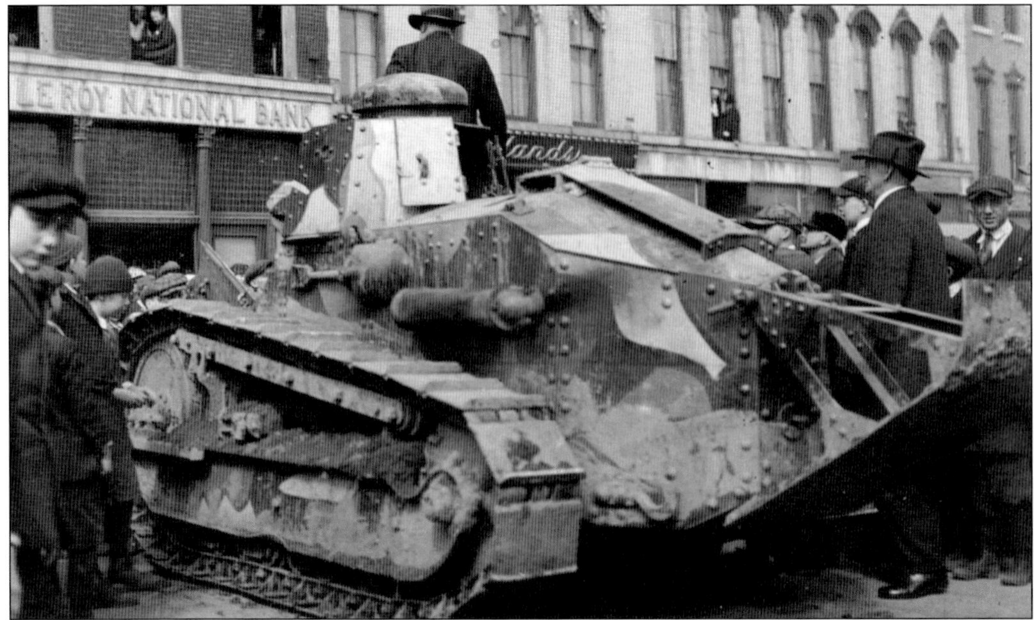

Tank on Main Street. On April 30, 1919, two tanks were traveling from Buffalo to Hornell in an effort to raise money for the Victory Loan drive. When they arrived in LeRoy, the seven-ton tank stopped in front of the National Bank. Mayor H. B. Ward climbed on top and apologized for "not having obstacles on Main Street to show what the tank could do."

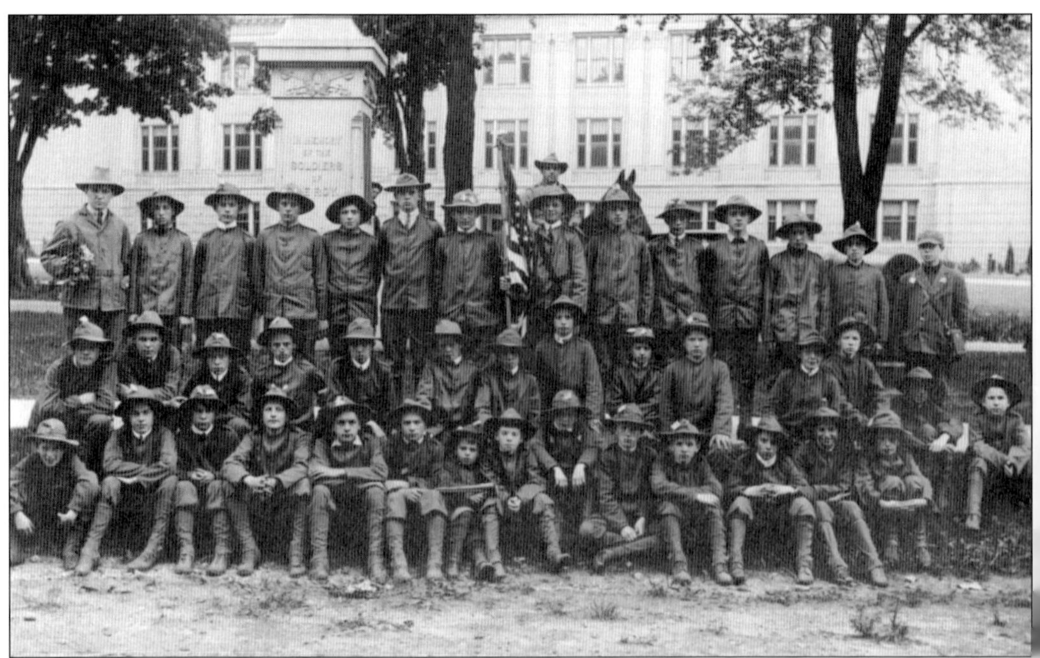

Boy Scouts. Early records do not indicate when the first LeRoy Boy Scout Troop was formed; however, as early as April 8, 1918, LeRoy Boy Scouts helped roll the Liberty Loan Ball into town (page 89). Troops 21 and 22 were chartered through the Genesee Council in Batavia in 1924. Daniel Carroll was the leader of Troop 21 and Winthrop Follansbee was the leader of Troop 22.

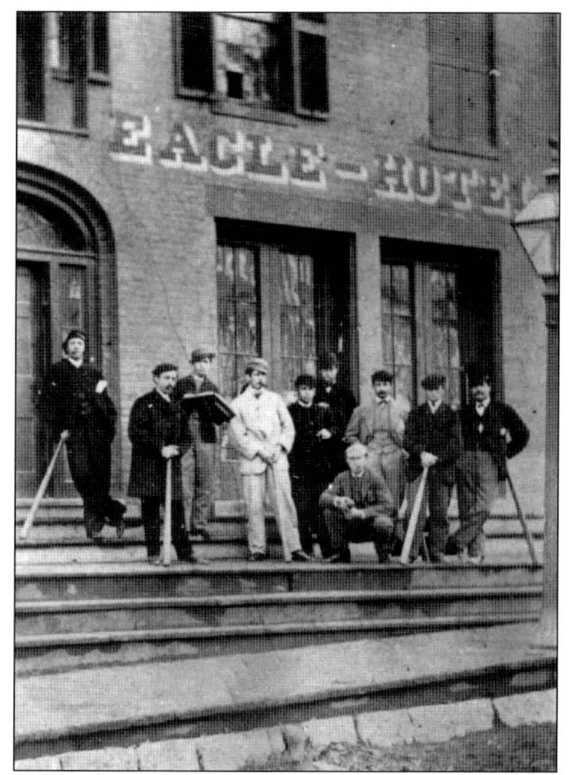

The Oatka Baseball Club, 1870. This photograph was taken on the front steps of the Eagle Hotel. Standing from left to right are Henry Chamberlain (catcher), Miles Lampson (second base), Francis Bartow (scorekeeper), Edward Comstock (third base), Manly Osborne (short stop), Bob Garvin (left field), Turner Comstock (center field), John Bissell (first base), "Orve" Waterman (right field), and seated, Frank Dillingham (pitcher).

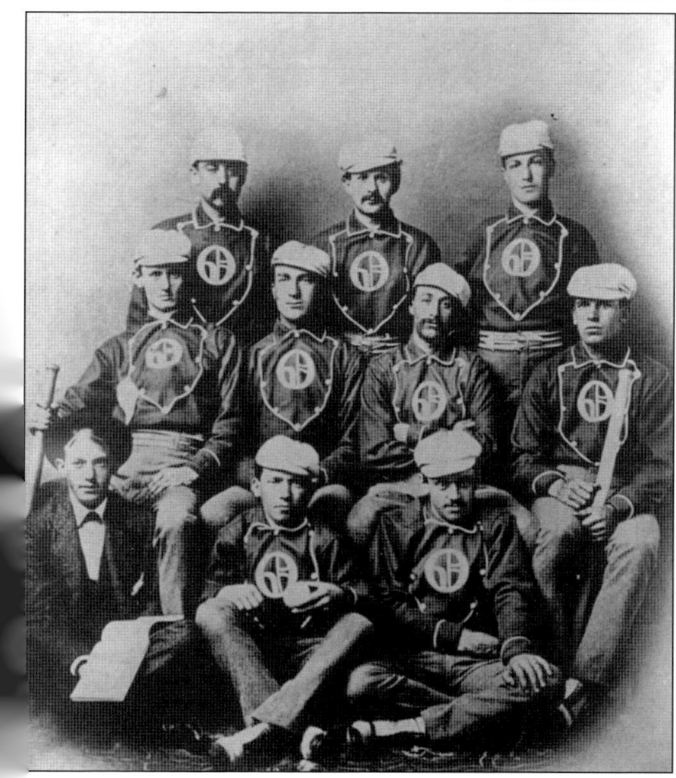

Oatka Baseball Club, 1873. LeRoy lost to East Bethany 100 to 74. The match game was played on Trigon Park. Over 1,000 people came to watch the game, which LeRoy lost, 15 to 11. Pictured from left to right are (first row) Charles Annin, "Jimmie" Jones, and James Lampson; (second row) Herbert Ferguson, Theodore Hascall, Henry Chamberlain, and Charles Wiard; (third row) Miles Lampson, Henry Fairchild, and Charles Taylor.

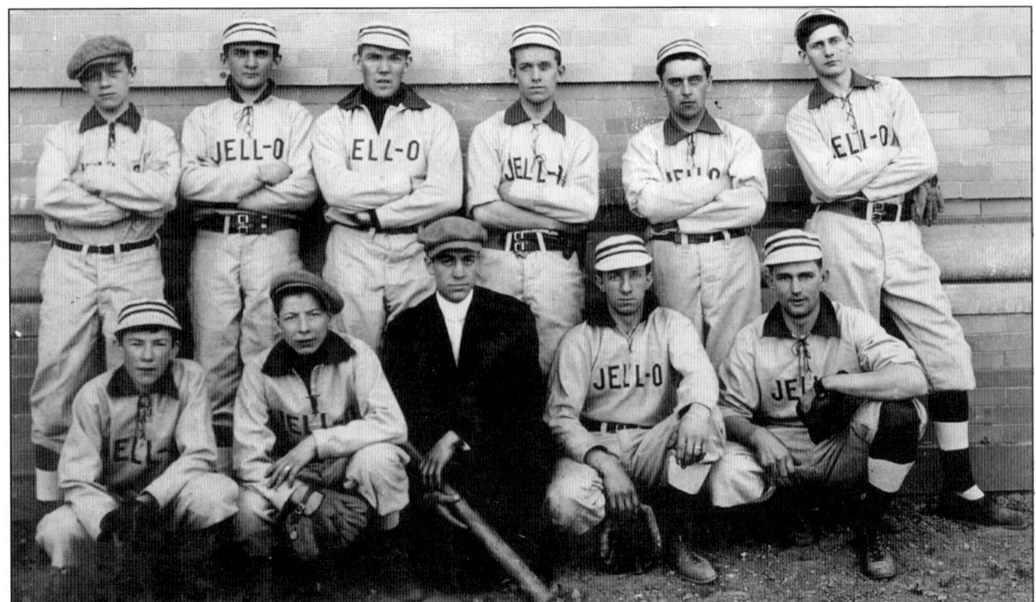

Jell-O Baseball Team. LeRoy had a semiprofessional league that included teams from several of the industries, including Lapp Insulator, LeRoy Bottling, Union Steel Chest, the *LeRoy Pennysaver*, and Jell-O. Donald Woodward, the youngest son of the owner of Jell-O, is pictured in the second row, third from the right. Sunday games were not allowed until 1940.

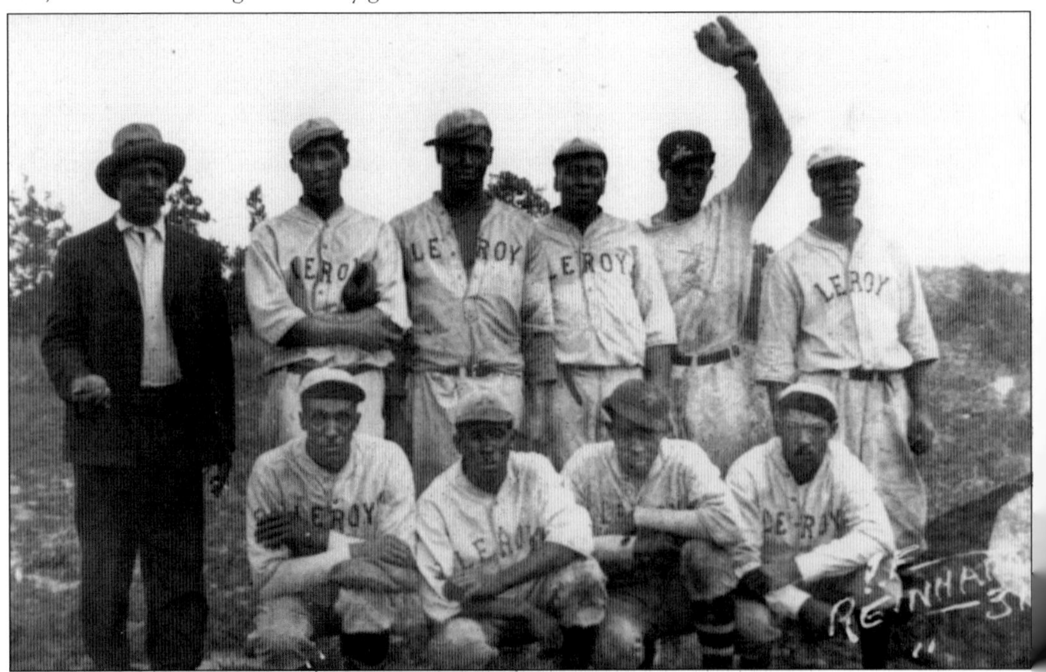

Nine Sticks of Dynamite, 1931. This all black baseball team was popular before World War II. Pictured here from left to right are (first row) unidentified, Clarence Perry, unidentified, and Arthur Redman; (second row) Russell Lewis (manager), Taylor Majors, Bill Majors, James Burrell Sr., Burnett Booten, and unidentified. The team played on Lake Street in the village. Another all black team, the Aces, played after World War II.

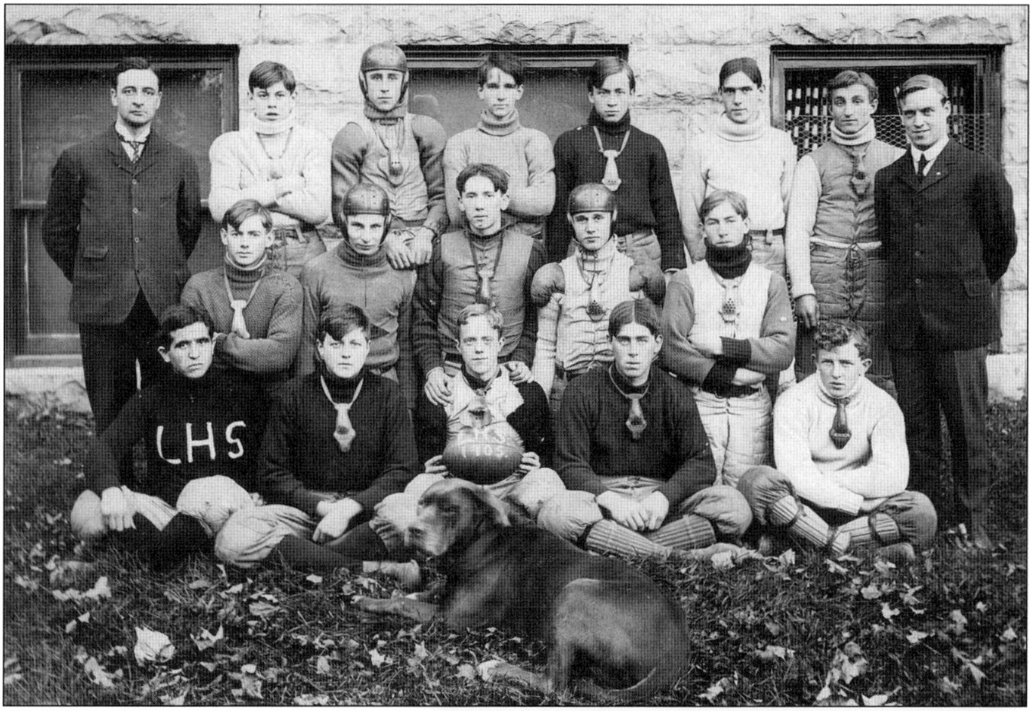

Football Team, 1905. High school football is an important part of LeRoy's history. Football was played as early as 1884 behind the LeRoy Academic Institute. Championship games against old rivals are indelibly written in the sports annals. The first recorded game between the LeRoy Monarchs and Caledonia was held October 20, 1900. Caledonia won 16 to 5. LeRoy lost the first game against Batavia in 1897 with a score of 80 to 0.

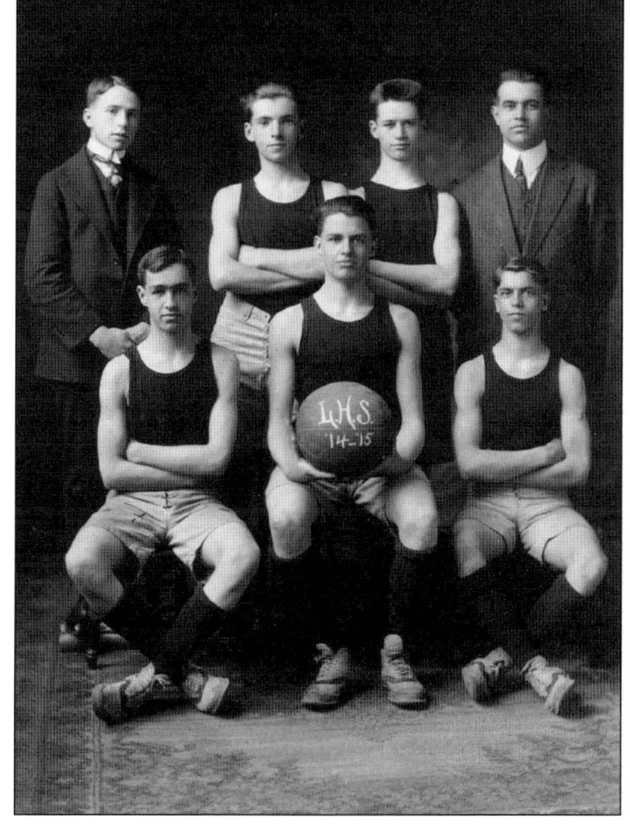

Basketball Team, 1914–1915. Basketball teams have been photographed for over 100 years and are included in the high school yearbook, the *Oatkan*. Photographed here are, from left to right, (first row) Merton Connor, Clarence McDowell, and Orton Munt; (second row) Norman McMillan, Clarence Walker, John Ripton, and Bill Welton.

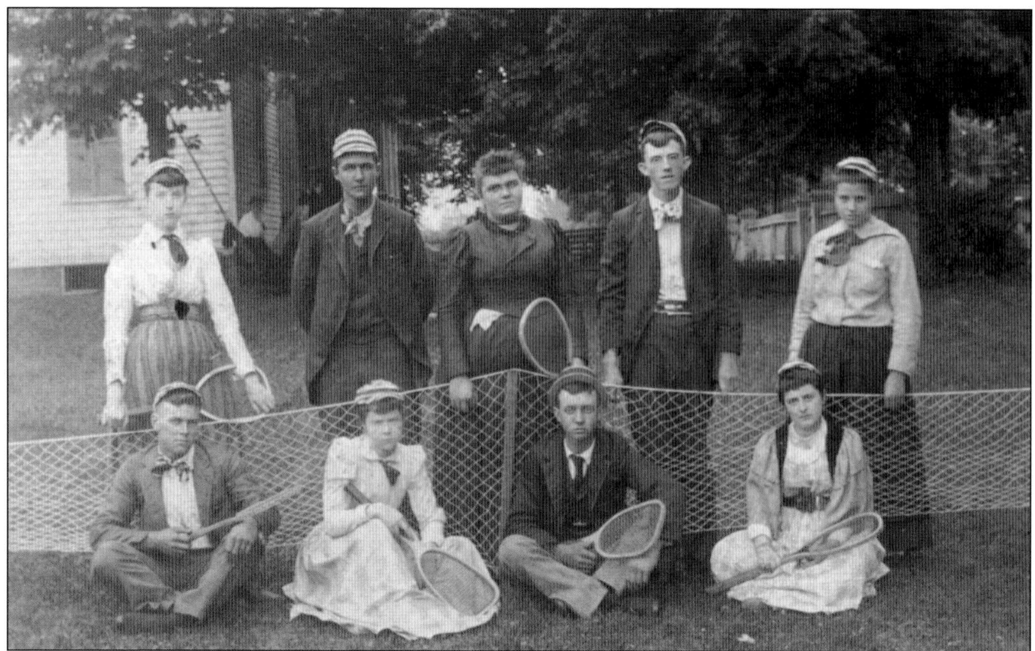

Fort Hill Tennis Club, 1890s. Tennis has been a popular sport in LeRoy. Ingham University students played tennis on the front lawn of University Hall. In 1924, Donald Woodward donated the clubhouse and tennis courts at Wolcott Street to the village. In the photograph are, from left to right, (seated) ? Lebarron, Lottie McPherson, Fred Brown, and Madge Nelson; (standing) Mary McPherson, Don Hebbard, Marion Hebbard Vallance, Arch McPherson, and Effie Anderson.

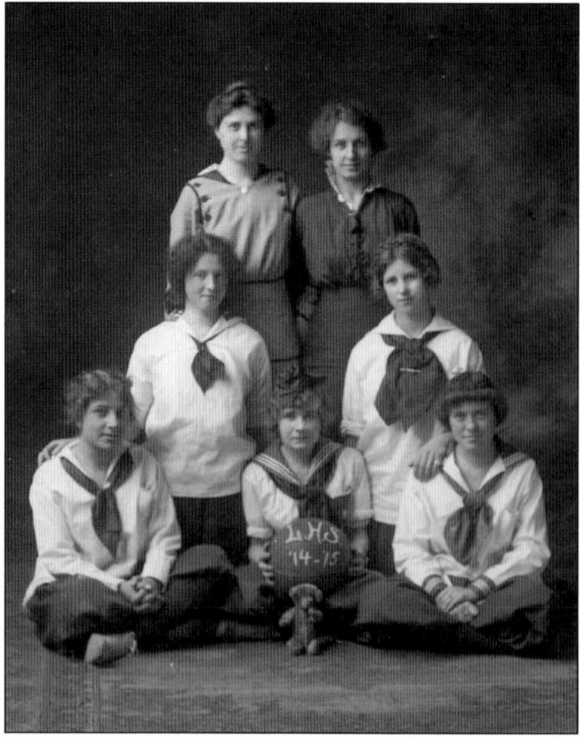

Girls Basketball Team, 1914–1915. From left to right are (first row) students Anna Randall, Frances Cromwell, and Bessie Reuben; (second row) Delores Carolan and Ruth DuBois. Pictured in the back are Mary Spink (the German teacher) and Miss Kemper (the American History teacher).

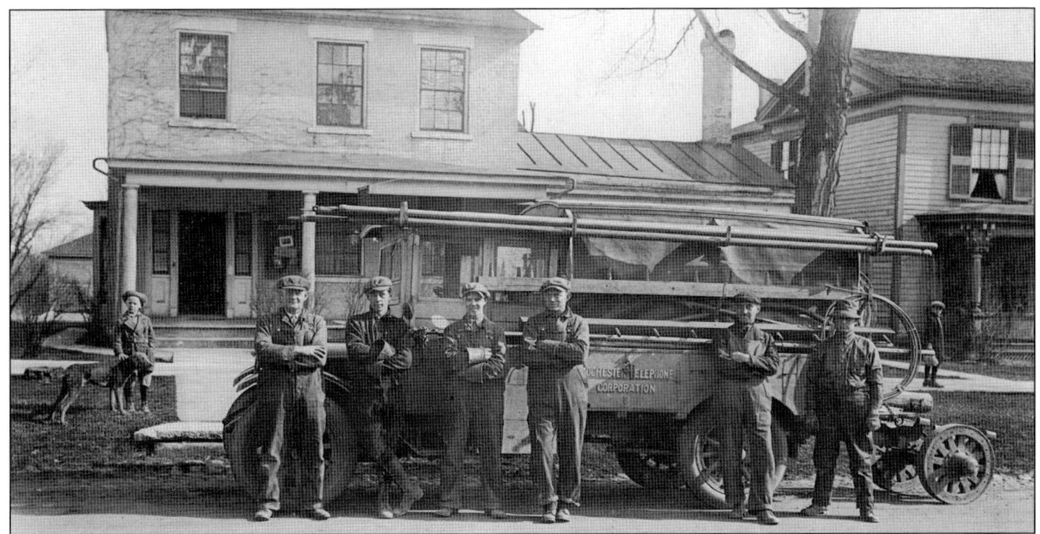

Rochester Telephone Company Workers. The LeRoy Telephone Company was established in 1891 and had 29 subscribers. When the Bell Telephone Company came to LeRoy, there were concerns about the "ugly" telephone poles, so they were painted bronze-green to make them less noticeable. The Home Telephone Company came to LeRoy in 1903. Included in this photograph is Charles E. White on the extreme left.

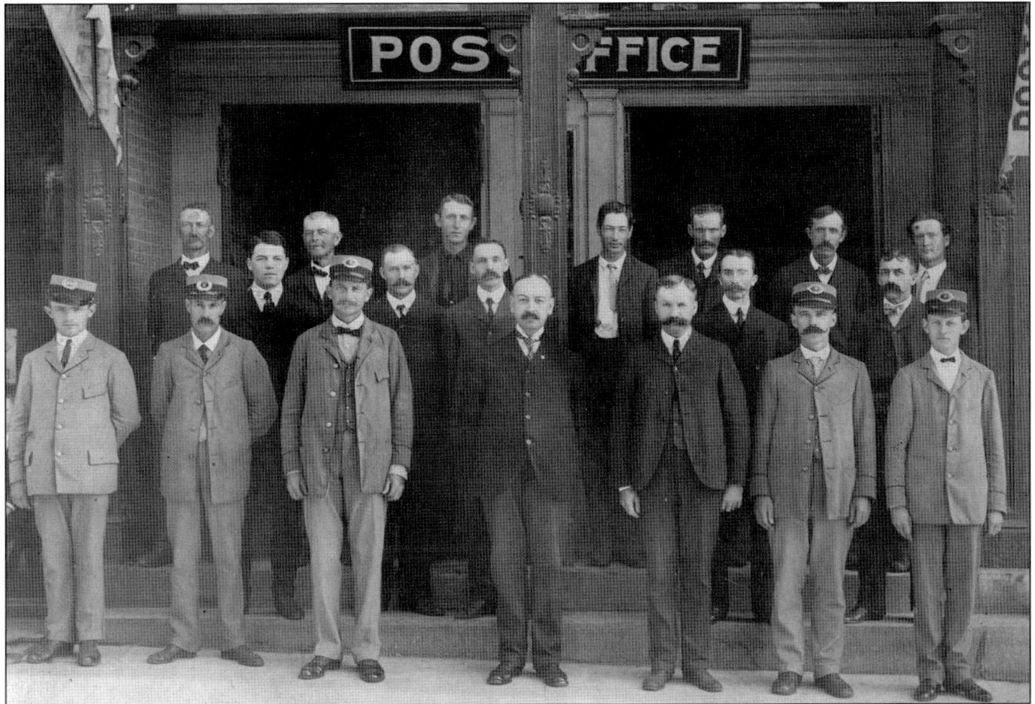

Post Office at the Arcade Building. The first post office in LeRoy was established on April 1, 1804, at the home of the first postmaster, Asher Bates. At one time, the post office was at the Eagle Hotel. This photograph shows the postmen standing outside the Arcade, which was in the Lampson Block. Before rural mail delivery, there were post offices at Fort Hill, Lime Rock, and South LeRoy.

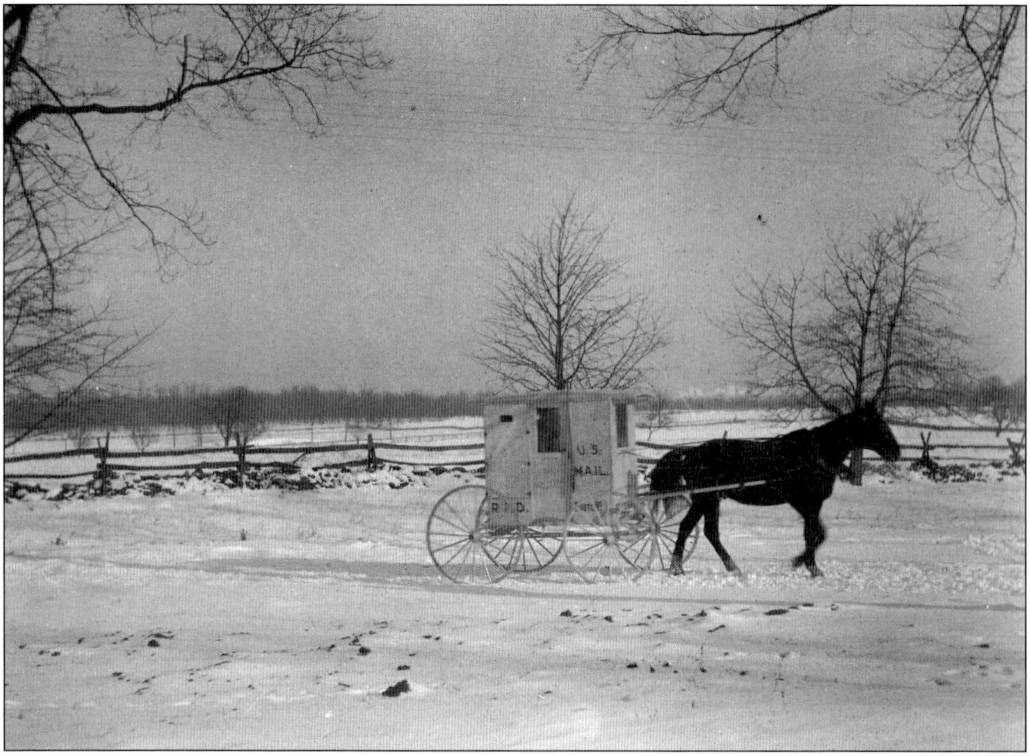

RURAL FREE DELIVERY (RFD). In 1901, RFD began in LeRoy. Perry Clark, shown in this photograph on Route 5 east of town, bought this mail wagon and drove the southern route. The northern route included Fort Hill.

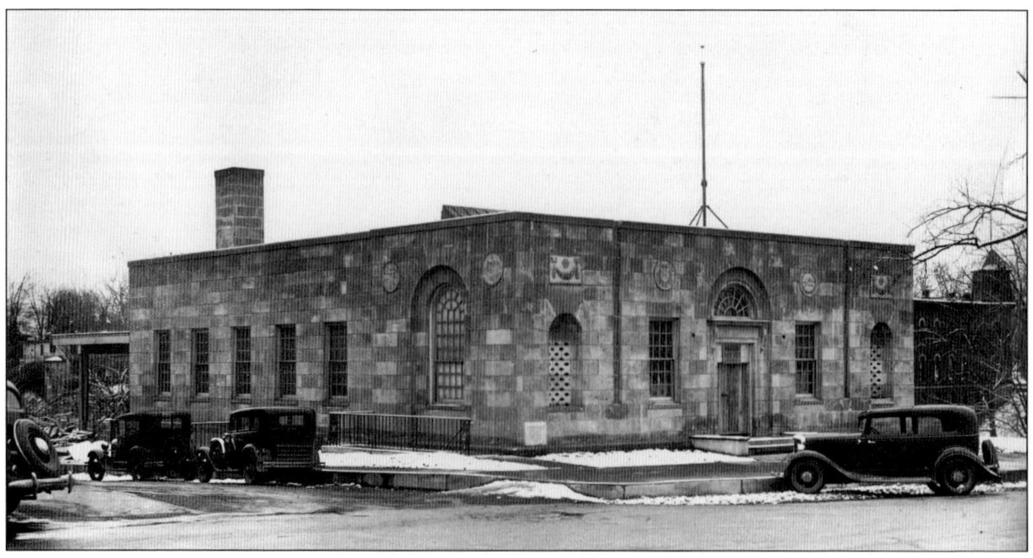

LEROY POST OFFICE. Constructed on the site of the former "Dock" building, the new post office was built under the guidance of Ernest Woodward. The truncated building shown in this photograph did not meet with Woodward's vision for a Colonial Revival building, so a gabled roof with clock tower was added. Woodward financed the clock. The building was dedicated on August 21, 1938. It was placed on the National Register of Historic Places in 1987.

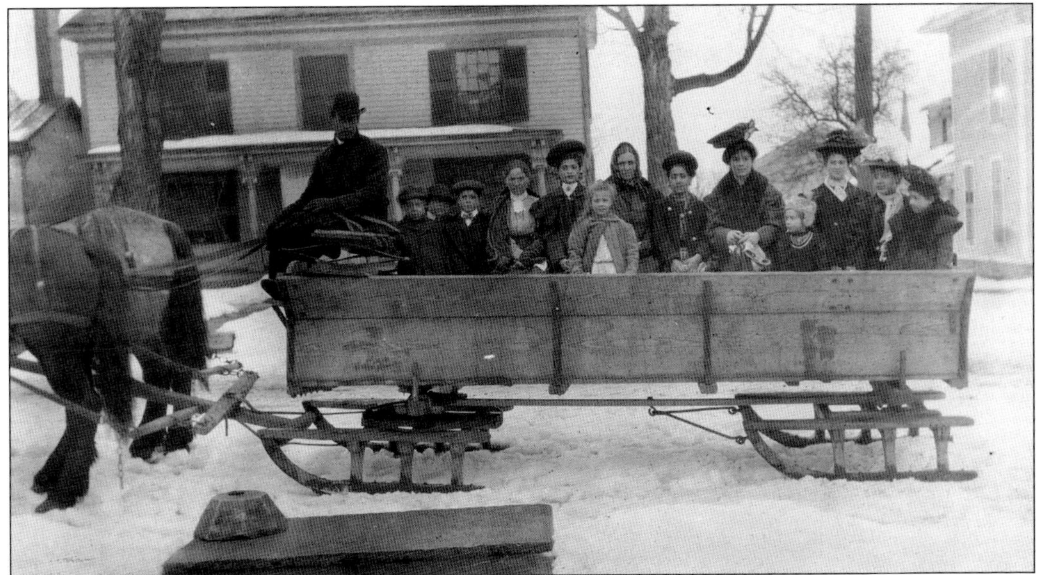

Sleigh Ride. The Keeney Farm hired many Italian families to harvest and sort beans. This photograph, taken on Christmas day in 1907, shows Will Alexander driving a bob sled with some of the Keeney workers on a winter sleigh ride.

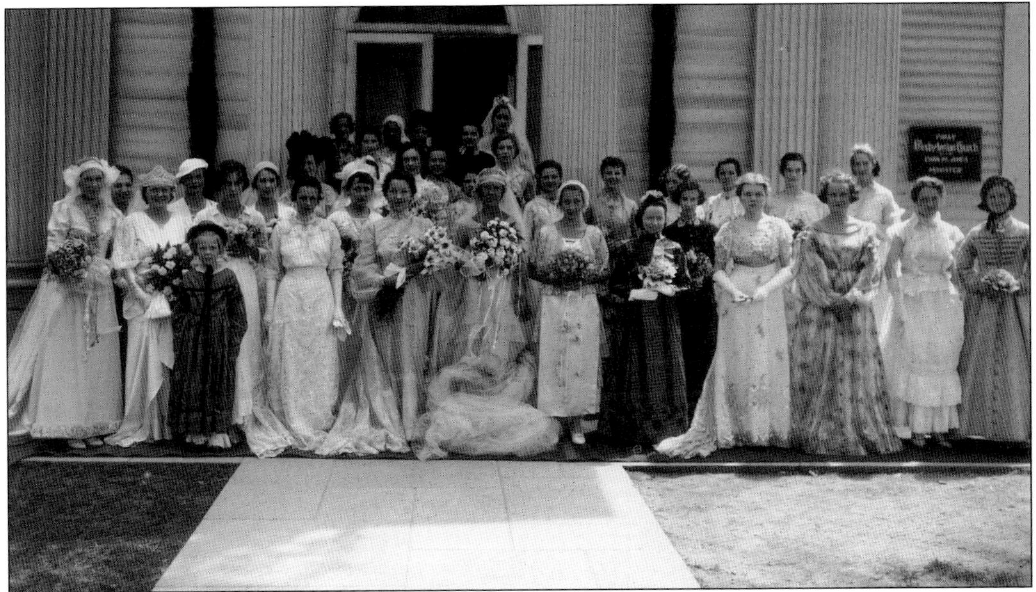

Century of Brides. In 1934, the Village of LeRoy celebrated its centennial. One of the most memorable events was the "Century of Brides" held at the First Presbyterian Church in July. Ladies wore family bridal gowns in a fashion show.

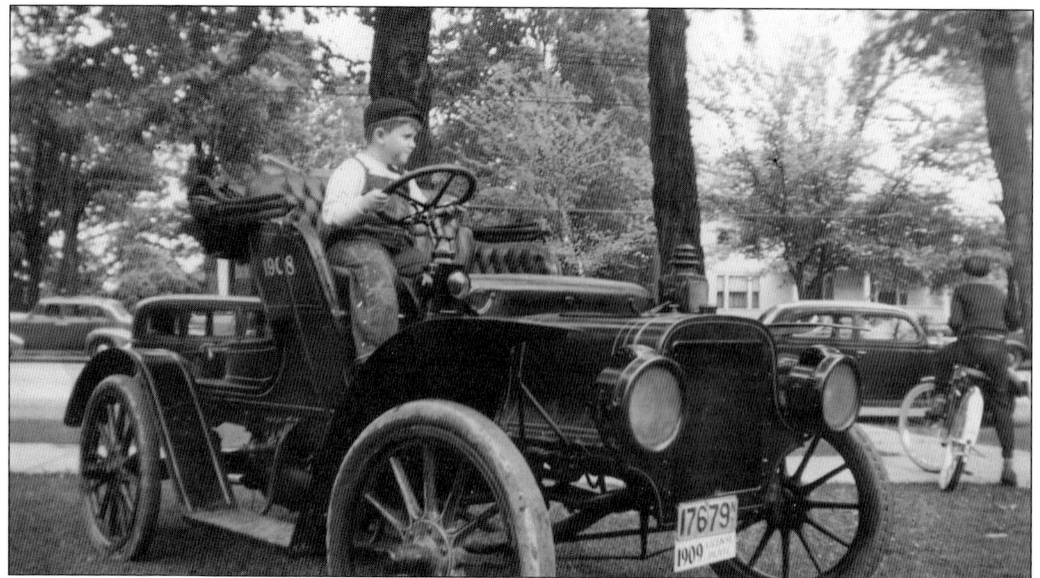

Seely Pratt in the 1908 Cadillac. In 1908, the Cadillac was purchased by Mrs. Cora Osborn for $900. Later the Kellogg family owned it, and it was often seen in parades. Before one of the parades, a young Seely Pratt climbed onto the seat and had his picture taken. The Cadillac was donated to the LeRoy Historical Society and is now in the On the Road exhibit.

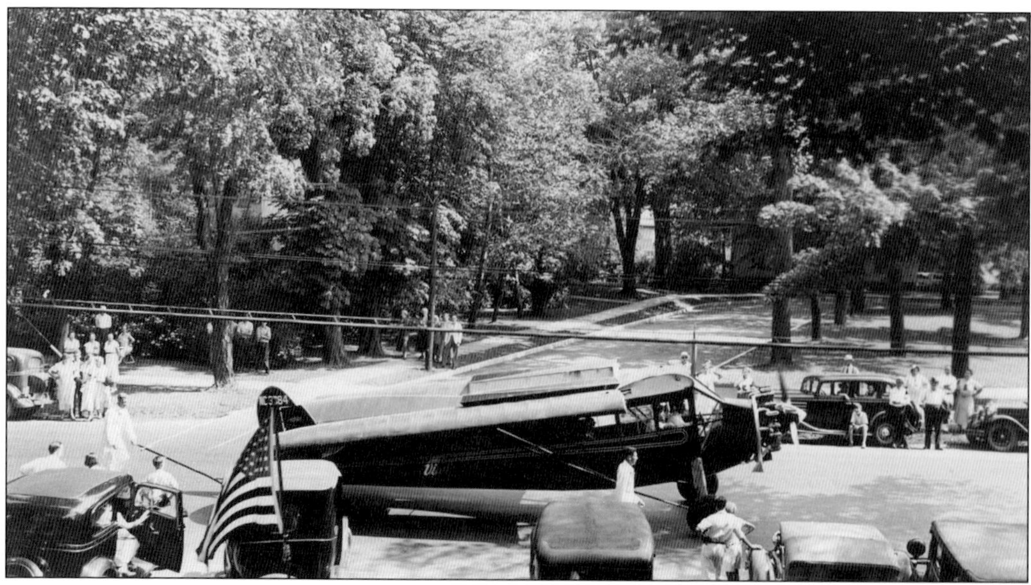

Airplane on Main Street. This Fairchild monoplane from the DW Airport was featured during LeRoy's Centennial Parade in 1934. The parade was two miles long, and the plane taxied down Main Street to the delight of the spectators.

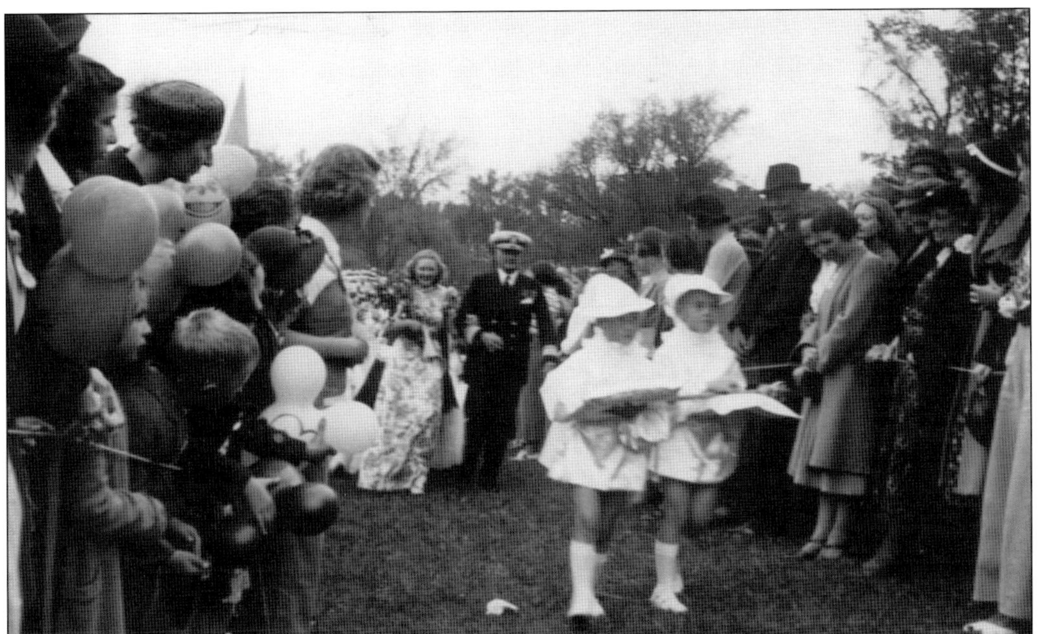

Apple Blossom Festival. LeRoy hosted the Western New York Apple Blossom Festival on May 21, 1938. Over 30,000 people arrived in LeRoy for the festivities, which included the coronation of the Apple Blossom Queen, Musette Haring. She was escorted by Admiral Ellis. Lionel Bradbury and William Rafferty, dressed in white satin page's costumes, carried her crown and scepter. A plane flown by Russell Holderman dropped apple blossoms and flowers on the crowd.

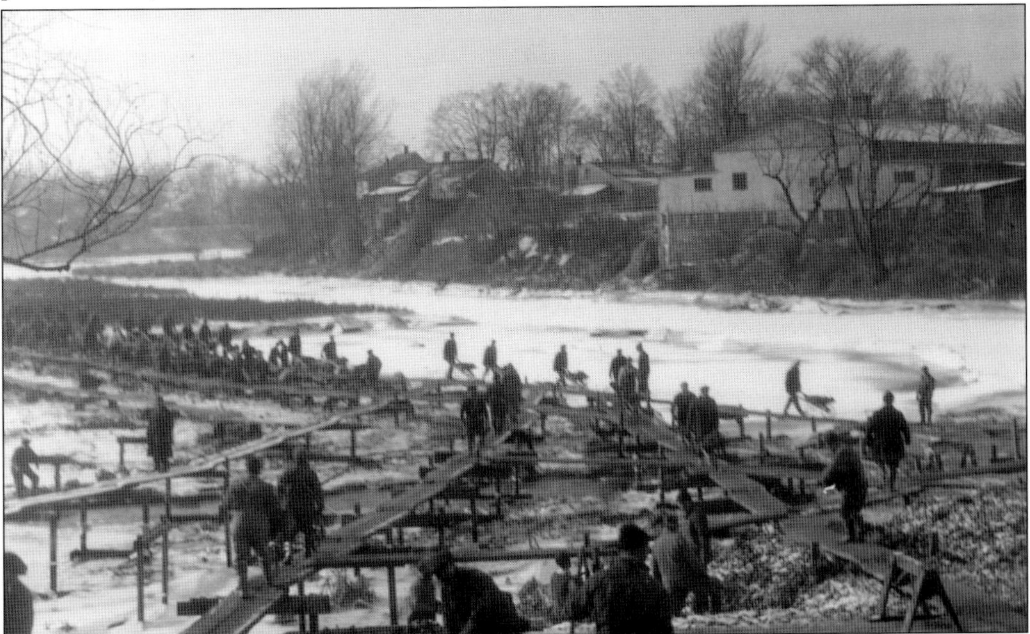

The Creek Project. In the winter of 1933, the Mill Pond was drained and unemployed workers were hired under the Federal Civil Works Program to dig out the creek. Hundreds of workers, most of them Italians from LeRoy, worked through one of the coldest winters on record. This picture was taken on December 21, 1933. The thermometer read three degrees below zero.

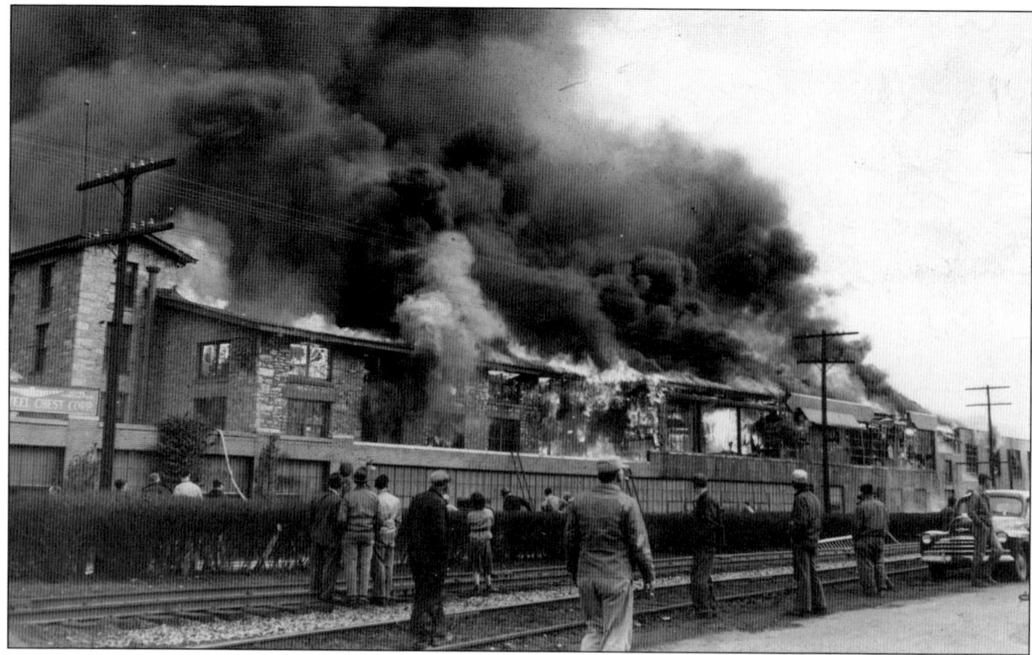

Union Steel Chest Fire. Fires have claimed many buildings in LeRoy. In 1855, almost the entire north side of Main Street was consumed. LeRoy Salt Company, LeRoy Plow Company, and the Keeney Bean Company all survived major fires. This fire on March 15, 1949, claimed the Union Steel Chest building, which was one of the oldest factory buildings in LeRoy.

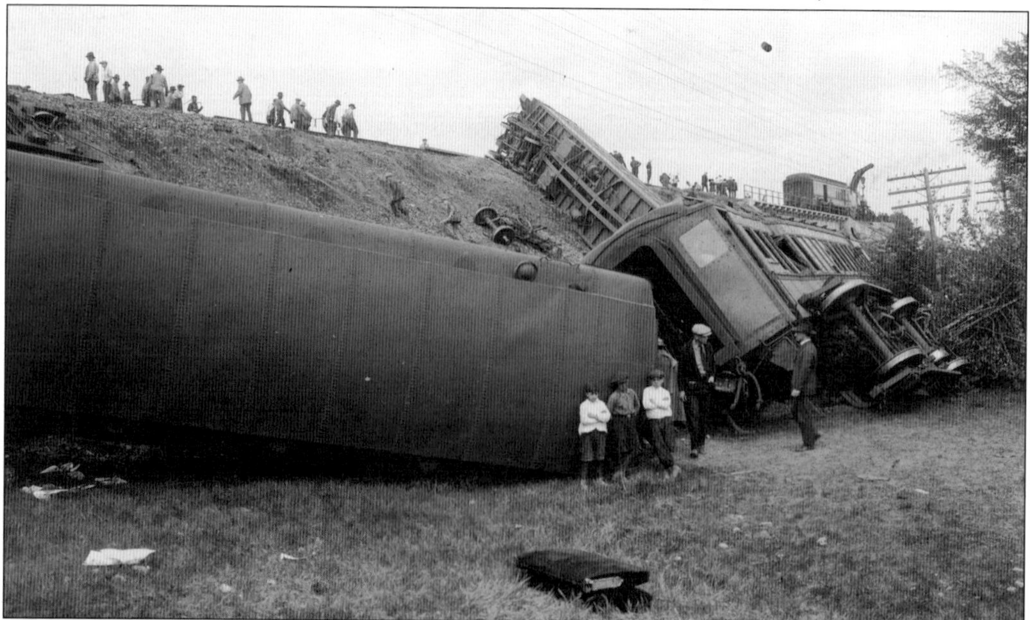

The Black Diamond Wreck. On May 13, 1922, as Thomas R. Brodie crossed the first set of railroad tracks at North LeRoy, a second train, traveling in the opposite direction, slammed into Brodie's car, killing him instantly. Five people were killed and 40 injured. This crossing in North LeRoy was the site of another fatal accident in 1893, when a train hit the Bovee family in their horse and carriage.

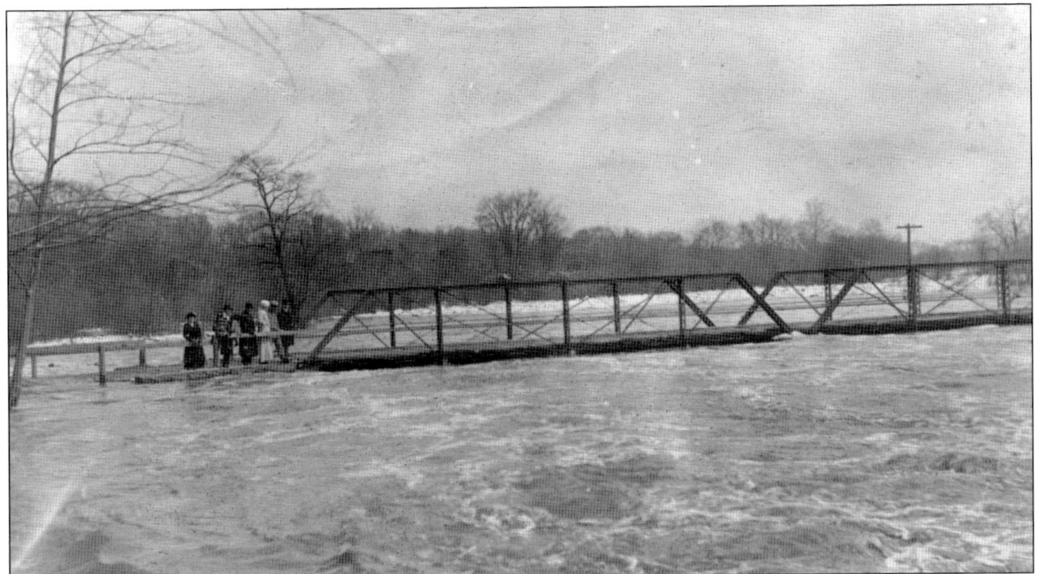

Flood at Red Bridge, 1916. One of the worst floods occurred in May 1916 when this picture was taken. Water over the spillway at the new dam at Lake LeRoy rose from 6 inches to 8.5 feet in 10 minutes. Water flowed a foot over Red Bridge, but it held. In March 1920, huge blocks of ice slammed into the bridge and carried two iron sections downstream.

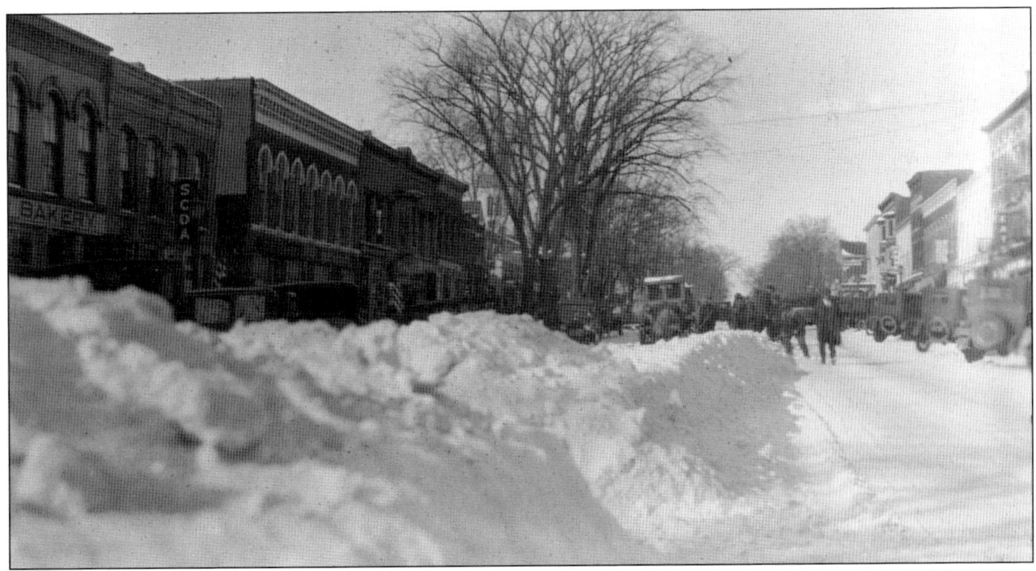

Snow Storm. Western New York is known for unpredictable snowstorms. LeRoy receives lake-effect snow from Lake Erie and Lake Ontario. This undated photograph was probably taken after the 1925 storm. It illustrates the method of snow removal at the time. The north side of Main Street was cleared first and the snow pushed to the south side. Then the south side was cleared.

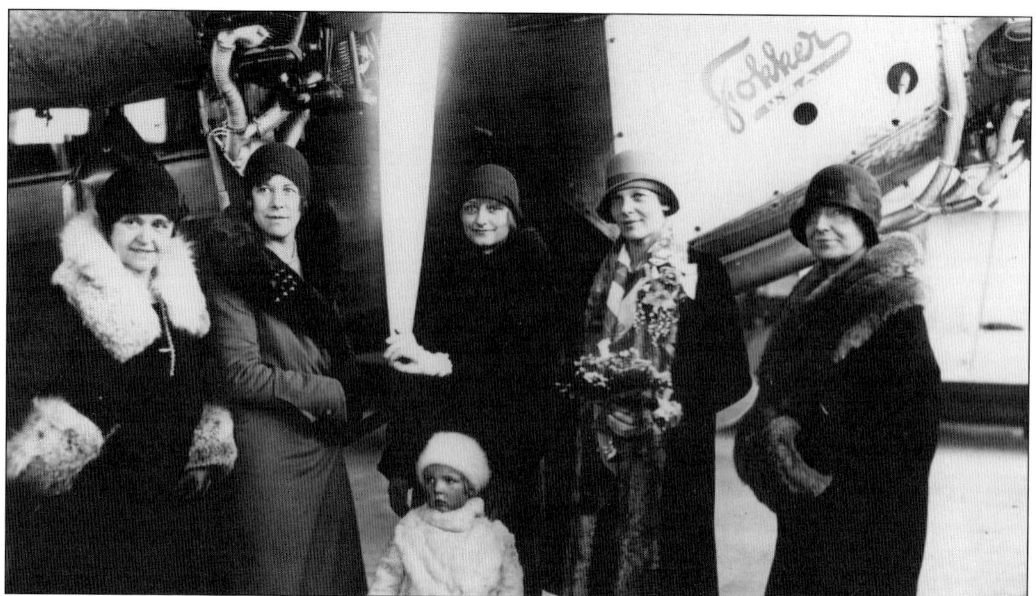

Amelia Earhart in LeRoy. On January 24, 1929, Amelia Earhart (second from right) came to LeRoy to visit the plane in which she made her historic flight across the Atlantic on June 17, 1928. The famous plane, known as the *Friendship,* was purchased by Donald Woodward and flown to LeRoy for the opening of his DW Airport in October 1928. He sold the plane to a South American cartel in 1929.

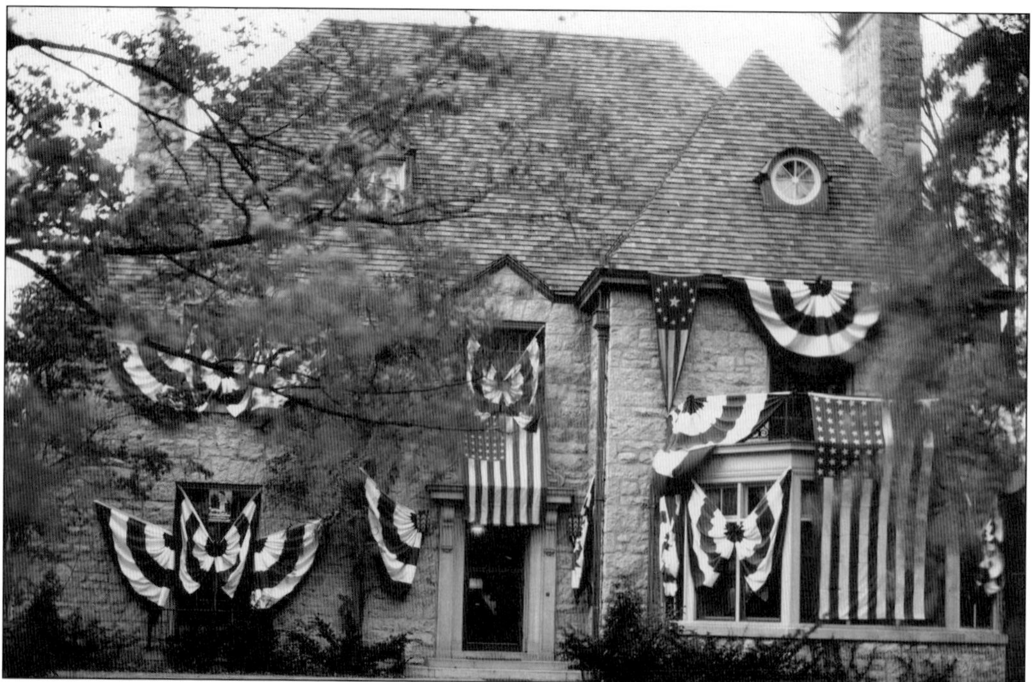

Eleanor Roosevelt's Visit. The first lady stopped in LeRoy on October 25, 1934, to support Caroline O'Day's campaign for U.S. Congress. Donald Woodward's wife, Adelaide, vice chairman of the Genesee County Democratic Party, hosted a tea at her house that was decorated with red, white, and blue bunting. Three thousand people and a Democrat donkey gathered on the front lawn.

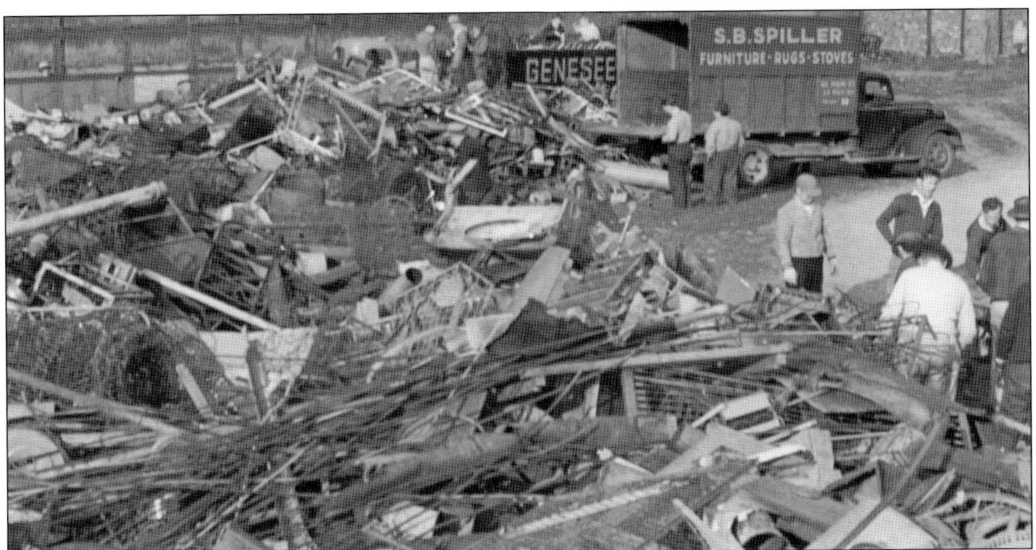

Scrap Drive. During World War II, LeRoy participated in the scrap drive. In 1942, to meet the quota, two cannons that once flanked the Soldiers Monument were dug up and added to the drive. The 16,000-pound cannons had been buried in 1925 after citizens complained that they were aimed at the First Baptist Church. The cannons helped LeRoy meet its goal of 50 tons of scrap.

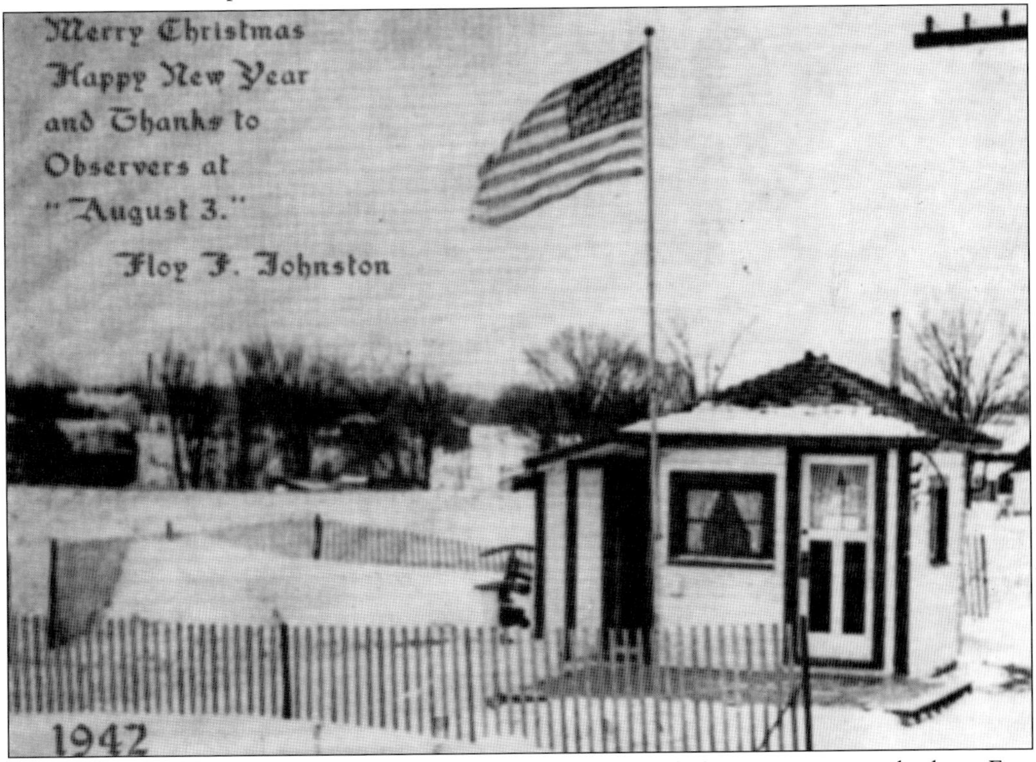

World War II Observation Post. During the war, a ground observer's post was built on East Bethany Road. The LeRoy post was manned 24 hours a day, seven days a week by over 150 volunteers who scanned the sky looking for enemy airplanes. Two of the volunteers were Gladys Zalacca and Della Nichols.

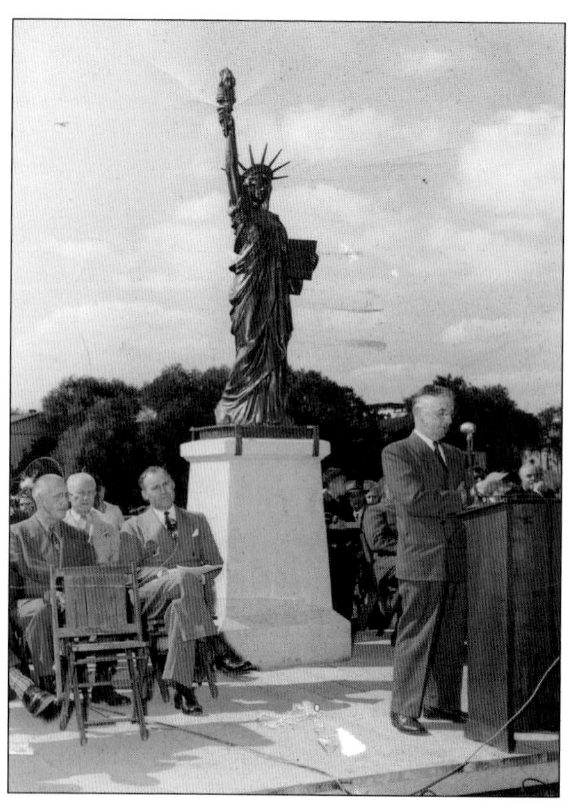

STATUE OF LIBERTY. The 8-foot statue is one of 25 that were cast in the United States. With a crowd of 5,000 people, the statue was dedicated on September 17, 1950, and presented to the Boy Scouts of LeRoy by the Loyal Order of Moose. The base was designed by Charles Ivan Cromwell. In 1986, it was restored with funds raised by Genesee Community College.

NEW YORK STATE THRUWAY EXIT 47. Work on the thruway started on July 11, 1946, at Liverpool near Syracuse. After a slow start, work resumed in earnest in 1951. Exit 47 in LeRoy opened August 26, 1954. Gov. Thomas E. Dewey cut the ribbon that opened the section between Exit 48 in Batavia and LeRoy. After 10 years of construction, the New York State Thruway was completed and opened on August 31, 1956.

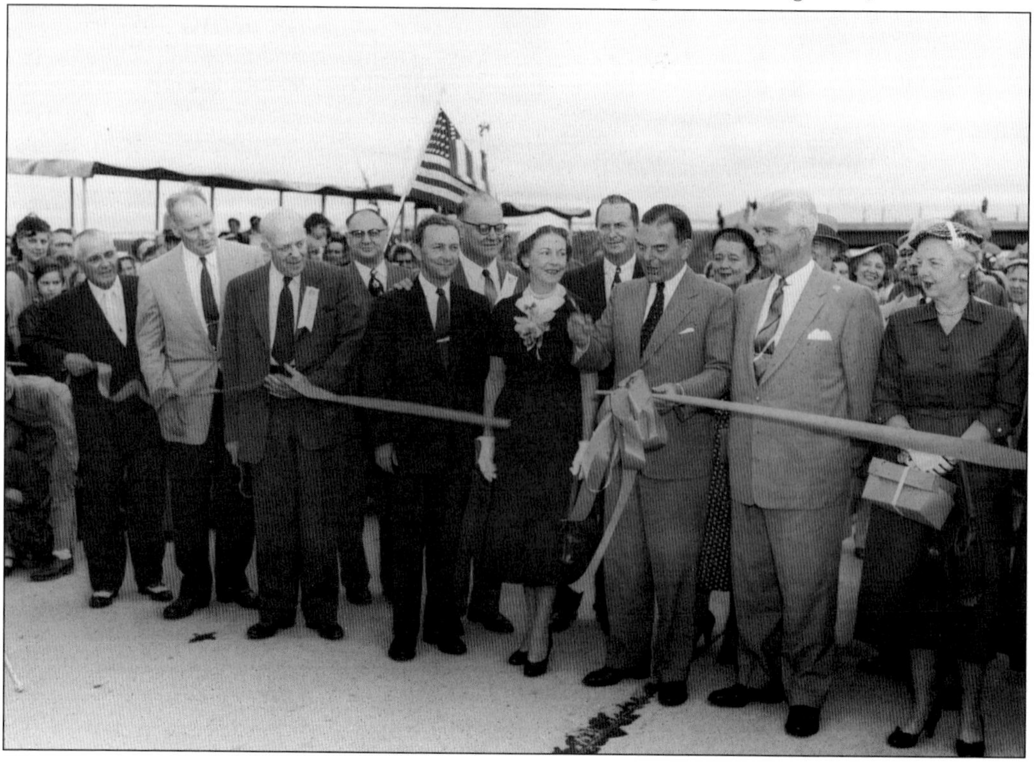

Seven

LeRoy in 1940

In 1939, Schuyler Wells, a prominent businessman, encouraged a group of interested citizens to hire photographer Oscar Wieggel to record the people, places, and organizations of LeRoy. Wieggel was given the use of an automobile and a dark room in a science classroom of the high school. Anyone could subscribe to the photographic record for a minimal fee. Over 500 images were included in the remarkable book. Captions were hand-lettered on archival quality velum and an index of people, places, and businesses was prepared. Two huge books were assembled. One was on display at the Woodward Memorial Library and the other was placed in storage at the Bank of LeRoy. Today the two books, the negatives, and contact prints are in the collection of the LeRoy Historical Society. The albums are a remarkable visual record of LeRoy made immediately before World War II. In the preface of the book, it is recorded that LeRoy had 26 industries. The high school had 1,192 students, and there were 8 rural school districts. There were 3 school buses that transported 50 students into town. Politically, LeRoy had 1,607 registered Republicans and 500 enrolled Democrats. In July 1940, there were 114 residents on relief, 9 receiving funds from the government sewing project, and 15 on the WPA project. The village was served by five locally owned groceries and meat markets as well as five neighborhood stores and four chain stores. Fruits and vegetables were sold house to house and three dairies provided pasteurized cream and milk. Town and village workers received 40¢ per hour. Twenty-five people commuted daily to Rochester. There were seven doctors, five lawyers, five dentists, five chiropractors, and one osteopath.

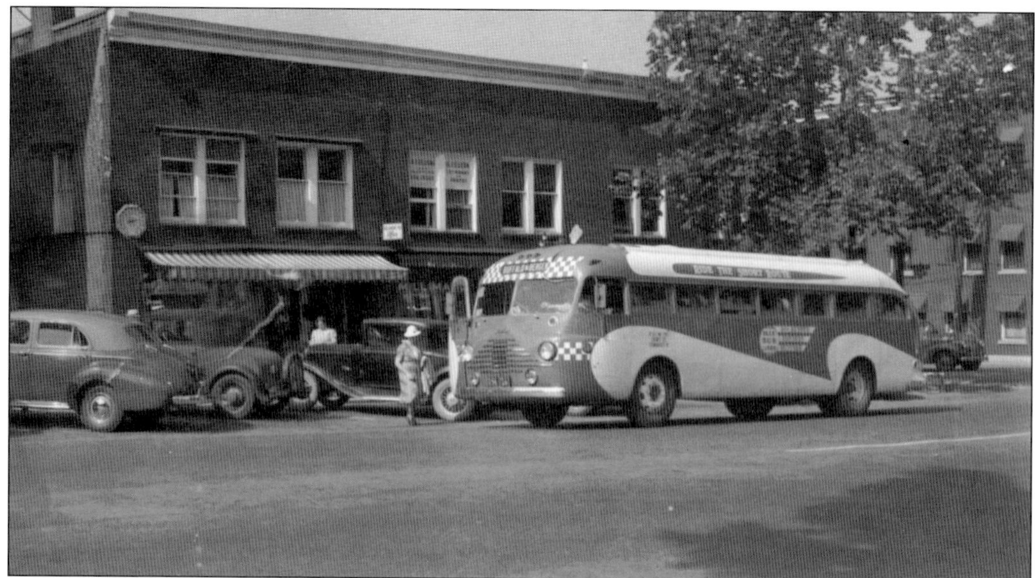

Blue Bus Station. In 1918, bus service between LeRoy and Batavia was established by Myron Russell, who operated two Studebaker buses. In 1927, he sold the business to the Western New York Bus Lines, which became known as the Blue Bus Line. Fourteen buses arrived daily at the station at the corner of West Main and Lake Streets. In 1940, Sidney Granger and his wife were the agents and proprietors.

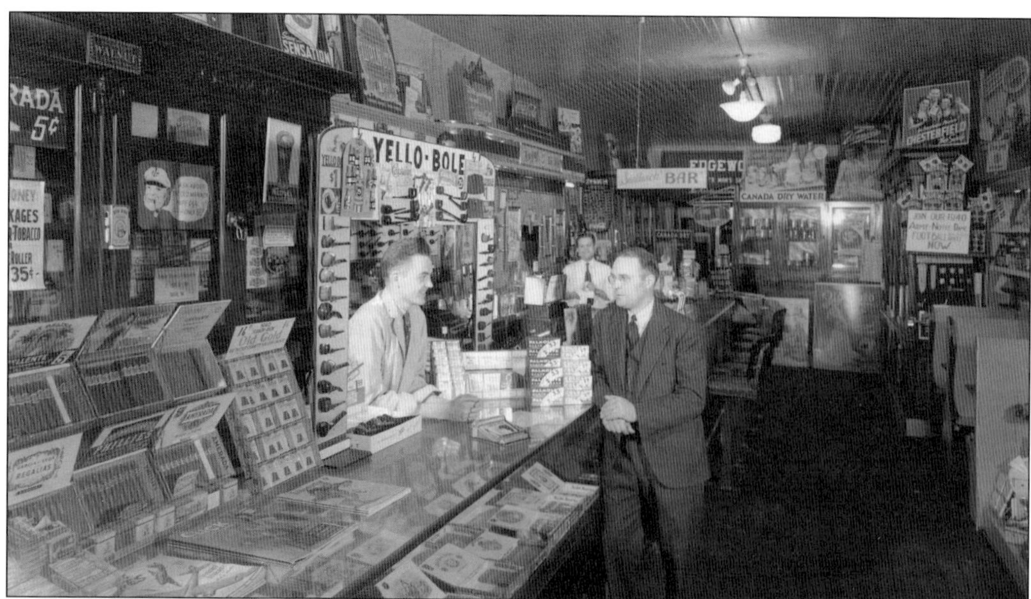

The Smoke Shoppe. John Graham, the proprietor, is standing behind the counter. He bought the shop from Anthony Reiselman in the 1930s. Reiselman manufactured corn fritters upstairs. He also named the store the Smoke Shoppe. At one time, LeRoy's only radio station was located on the second floor. In 1968, the shop was purchased by Ruth and Ross Harvie, and they operated it for 12 years. Today it is a gift shop.

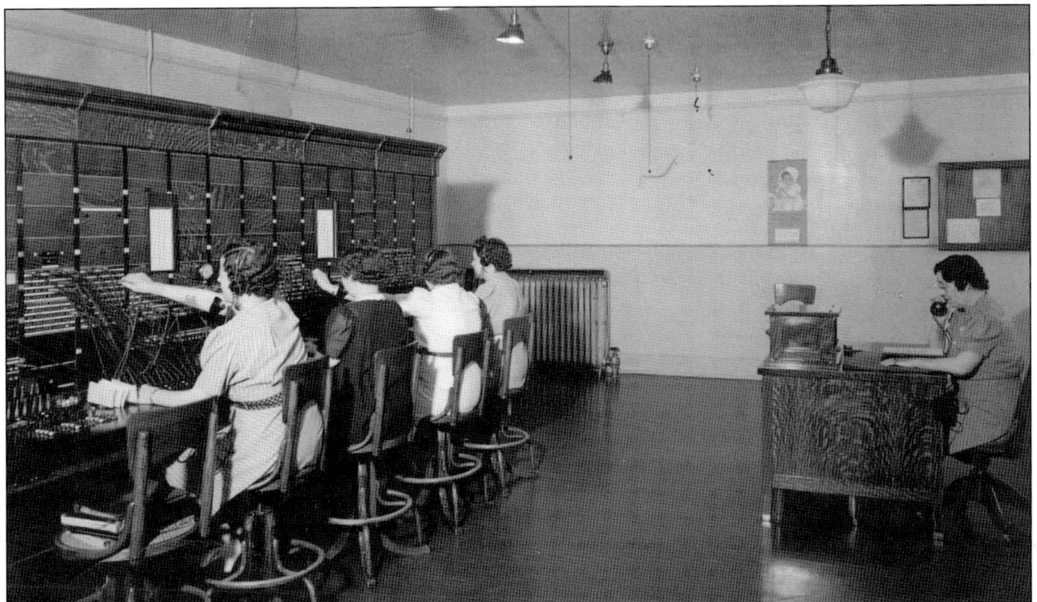

Rochester Telephone Switchboard. The switchboard operators were known as the "hello girls." In 1964, the switchboards were replaced with the Direct Distance Dial system. LeRoy's prefix 967 was in area code 716. In 1978, the prefix was changed to 768. The area code was changed to 585 in 2001. The operators in this photograph are, from left to right, Ethel Carney, Mrs. D. J. Crocker, Mrs. Philibin, Mrs. MacPherson, and Mrs. Robinson.

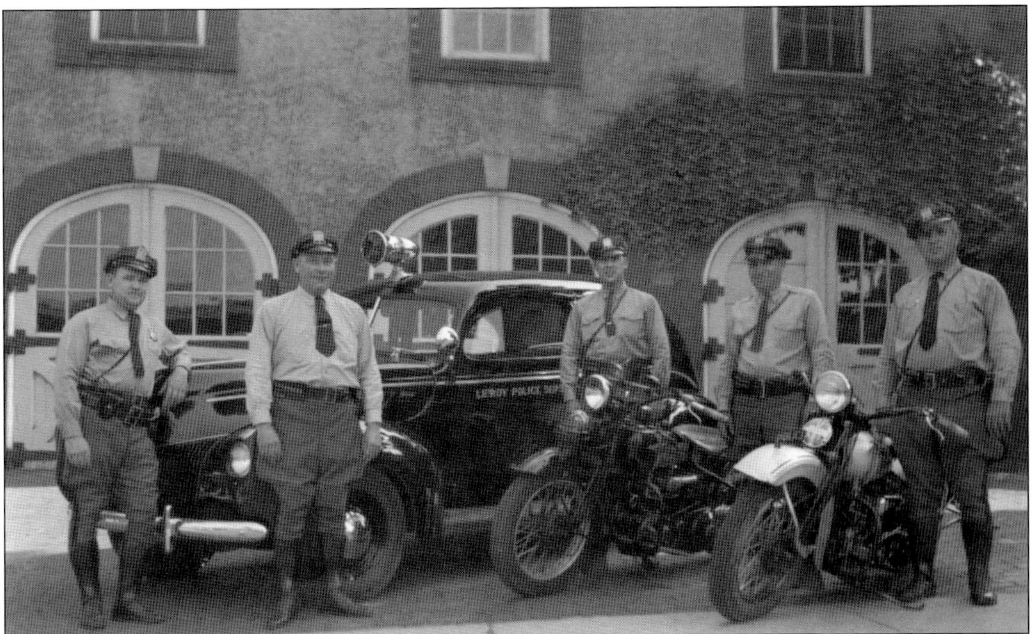

LeRoy Police Department. Little is known about the early history of the police department. One of the most unusual events occurred on August 1, 1922, when officer Raymond Dampier stopped Henry Ford's car for speeding. Ford challenged the ticket unsuccessfully and he erected warning signs at the edge of town. Standing in the photograph are, from left to right, Capt. Fred Rider, Joseph Scanlan, Robert Garlock, Alfred Messore, and Calvin "Tuffy" Lathan.

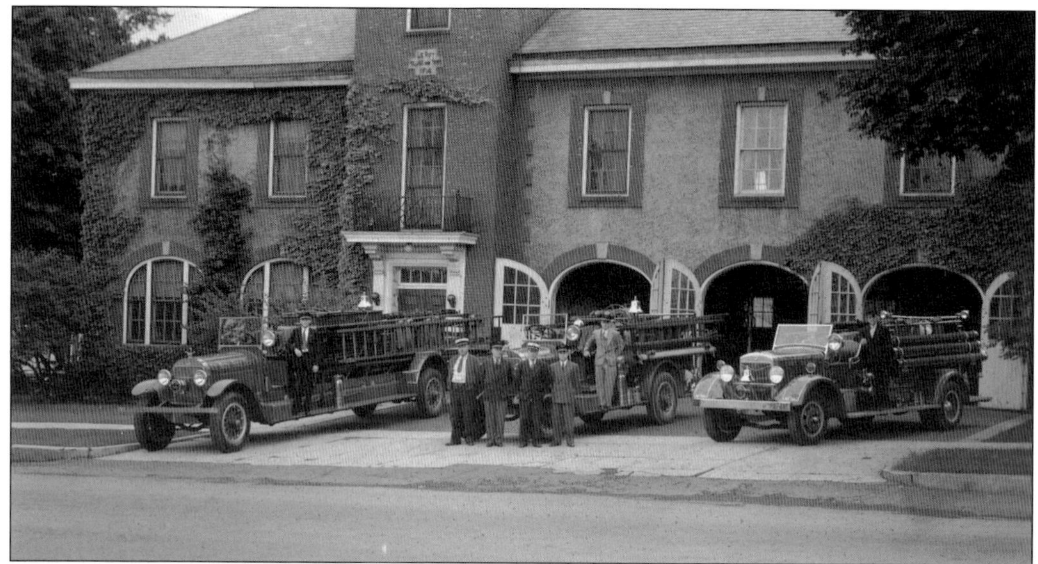

LeRoy Fire Department. In 1918, the fire department bought its first piece of motorized equipment, a Ford Model T chemical and hose truck. This picture was taken in front of the Municipal Building designed by Claude Bragdon and built in 1913. The trucks are parked in the old truck bays. Standing in the photograph are, from left to right, L. B. Mooney, J. W. Scanlan, T. R.Chapman, E. J. Snyder, S. E. Beadle, H. L. Heddon, and J. Kibler.

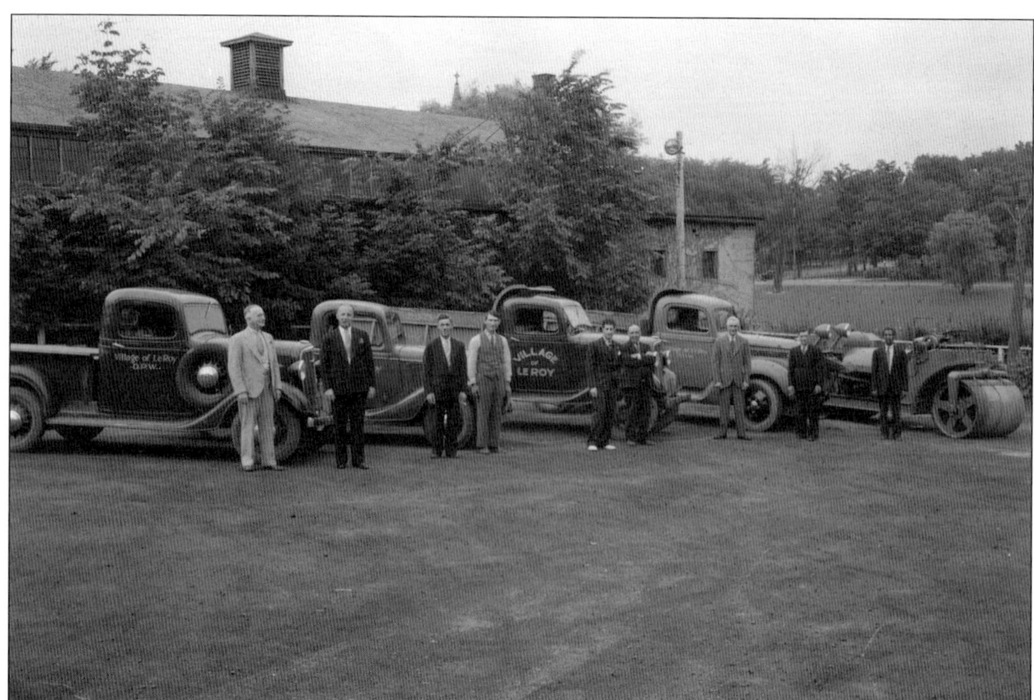

LeRoy Department of Public Works. This photograph was taken on Bank Street and includes the members of the Department of Public Works: (from left to right) F. J. O'Melia, J. J. Scinta, A. C. Barone, E. W. Preston, T. J. Scott, G. Joy, H. B. Cook, J. F. Cravotta, and G. Perry.

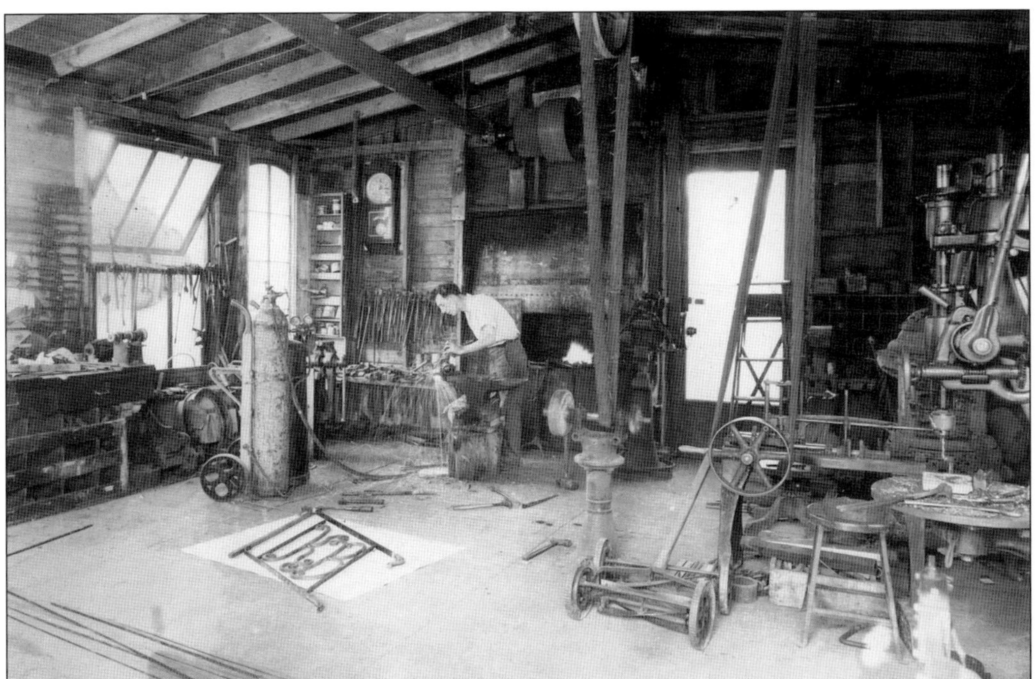

Blacksmith Shop. Located at 115 North Street, the blacksmith shop was established in 1905 and operated by T. Arthur Thompson. Samuel Arrington lived next door. He was a blacksmith for LeRoy Lime and Crushed Stone Company. The first blacksmith in LeRoy was Richard Waite.

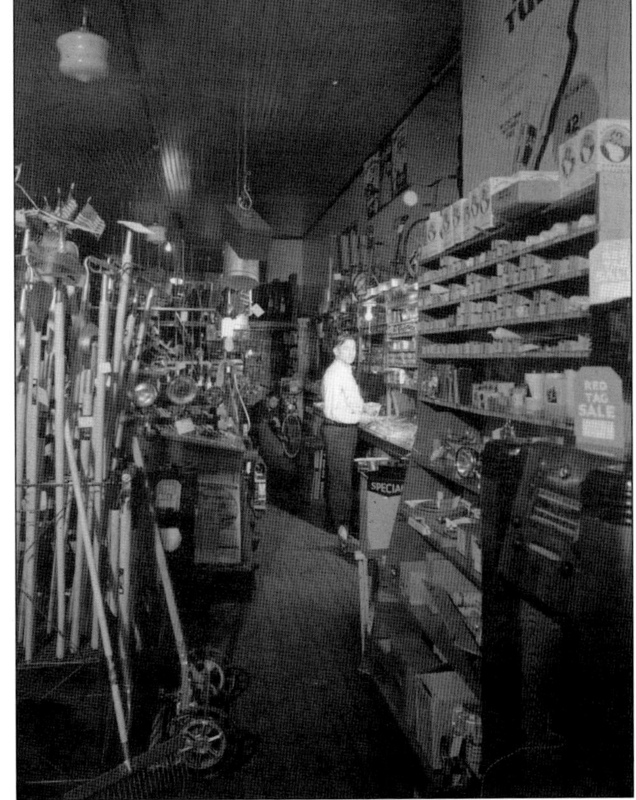

Western Auto Store. First open to the public in April 1938, the Western Auto Store was located at 41 Main Street. It was operated by G. F. Longwell. J. D. Holzschuh was in charge of the store until January 1951. It is now the LeRoy Hardware Store, operated by Bruce Stisser.

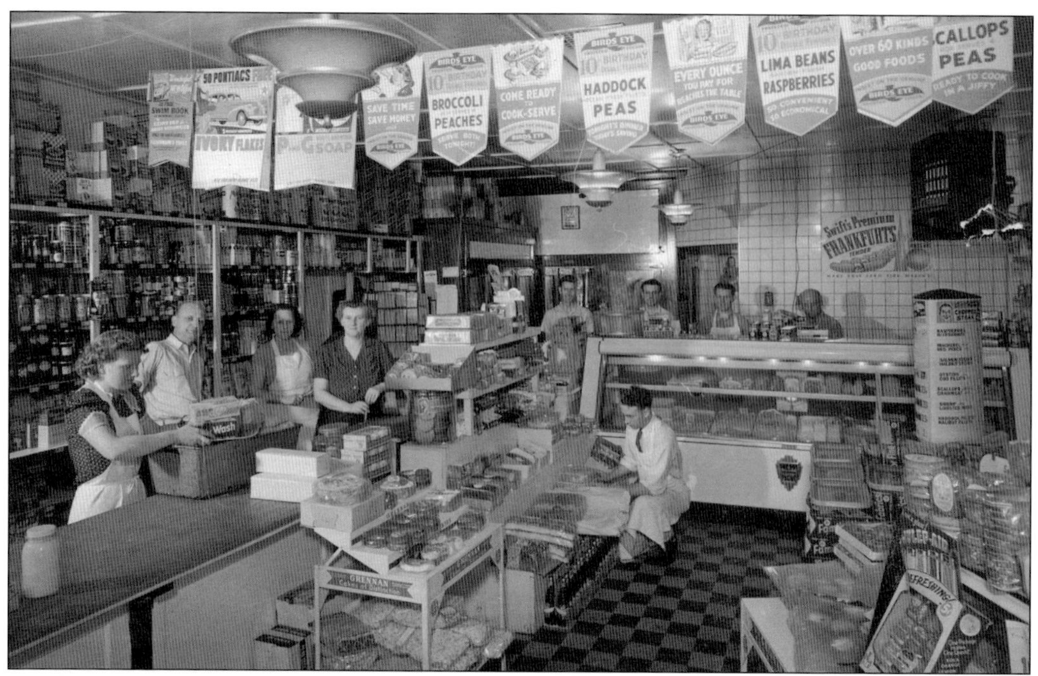

WILLARD'S GROCERY STORE. Frank Willard established the grocery store in 1920 at 23 Main Street. In 1940, the advertisement in the *LeRoy Gazette* noted that Willard's provided food "for particular people." Breakfast bacon was selling for 21¢ a pound and rib roast for 30¢ a pound. They also sold Mrs. Longs home baked pies, breads, and rolls. Willard's is now the dental office of Dr. Anthony Gugino.

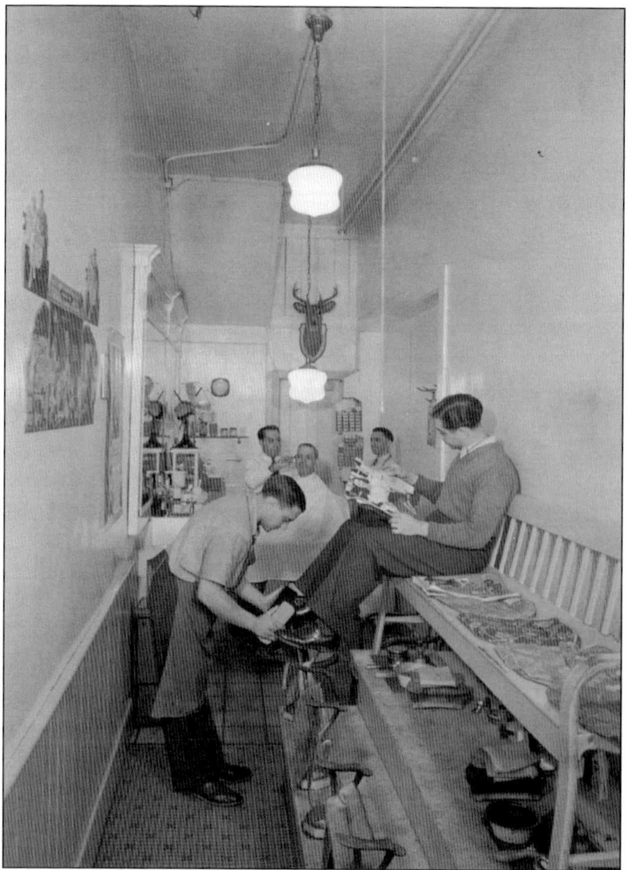

MARTINA'S BARBER SHOP. Located at 35 Main Street, this shop was as wide as the front door. Pictured in the back are A. S. Martina (left), the proprietor; S. L. Rose (center); and R. Campesi. In the front are S. T. Campesi (left) and A. J. Campesi. Later, Joe Antinore operated the barbershop. It was acquired by Vic Blood's Furniture Store and eventually razed.

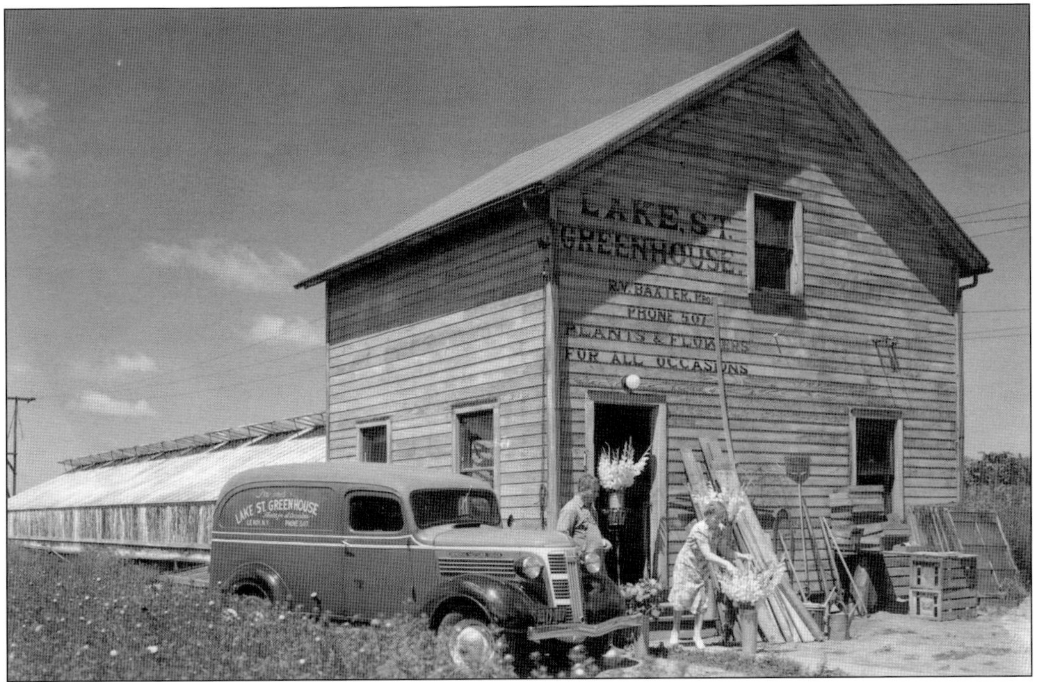

Lake Street Florist. Established at 81 Lake Street, the greenhouses were operated by William Baxter and then in 1936 by Frank Paolone and his sister Lena. The business was sold to Donald Rockcastle in 1981. One of the greenhouses came from the Donald Woodward estate. The property was sold to a landscaping business and the greenhouses fell into disrepair and were razed.

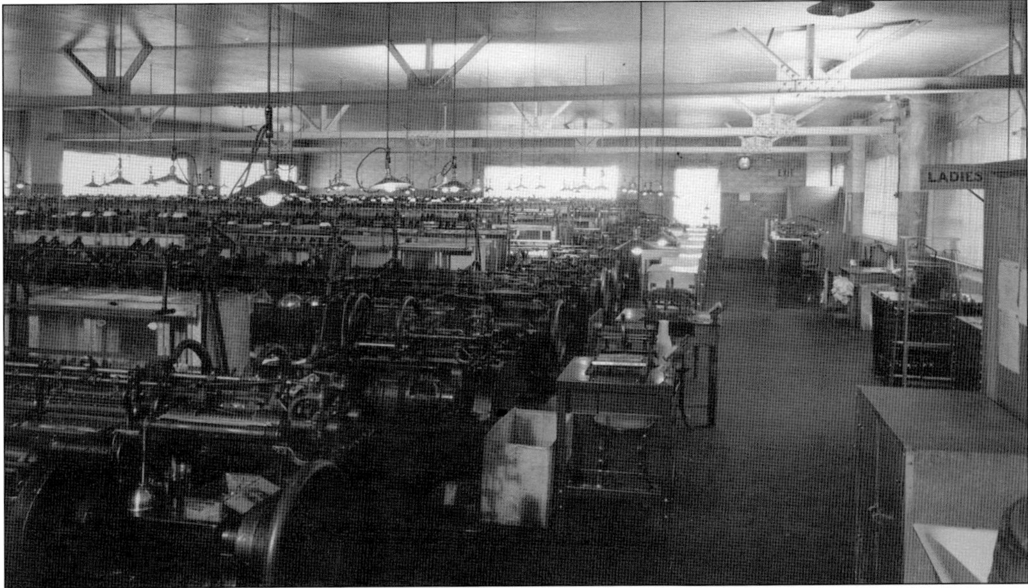

Veitel Hosiery. Founded by Franz Veitel in 1936, the factory was located behind his home at 26 West Main Street. Veitel manufactured silk stockings until World War II, but because silk was needed for parachute production, the company switched to nylon and rayon. The stockings were specialized with hand-painted butterflies and flowers. Franz Veitel presented Mamie Eisenhower with a pair of Veitel stockings for President Eisenhower's inauguration.

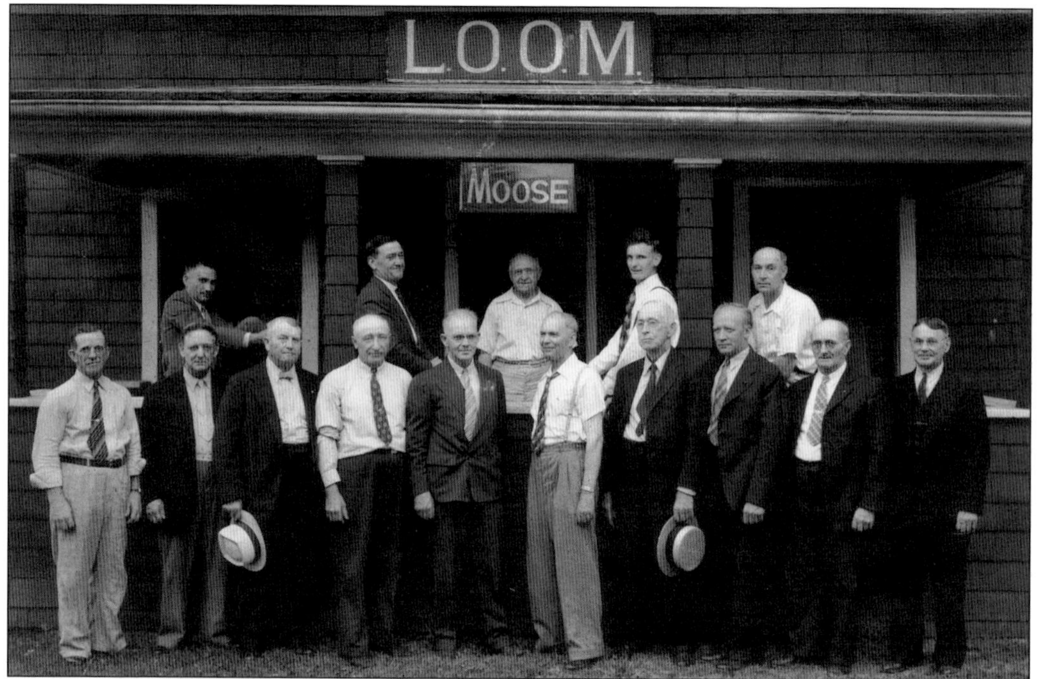

Loyal Order of Moose. Through the years, LeRoy has had many fraternal and service organizations, including the Olive Branch Lodge of Free and Accepted Masons, founded in 1815. The Odd Fellows were organized in 1895. The Knights of Columbus were established in 1945. The Loyal Order of Moose were chartered in 1914 and in 1928 purchased the clubhouse on Bank Street. The LeRoy Rotary Club was founded in 1940.

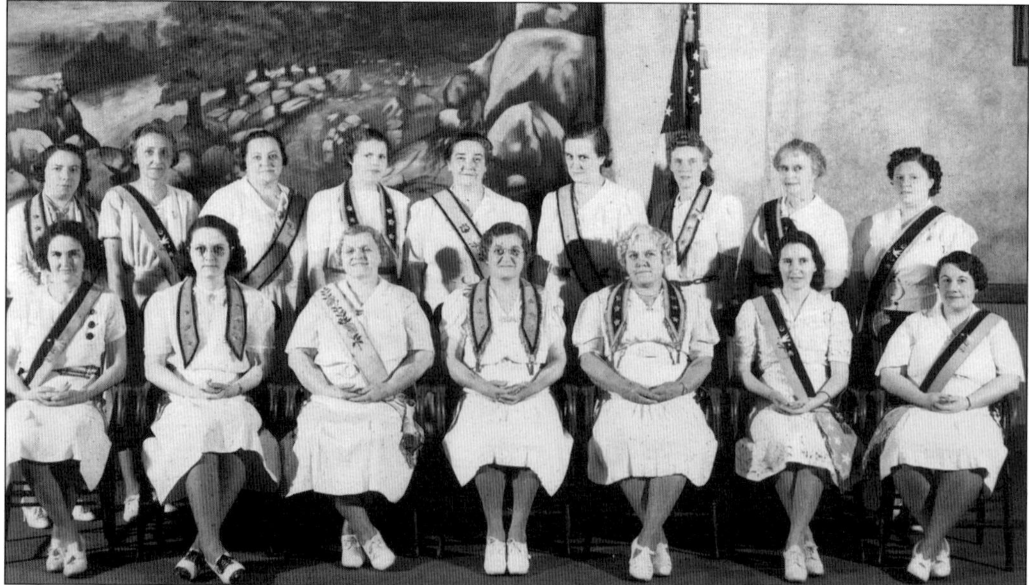

Rebekah Lodge. The Rebekah Lodge, affiliated with the Odd Fellows, was established in 1907 and later consolidated with the lodges from Pavilion, Bergen, Batavia, and Stafford. Other women's organizations included the Order of Eastern Star, the History of Art Club, the Women's Club, the Ladies of the Moose, the Mothers' Club, and the Daughters of the American Revolution.

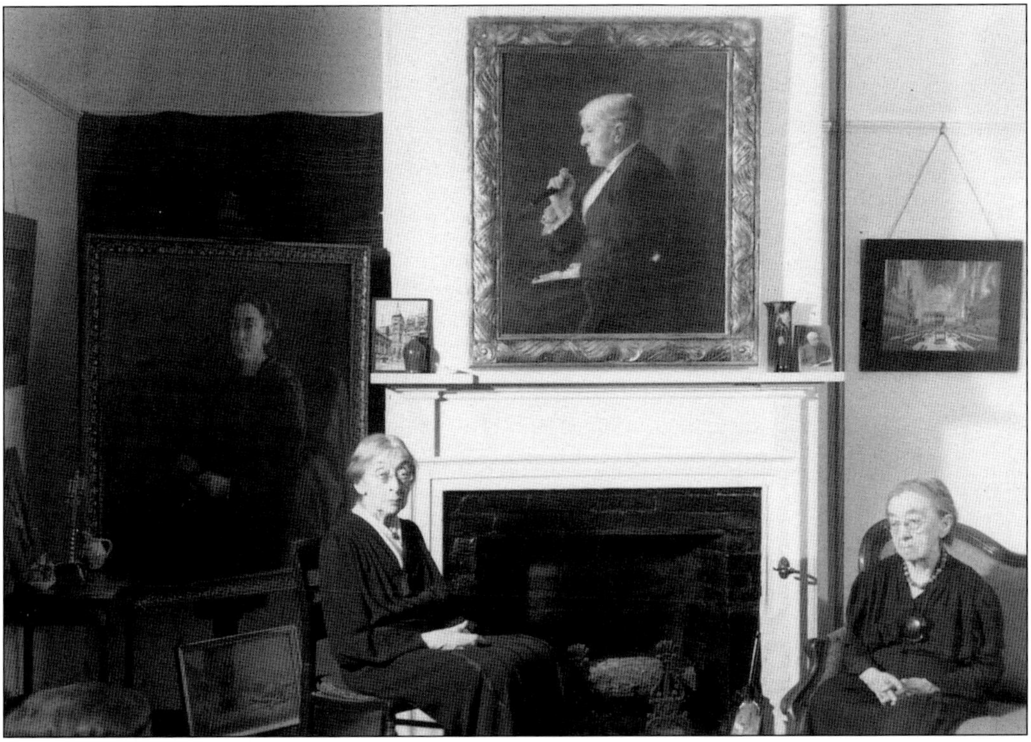

THE TAYLOR SISTERS. Ida Taylor, on the left, was a graduate of Ingham University and was a very well-known artist in the Rochester area. On the right is Isabella Taylor, a graduate of Smith College. The painting to the left is Ida's self-portrait. Over the mantle is the portrait of Cornelia Taylor, Ida's mother. The sisters lived in the Taylor family home on the point of Wolcott Street and Summit Street.

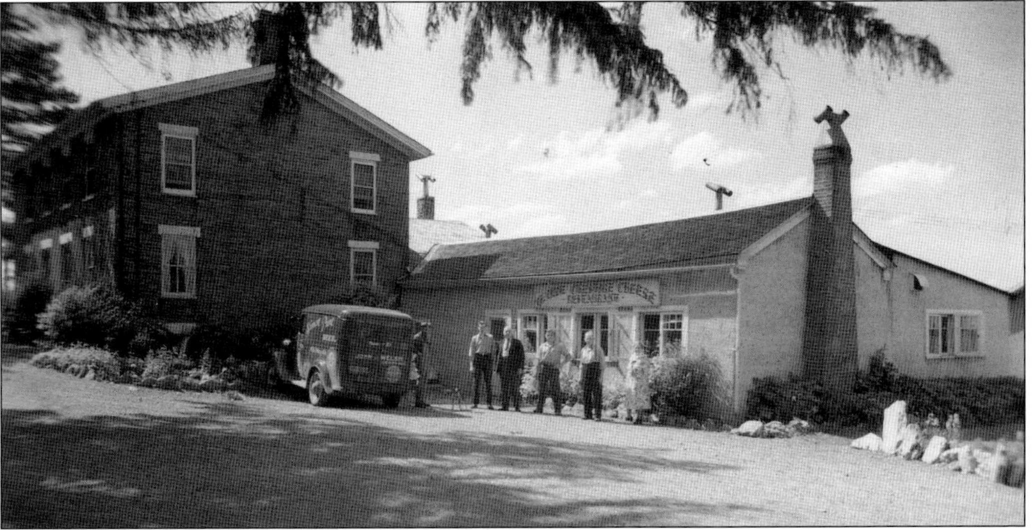

THE CHESHIRE CHEESE. This brick house on Randall Road was built in 1827. In 1933, Sidney Habgood named the restaurant Ye Olde Cheshire Cheese. It was in operation until the early 1970s. Standing in the photograph are (from left to right) L. C. Verney, C. J. Habgood, S. Habgood, H. A. Pickell, W. H. Habgood, and Mrs. W. H. Habgood.

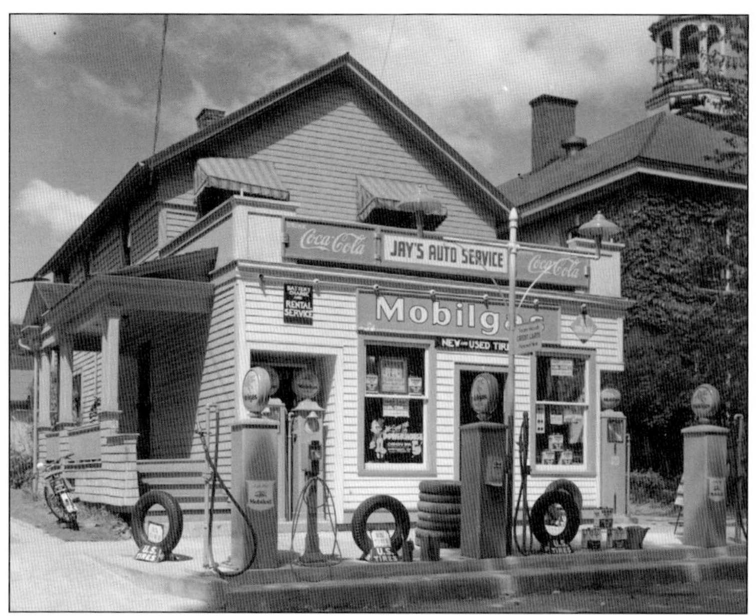

JAY'S AUTO SERVICE. With the popularity of the automobile, gas stations and auto mechanics were important. The first automobile garage in LeRoy was in a barn on Craigie Street owned by the McPherson brothers. The mechanic was Lewis Alexander. In 1940, Jay's Auto Service was owned by Jay Serusa and was on Clay Street about where the driveway to the back of the Municipal Building is located.

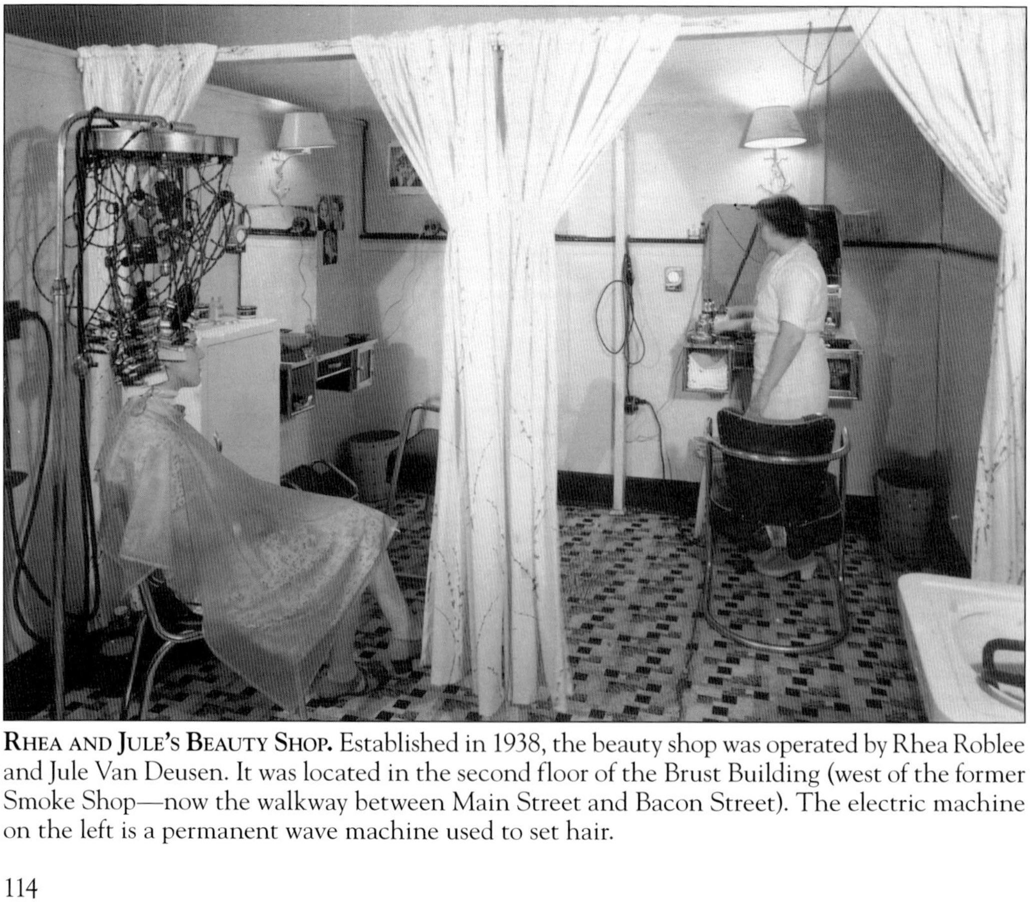

RHEA AND JULE'S BEAUTY SHOP. Established in 1938, the beauty shop was operated by Rhea Roblee and Jule Van Deusen. It was located in the second floor of the Brust Building (west of the former Smoke Shop—now the walkway between Main Street and Bacon Street). The electric machine on the left is a permanent wave machine used to set hair.

Eight

The Vanishing Landscape

Towns and villages change. Progress often requires demolition. Fires and neglect claim homes, barns, and buildings. And although LeRoy is remarkable because of its historical landscape, it has not survived unscathed. The tree-lined streets have succumbed to Dutch Elm disease and the brutal tree trimming necessary to maintain telephone and power lines. And it is not only the buildings and trees that have disappeared, but also industry and organizations that once thrived in LeRoy. It is easy to forget that LeRoy once boasted six railroads, the largest malt processing plant, a university for women, "America's Most Famous Dessert," and the best private airport in the nation, not to mention an Odd Fellows Club, the Oatka Falls Grange, the Women's Club, a Red Cross Chapter . . . the list goes on. Some communities disappear and others are absorbed into larger metropolitan regions. That has not happened to LeRoy. It still retains its unique identity. No one knows what the future holds for a small community like LeRoy, but its unique heritage—even that which has vanished—can be shared in this book. This last chapter captures a bit of the vanishing LeRoy landscape with a hope that a look back will enable LeRoy to plan for the future.

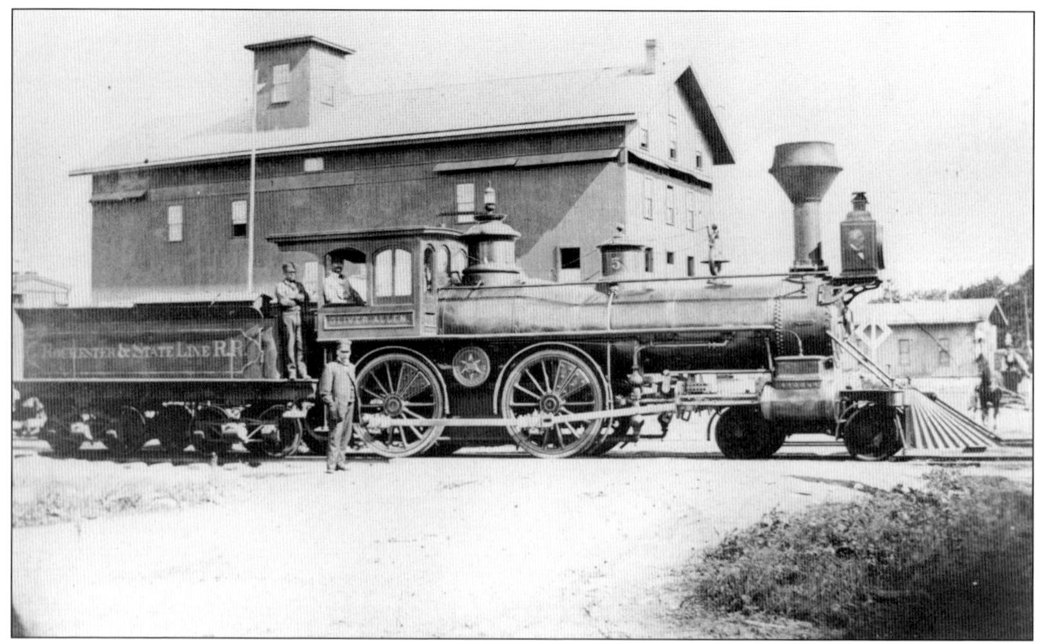

The Oliver Allen, 1881. Known as Engine No. 5, it was manufactured at the Brooks Locomotive Works in Dunkirk, New York. Pictured at the Lake Street crossing near the station, it ran between Rochester and the coal fields in western Pennsylvania. It was named for Oliver Allen II, president of the railroad. In 1879, it overturned in Great Valley but returned to service. The lantern belongs to the Rochester Historical Society.

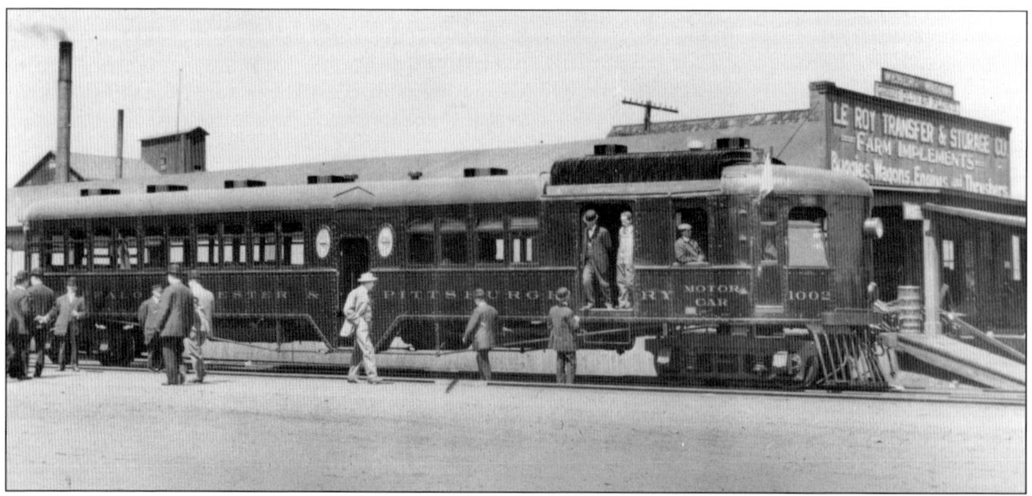

The Comet. The Comet, introduced in 1910, was one of two electric-diesel-powered cars that ran commuter service between LeRoy and Rochester. The Meteor was introduced in 1911. The railroads provided passenger service until 1953.

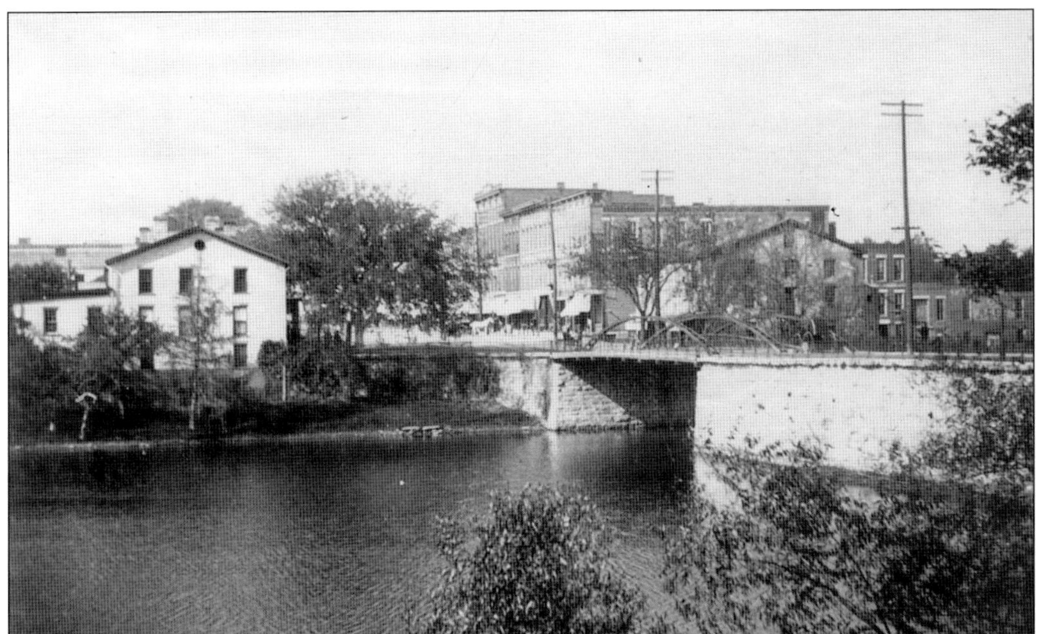

The Iron Bridge. In 1853, the Main Street bridge was washed out by a flood. For two years, traffic was diverted to the Lodi bridge at Clay Street. In 1855, the iron arch bridge with a wooden deck was completed. It also carried water lines from the west side of town to the east side. The iron bridge was replaced in 1909 by the first cement bridge.

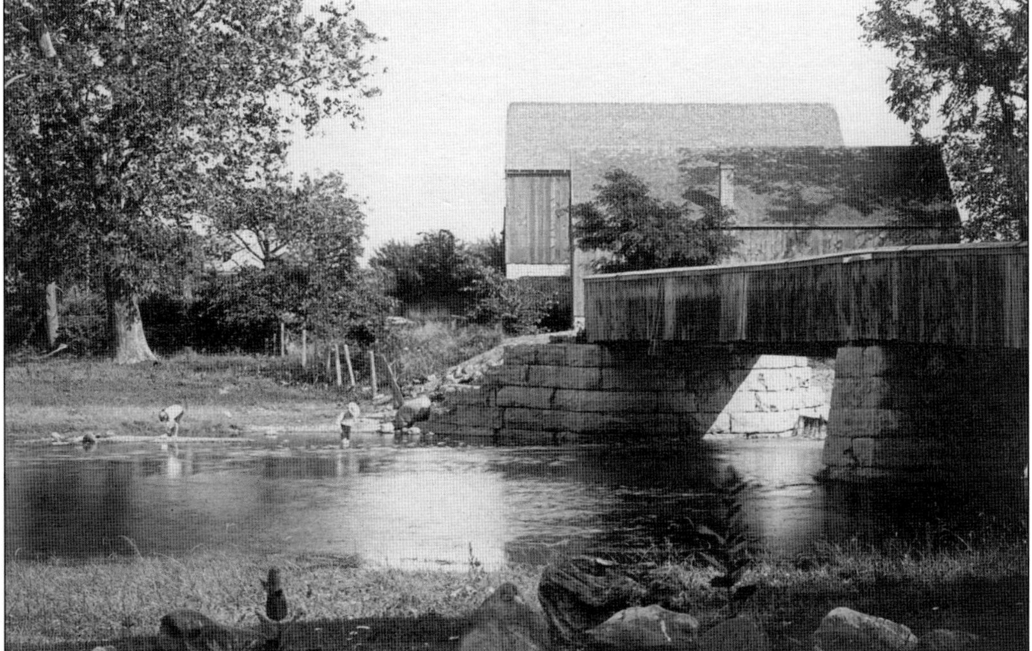

Red Bridge. This red wooden bridge spanned the Oatka Creek at Munson Street. It was replaced with the iron spans of the old Lodi bridge from Clay Street. The Haskins Mill dam was south of the bridge and provided a summer swimming hole for many years. The bridge remained known as Red Bridge until it was replaced by the modern Munson Street bridge.

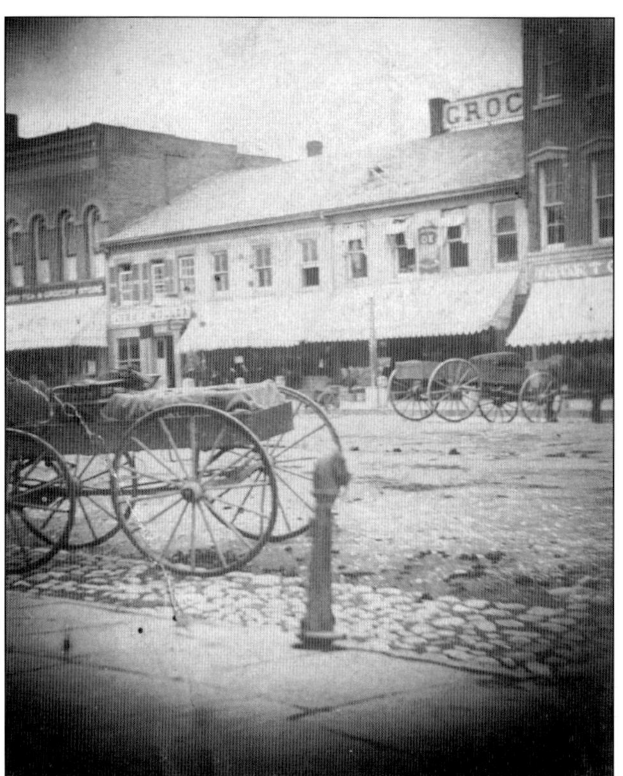

North Side of Main Street. This is one of the oldest photographs of the north side of Main Street. In the foreground is one of several iron horse posts that lined Main Street. They were cast by Coleman and Webb Foundry of LeRoy. Darius Hinkston carved the pattern for the horse head and Mr. Starr designed the posts.

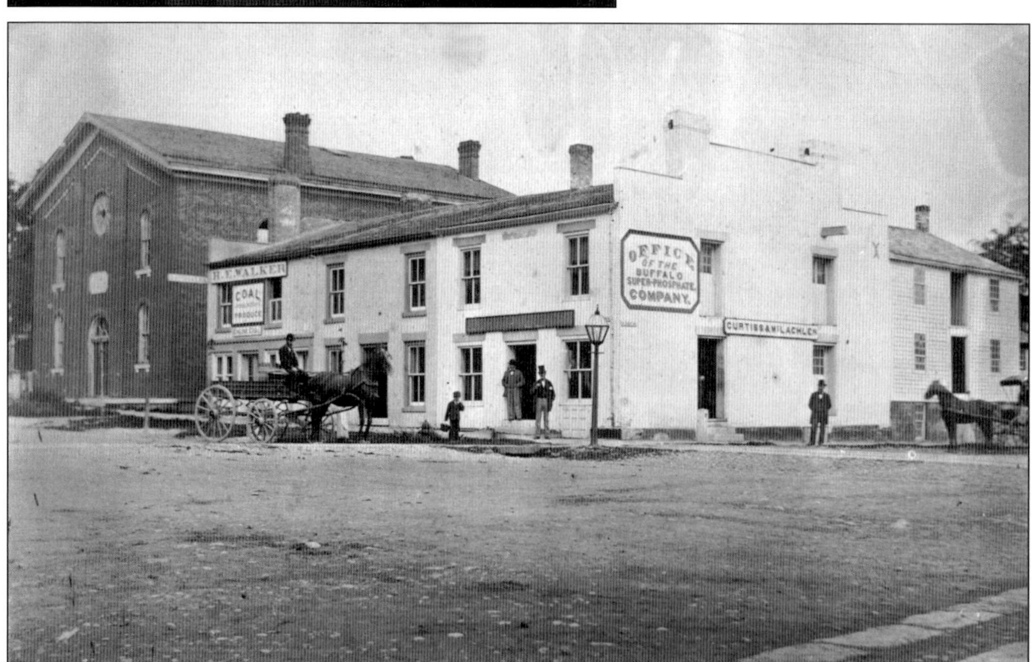

The Corner of Lake and Main Streets. The corner building was enlarged in the early 1900s and was known as the Milliman Block. The large brick building to the left was originally the Universalist Church built in 1859 on the site of the Round House. The church was sold and became the Masonic Lodge until both buildings were razed in 2008 for a Walgreens Drug Store.

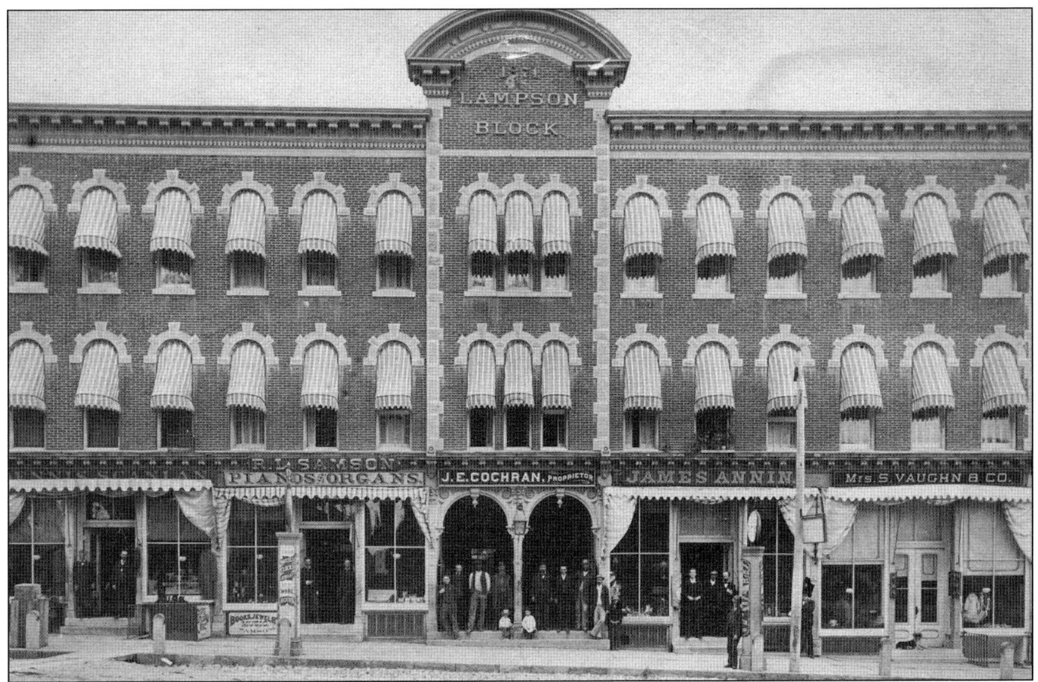

LAMPSON HOUSE. In 1873, William Lampson built the largest commercial building on the north side of Main Street. An open arcade ran through the middle of the main floor, and the upper floors provided meeting rooms and the best hotel rooms in town. The building survived a major fire in 1903 and was rebuilt. The building was destroyed by fire in 1945.

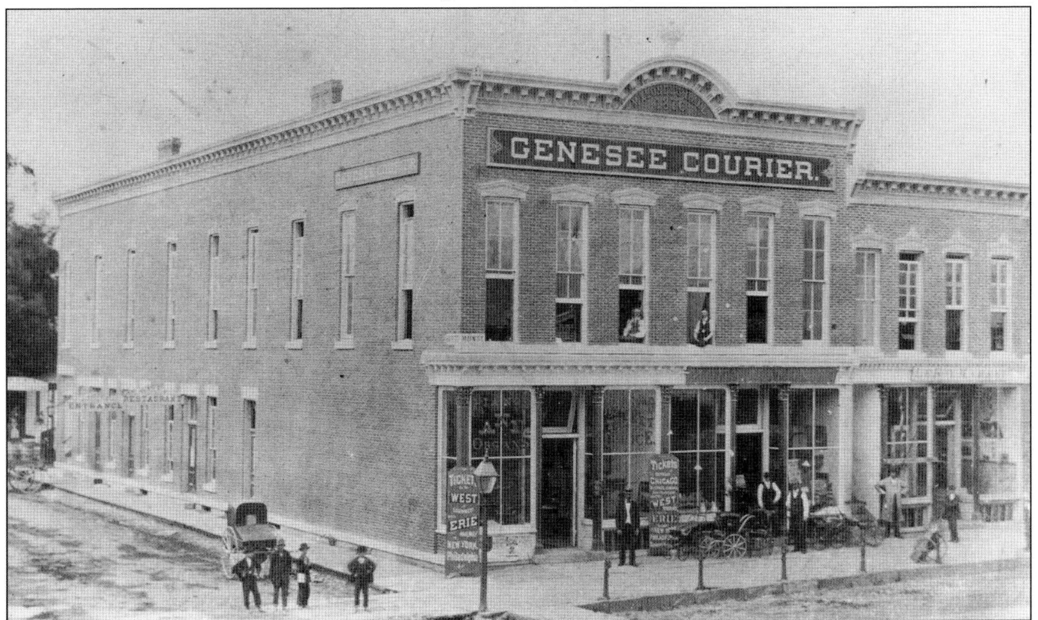

MALONEY BLOCK. Built in 1876, Maloney Black was on the corner of Main Street and Bank Street. It replaced the Starr Block after a fire in 1875. The Maloney Block housed the opera house and the *Genesee Courier.* It burned in 1960 and was razed. The corner is now occupied by the Bank of Castile and Tompkins Insurance.

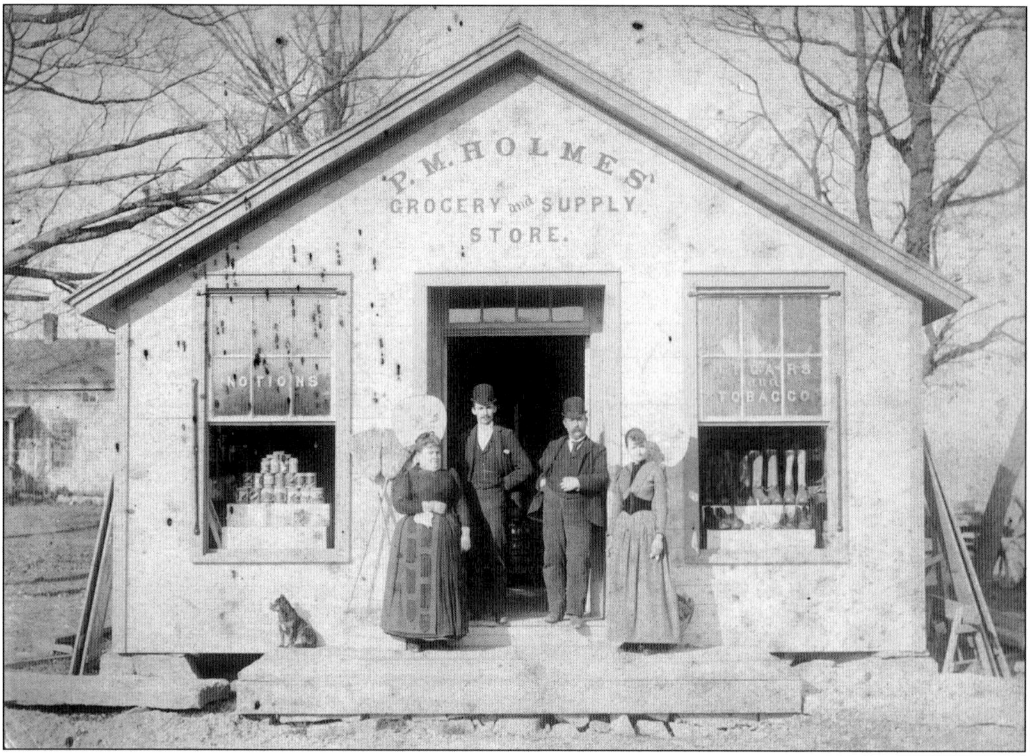

HOLMES STORE IN LIME ROCK. George Holmes owned limestone quarries and limekilns in Lime Rock. Harry Holmes built the log cabin on Route 5 in Lime Rock. It is not known exactly where the store was located, but the picture was probably taken about 1900.

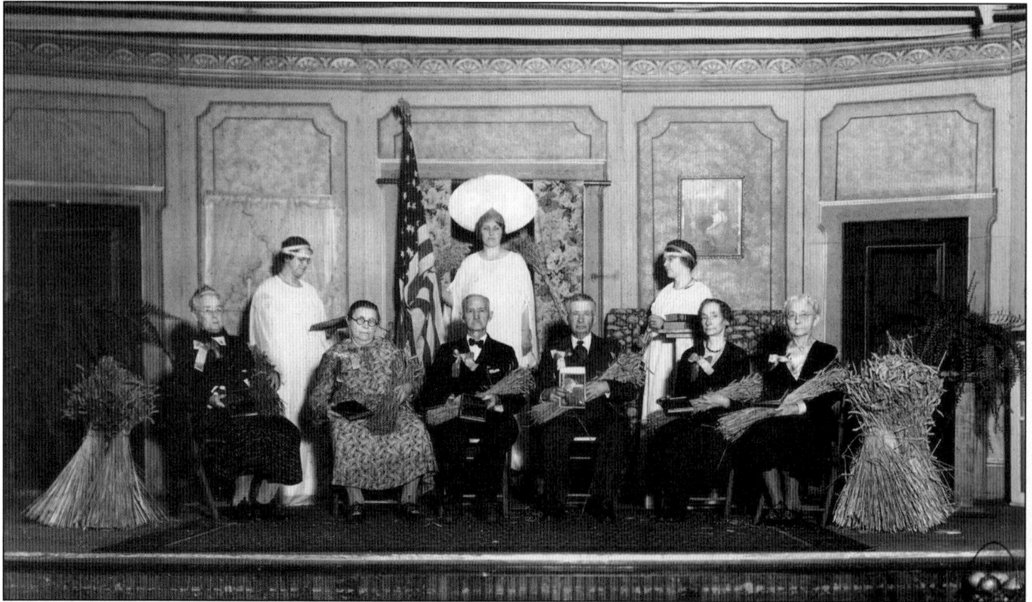

THE OATKA FALLS GRANGE. The Grange Hall is located on Parmelee Road and was built around 1879. It is now a private residence. The Oatka Falls Grange was organized in 1876 under the guidance of Dwight Pierson.

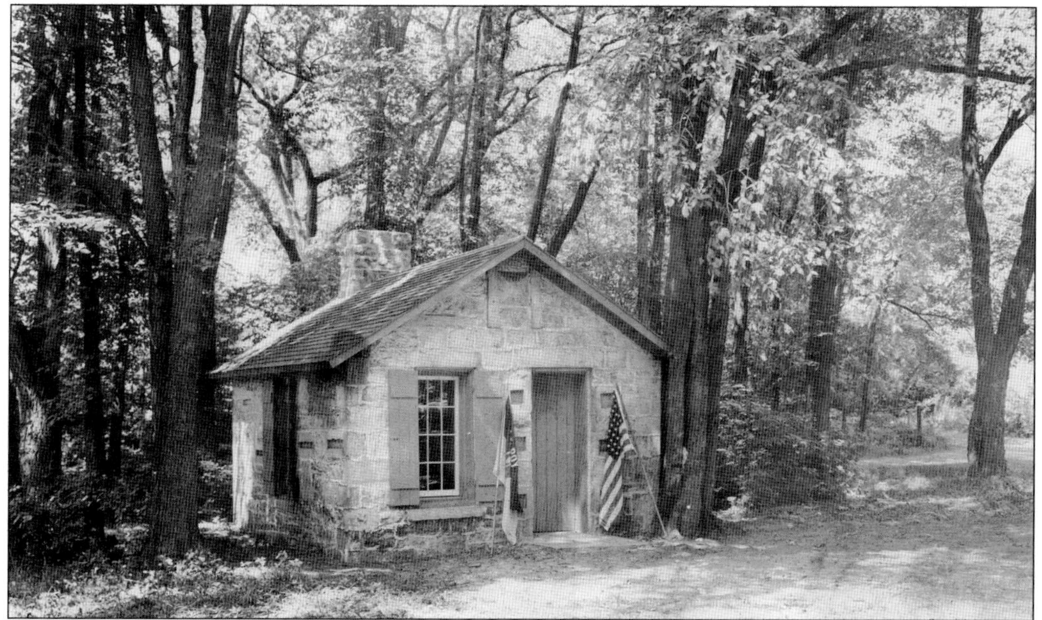

The Girl Scout Cabin. Girl Scouts were established in LeRoy as early as 1920 under the leadership of Ruth Keeney and Mary Sampson. This limestone building was located on the west side of the Oatka Creek near Red Mill Road. Originally it was the office and powder house for a limestone quarry. It was donated to the Girl Scouts by Frank LaBounty. It fell into disrepair and was later razed.

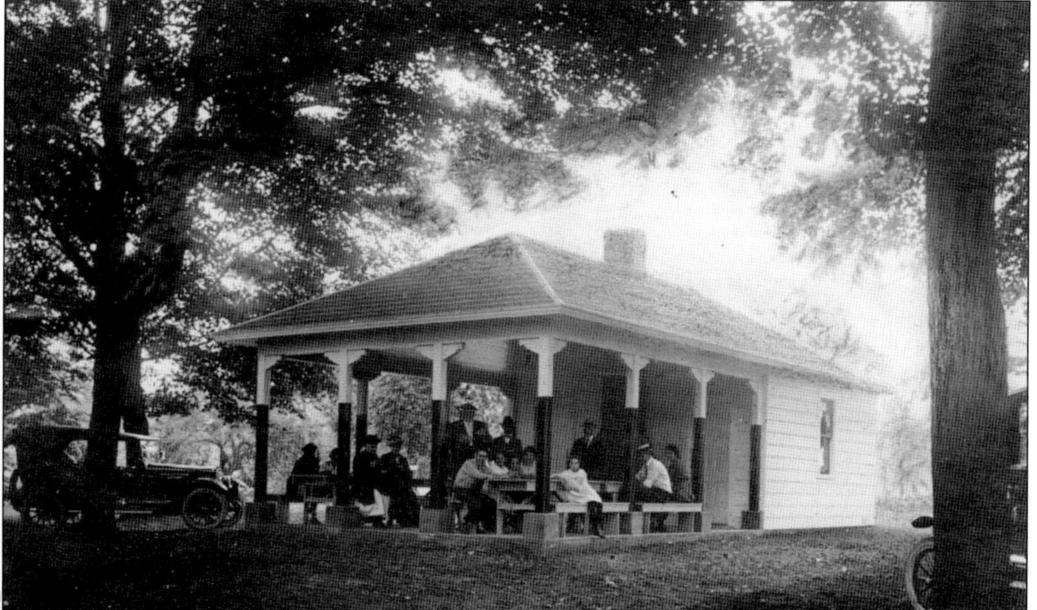

The Grove. Advertised as a modern service to motorists, the Grove offered free camping for tourists with tent platforms and electric lights. Lavatories were in this pavilion. The Arbor tearoom opened at the Grove in 1922. An eight-unit motel was built in 1936. In 1981, Phyllis Haywood and Anita Harris remodeled the office into a dress shop called The Studio. The building was razed in 1999.

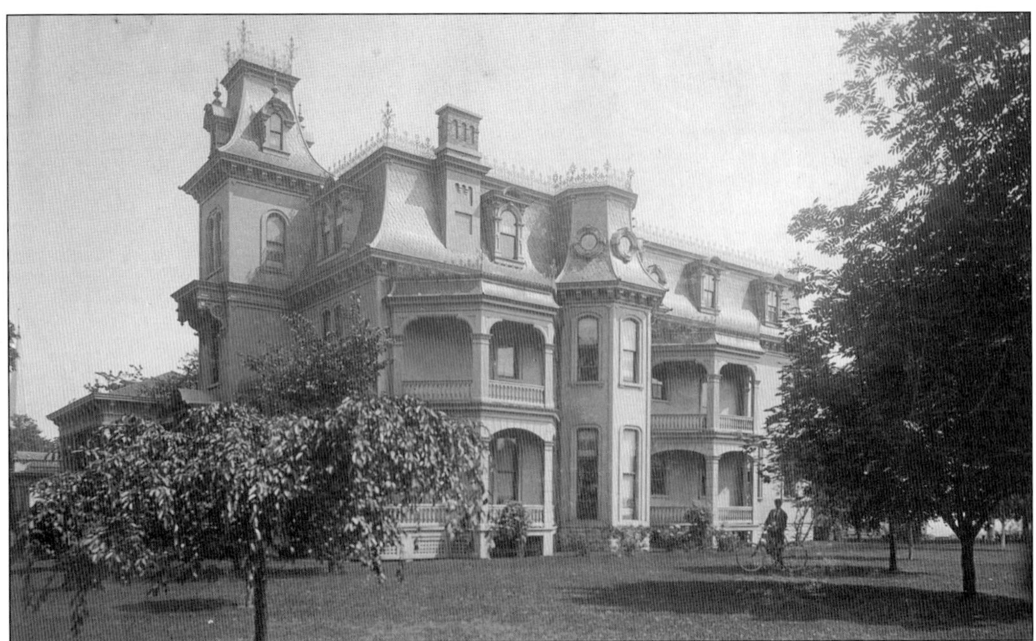

Lampson-Butler Mansion. Located on the south side of West Main Street, this home was built in 1872 by Miles Merritt for William Lampson. In 1897, Edward Butler, owner of the *Buffalo Evening News*, bought the house. It was known as West Lawn. After a long battle to save the building, it was razed in 1962 and replaced by Acme Supermarket. The carriage house is used by the Knights of Columbus.

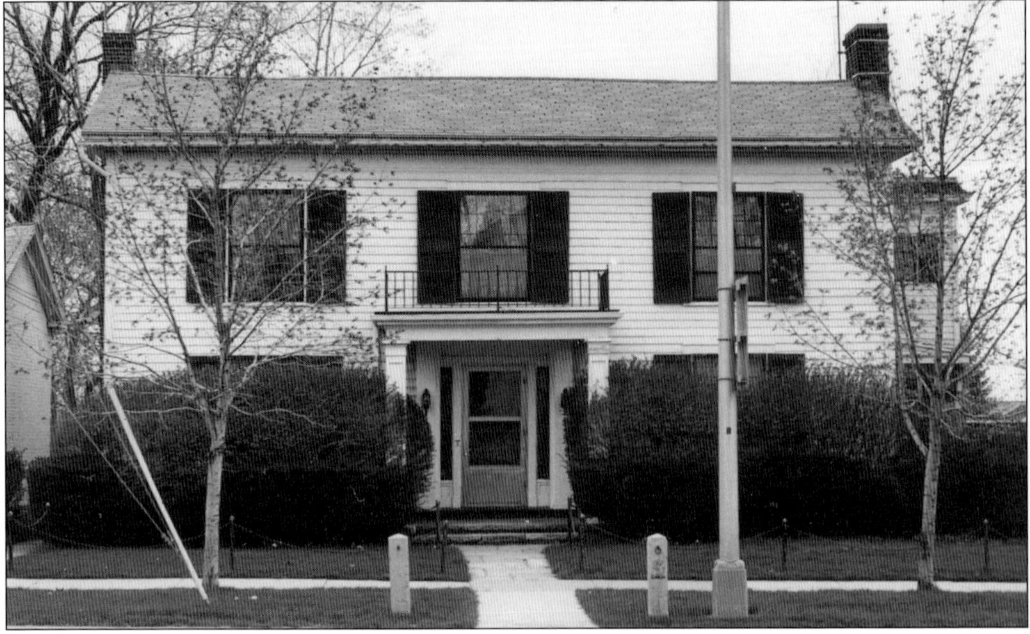

14 West Main Street. Known recently as the Welsh House, this structure was built in 1826 for Charles Darling. After a series of owners, including dressmakers Mary and Jennie Daley, the house was purchased by Dr. Paul Welsh in 1936, and it served as his home and office. This fine example of Federal architecture was razed in 2008 for a Walgreens Drug Store.

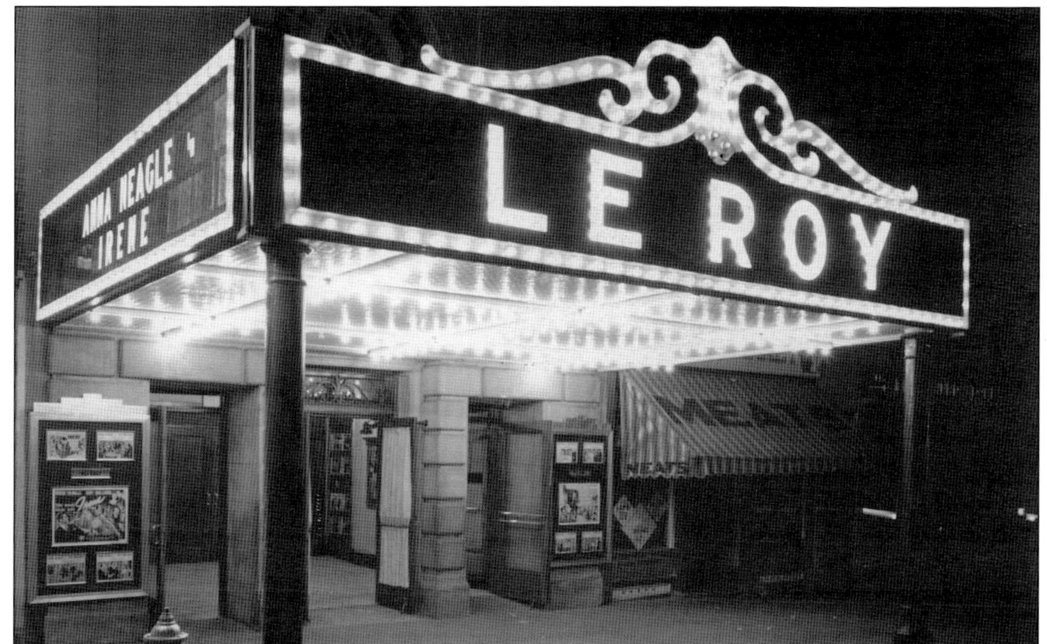

LeRoy Theater. In 1932, Ralph Blouvet purchased the Bank of LeRoy building. Charles Cromwell designed the new interior with seats for 494 people and 150 seats in the balcony. In 1941, the theater was renovated again. The interior was designed by Oscar Glass of New York City, who also designed the Ziegfield Theater. The marquee was removed in 1976. The theater is now the Church of the Living Waters.

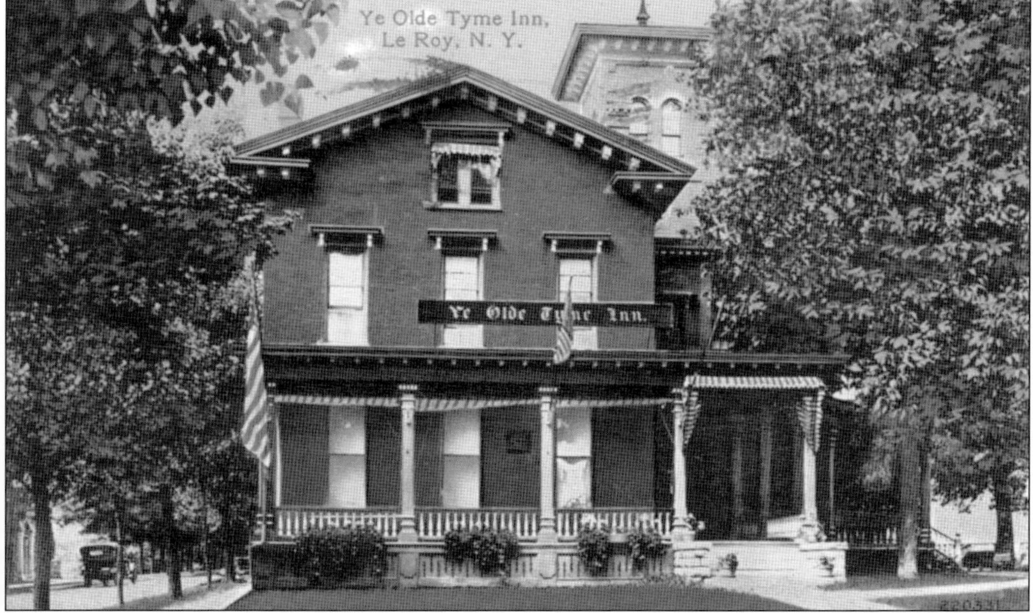

Ye Olde Tyme Inn. This building stood on the corner of Church and East Main Streets. Built in the early 1800s, the back portion was part of the Triangle Tract land office. In 1918, the Kellogg family transformed the 29-room house into Ye Olde Tyme Inn. It was later used as a community center but was razed in 1936, and the site is the parking lot for St. Mark's Episcopal Church.

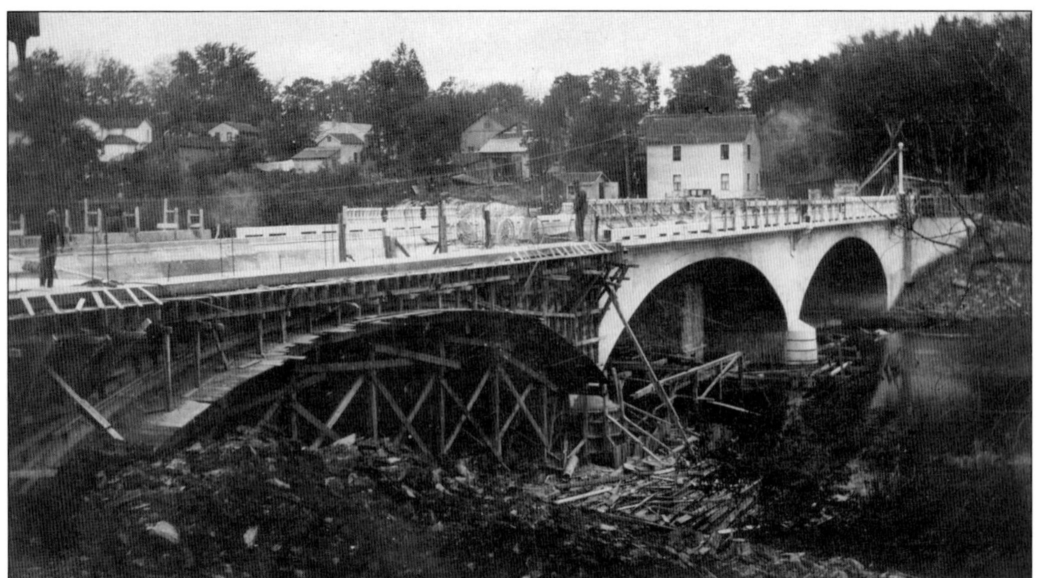

CLAY STREET BRIDGE , 1924. There have been six bridges on this site. The first was built in 1840. The second was built a few years later. The third was an iron-span bridge built in 1894. The fourth was built in 1913. It was dismantled and rebuilt at Red Bridge. The 1924 cement bridge was replaced in 1990. The recent bridge features cement panels that imitate the old three-arch design.

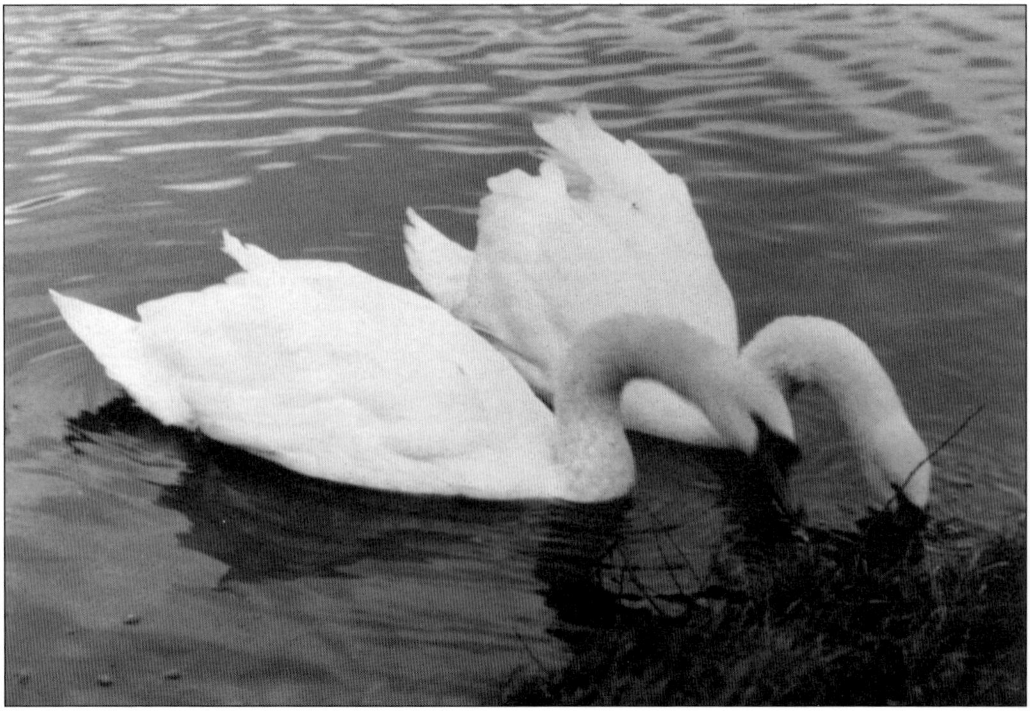

THE SWANS. In 1939, a pair of Royal Swans were acquired for the creek. A contest was held and they were named King George and Queen Elizabeth after the English monarchs. At one time, the LeRoy historian Marion Russell proposed that the sports teams of the school be called the Swans.

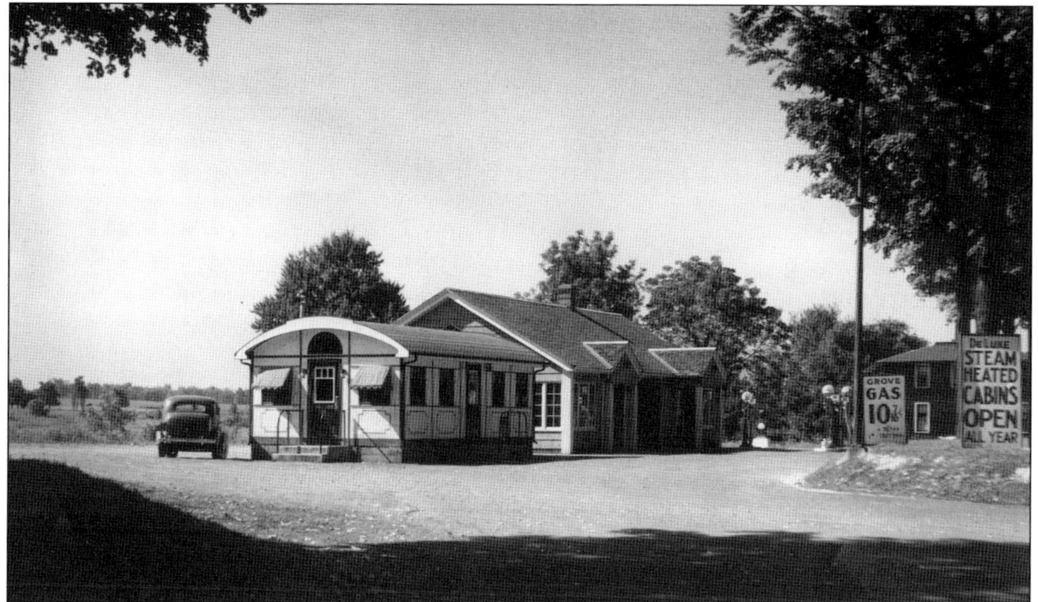

The Diner. Located near the Grove Motel on West Main Road, the diner was eventually moved downtown in front of the LeRoy Dining Grill. The other diner in the village was located on Lake Street adjacent to the Wiss Hotel. Known as the Conklin Diner, it was a Ward Dining Car manufactured in Silver Creek, New York. It was razed in the 1990s.

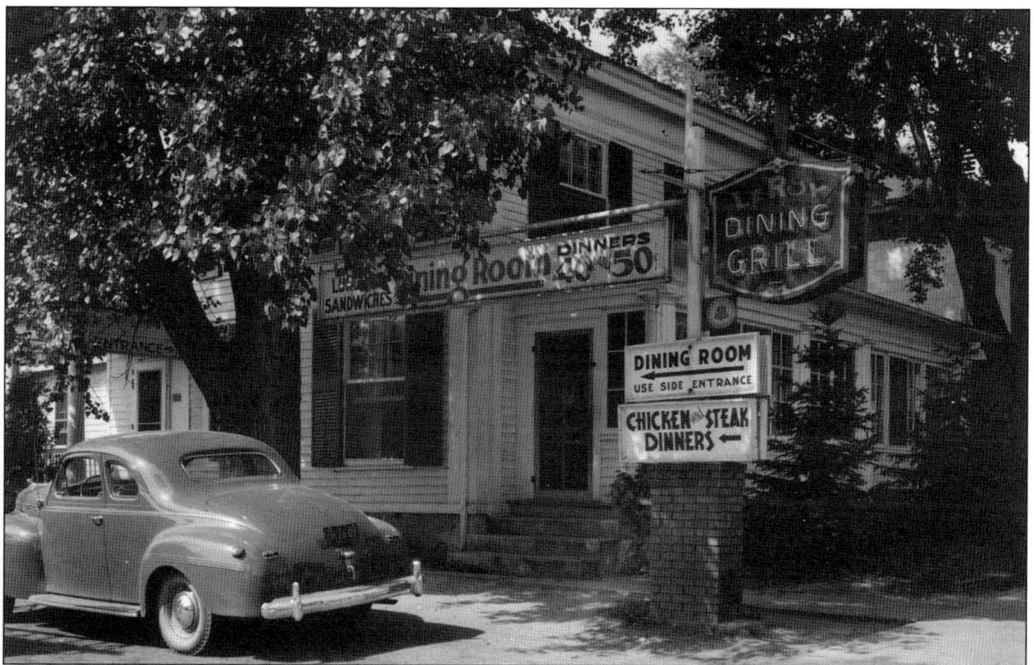

LeRoy Dining Grill. In 1927, Jake Lally opened a new restaurant, Lally's, in the former home of Dr. William McPherson at 63 Main Street. After Lally retired, the restaurant became known as the LeRoy Dining Grill. It was also known as the White House Restaurant. The front porch was replaced with the diner from the Grove Motel, and it was called the Sterling Diner. It was razed in 1980 to make room for a McDonald's restaurant.

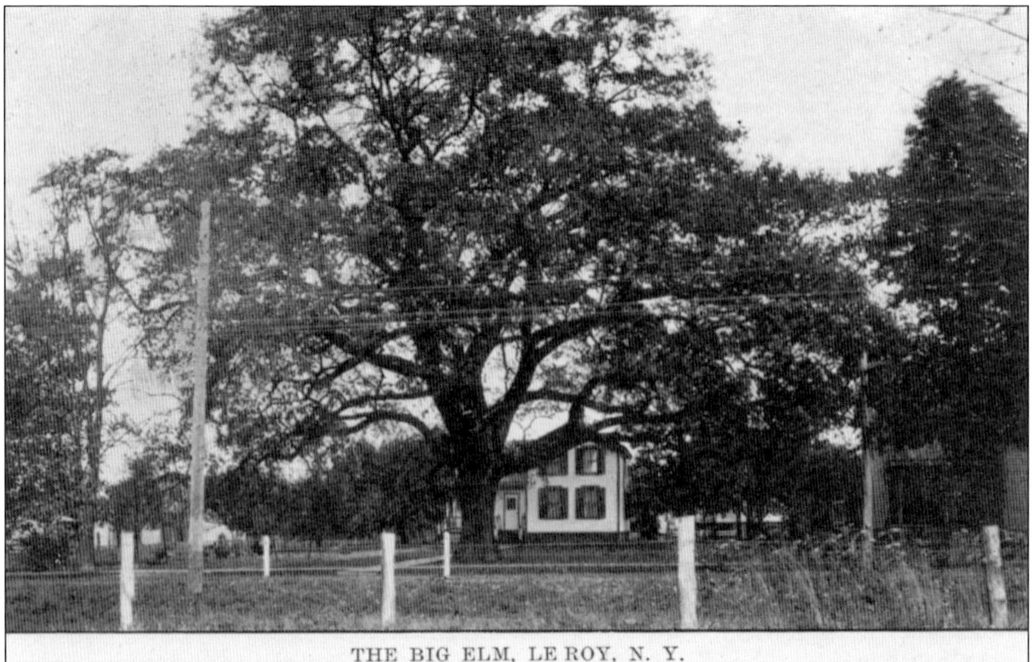
THE BIG ELM, LE ROY, N. Y.

THE ELM TREE. Around 1820, George Platt began trimming a young elm tree in a cleared field on Summit Street. As it grew, it became a landmark in LeRoy and it appeared on postcards. Nearly 140 years later, in 1960, the tree succumbed to Dutch Elm disease and was cut down. The trunk was 18 feet in circumference.

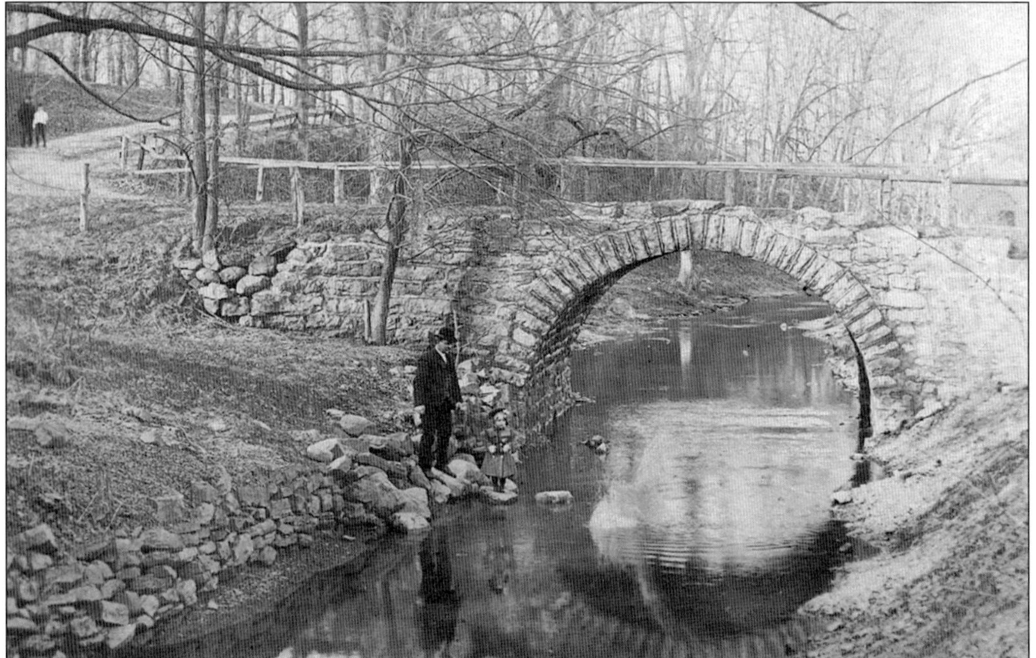

LOVER'S LANE. This stone arch was originally part of the Haskins' mill race on the west side of the creek near Red Bridge—now Munson Street. The ruins of the mill and the arch were razed when the Munson Street bridge was built.

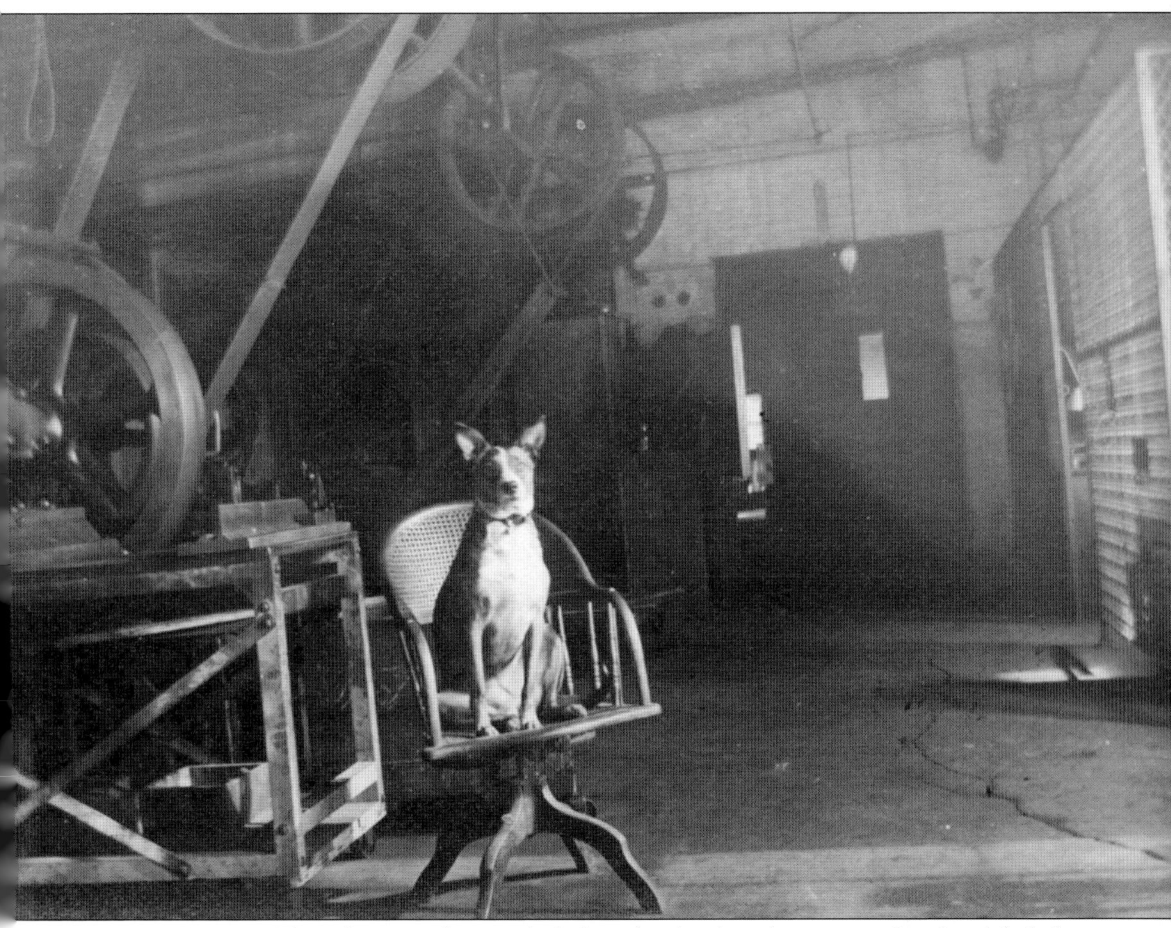

Man's Best Friend. This photograph is included in this book to be a reminder that labeled photographs are more valuable than those without labels. The handwritten note on the back says "perhaps LeRoy Plow." No one bothered to write down the dog's name. A few people who work at the LeRoy Historical Society named her Babe. William James Harris wrote, "Faces fade, and the people we once knew, some of them, are gone forever. Children grow up and go away. The old house is torn down. The pets die or disappear. The time to take the picture is when you see it. The historic value to things, fixed in the form of a picture, is beyond price."

Find *Your* Place in History.

www.arcadiapublishing.com

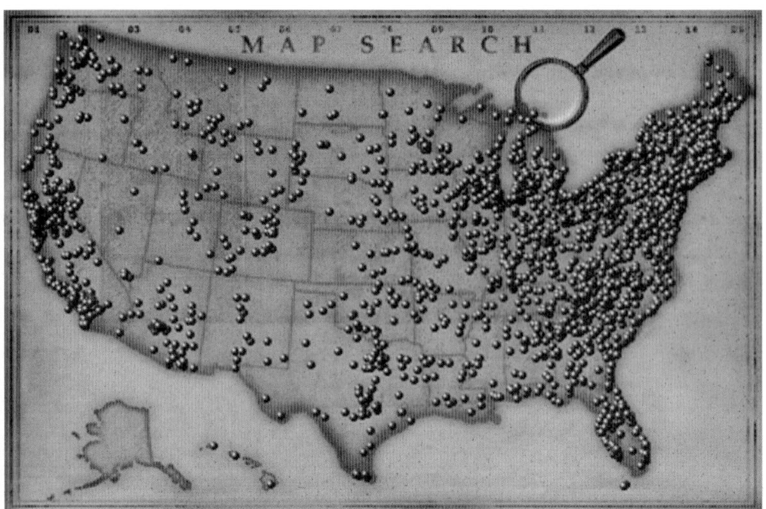

Discover books about the town where you grew up, the cities where your friends and families live, the town where your parents met, or even that retirement spot you've been dreaming about. Our Web site provides history lovers with exclusive deals, advanced notification about new titles, e-mail alerts of author events, and much more.

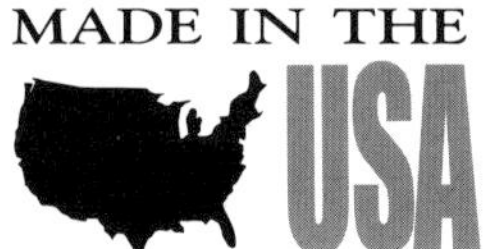

Arcadia Publishing, the leading local history publisher in the United States, is committed to making history accessible and meaningful through publishing books that celebrate and preserve the heritage of America's people and places. Consistent with our mission to preserve history on a local level, this book was printed in South Carolina on American-made paper and manufactured entirely in the United States.

This book carries the accredited Forest Stewardship Council (FSC) label and is printed on 100 percent FSC-certified paper. Products carrying the FSC label are independently certified to assure consumers that they come from forests that are managed to meet the social, economic, and ecological needs of present and future generations.

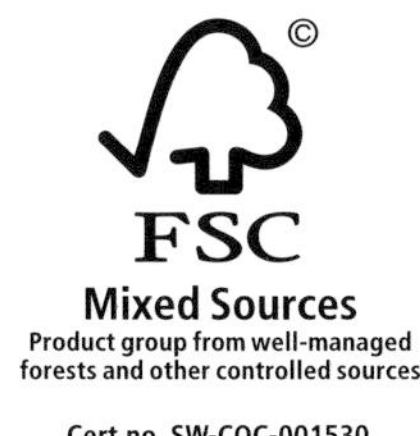